AWKWARD

AND

DEFINITION

The High School Comic Chronicles of

Ariel Schrag

A Touchstone Book
Published by Simon & Schuster
New York   London   Toronto   Sydney

Touchstone
A Division of Simon & Schuster, Inc.
1230 Avenue of the Americas
New York, NY 10020

First Touchstone trade paperback edition April 2008

TOUCHSTONE and colophon are registered trademarks of Simon & Schuster, Inc.

For information about special discounts for bulk purchases,
please contact Simon & Schuster Special Sales at
1-800-456-6798 or business@simonandschuster.com.

Manufactured in the United States of America

10 9 8 7 6 5 4 3 2 1

Library of Congress Cataloging-in-Publication Data is available.

ISBN-13: 978-1-4165-5231-4
ISBN-10:   1-4165-5231-6

AWKWARD

·By Ariel Schrag·

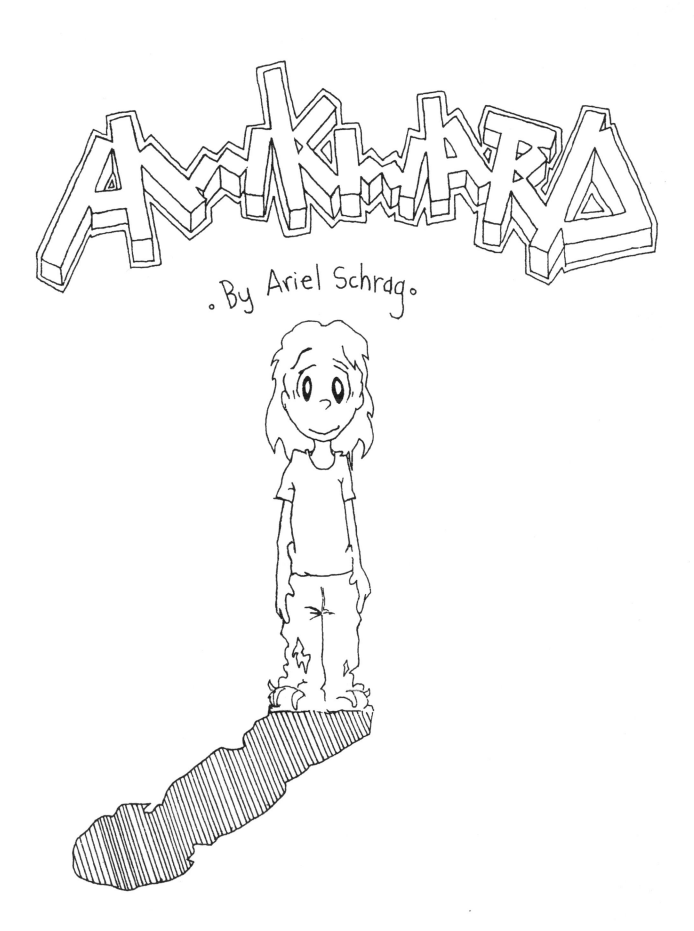

for Julia

definition number one awkward

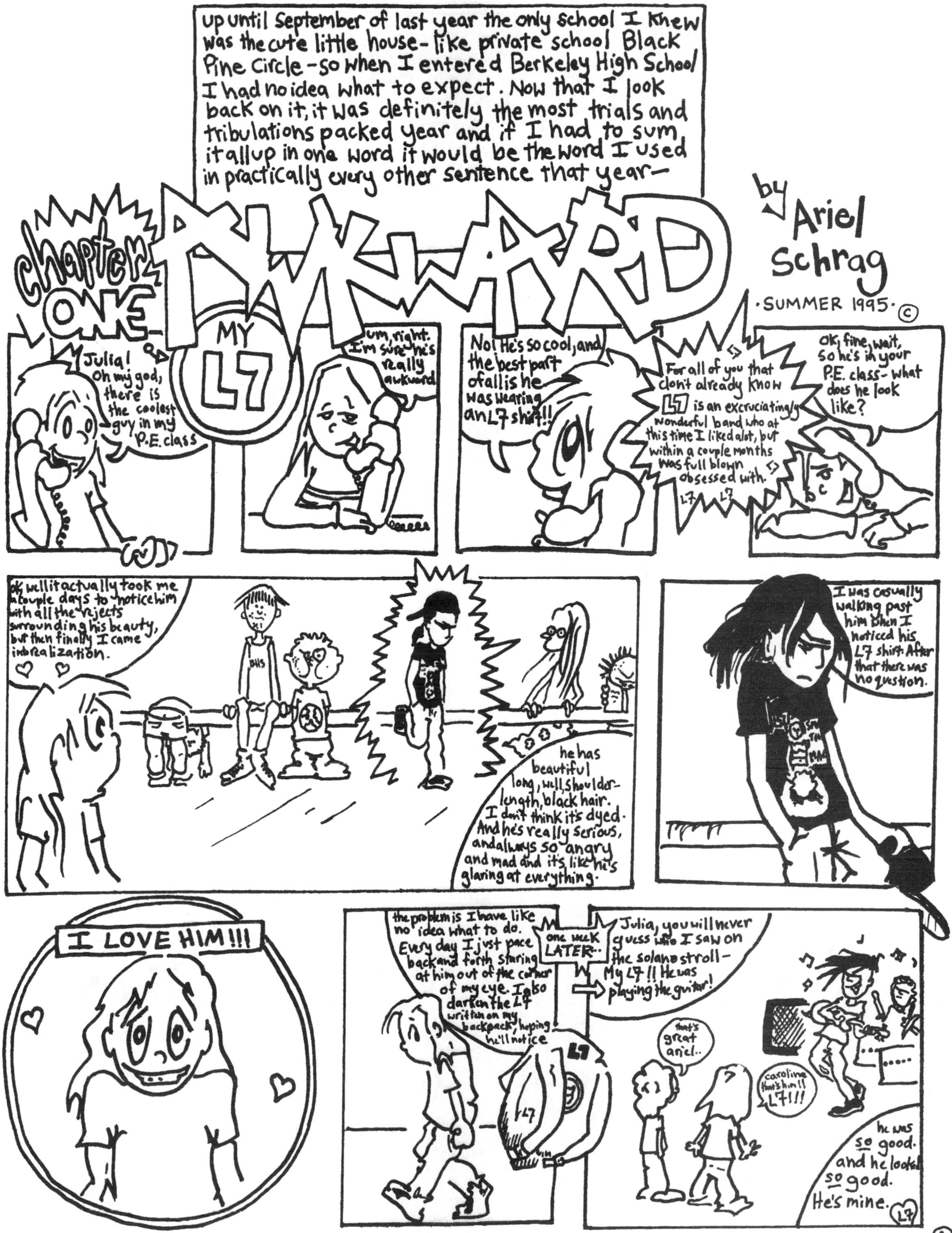

up until September of last year the only school I knew was the cute little house-like private school Black Pine Circle-so when I entered Berkeley High School I had no idea what to expect. Now that I look back on it, it was definitely the most trials and tribulations packed year and if I had to sum it all up in one word it would be the word I used in practically every other sentence that year-
chapter ONE
AWKWARD
by Ariel Schrag
·SUMMER 1995· ©
Julia! Oh my god, there is the coolest guy in my P.E. class
MY L7
um, right. I'm sure he's really awkward
No! He's so cool, and the best part of all is he was wearing an L7 shirt!!
For all of you that don't already know L7 is an excruciatingly wonderful band who at this time I liked alot, but within a couple months was full blown obsessed with.
L7 L7
ok, fine, wait, so he's in your P.E. class- what does he look like?
ok well it actually took me a couple days to notice him with all the rejects surrounding his beauty, but then finally I came into realization.
BHS
he has beautiful long, well, shoulder-length, black hair. I don't think it's dyed. And he's really serious, and always so angry and mad and it's like he's glaring at everything.
I was casually walking past him when I noticed his L7 shirt. After that there was no question.
I LOVE HIM!!!
the problem is I have like no idea what to do. Every day I just pace back and forth staring at him out of the corner of my eye. I also darken the L7 written on my backpack, hoping he'll notice
L7
L7
one week LATER..
Julia, you will never guess who I saw on the solano stroll- My L7!! He was playing the guitar!
that's great ariel..
caroline that's him!! L7!!!
he was so good. and he looked so good. He's mine.
L7

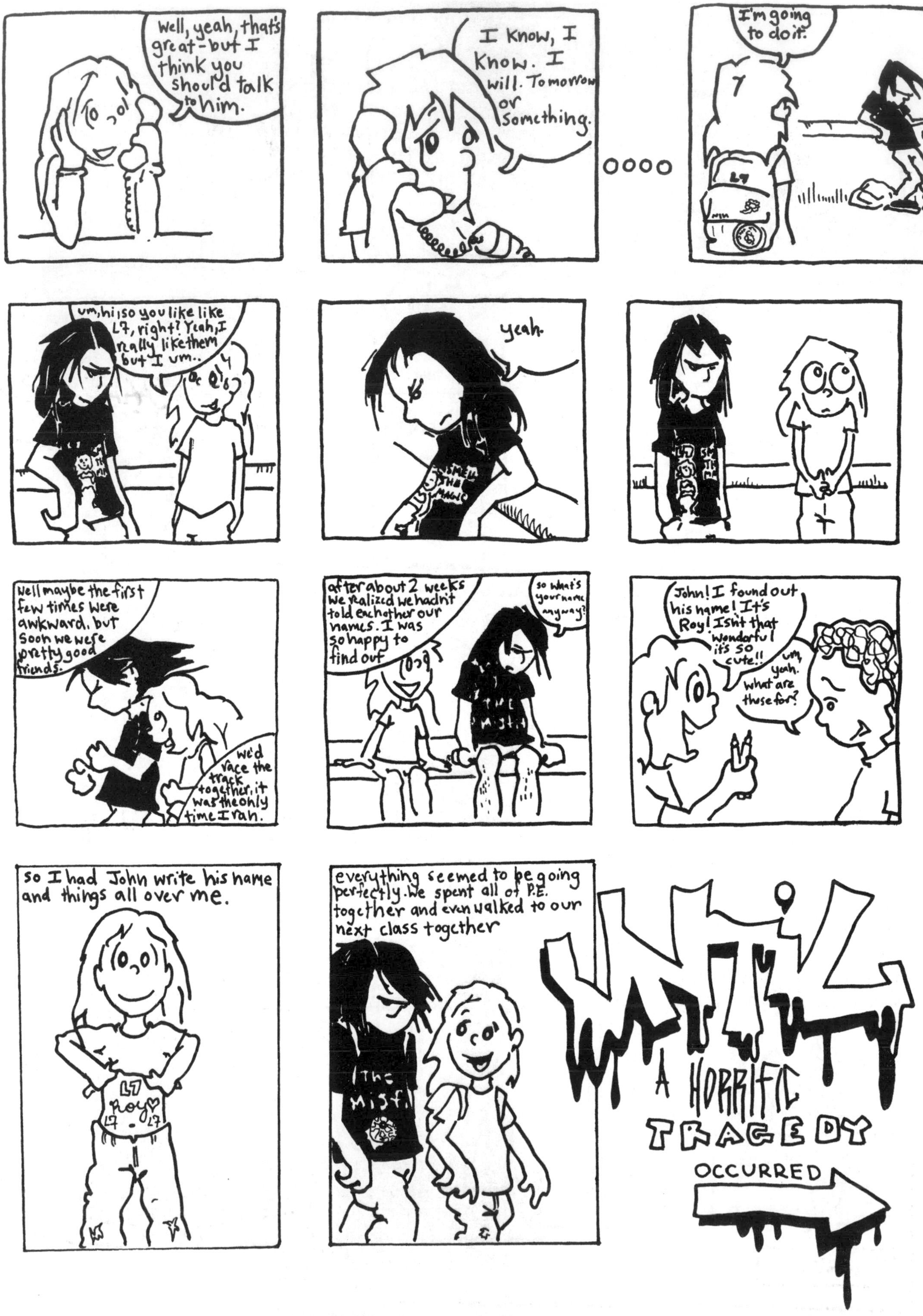
Well, yeah, that's great-but I think you should talk to him.
I know, I know. I will. Tomorrow or something.
OOOO
I'm going to do it.
L7
um, hi, so you like like L7, right? Yeah, I really like them but I um...
yeah.
Well maybe the first few times were awkward, but soon we were pretty good friends.
we'd race the track together, it was the only time I ran.
after about 2 weeks we realized we hadn't told each other our names. I was so happy to find out
so what's your name anyway?
John! I found out his name! It's Roy! Isn't that wonderful it's so cute!!
um, yeah. what are those for?
So I had John write his name and things all over me.
L7
Roy
L7
L7
everything seemed to be going perfectly. We spent all of P.E. together and even walked to our next class together
UNTIL
A HORRIFIC
TRAGEDY
OCCURRED

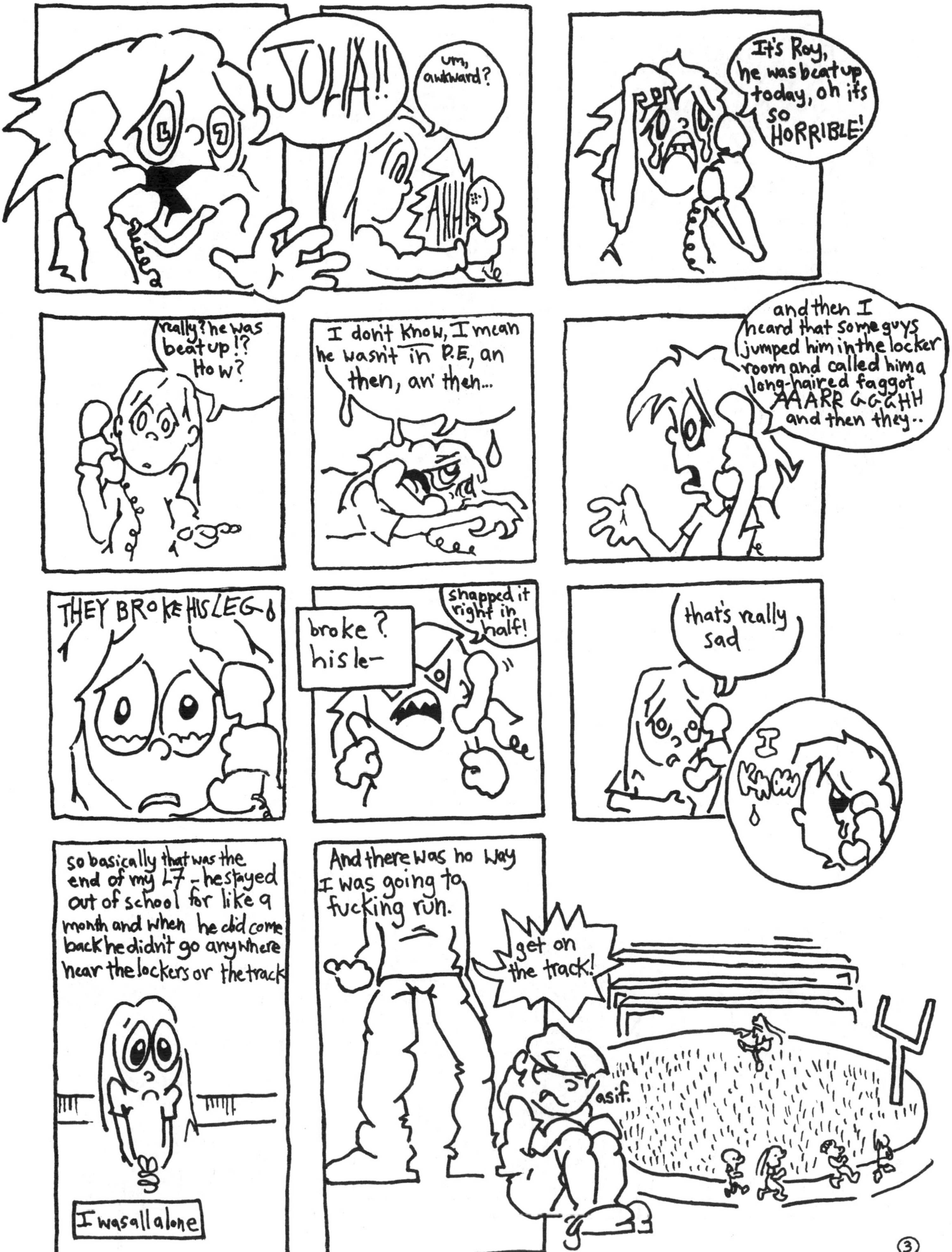

JULIA!!
um, awkward?
AHH!
It's Roy, he was beat up today, oh its so HORRIBLE!
really? he was beat up!? How?
I don't Know, I mean he wasn't in P.E, an then, an' then...
and then I heard that some guys jumped him in the locker room and called him a long-haired faggot AAARRGGGHH and then they..
THEY BROKE HIS LEG
broke? his le-
snapped it right in half!
that's really sad
I
so basically that was the end of my L7 - he stayed out of school for like a month and when he did come back he didn't go anywhere near the lockers or the track
I was all alone
And there was no way I was going to fucking run.
get on the track!
as if.

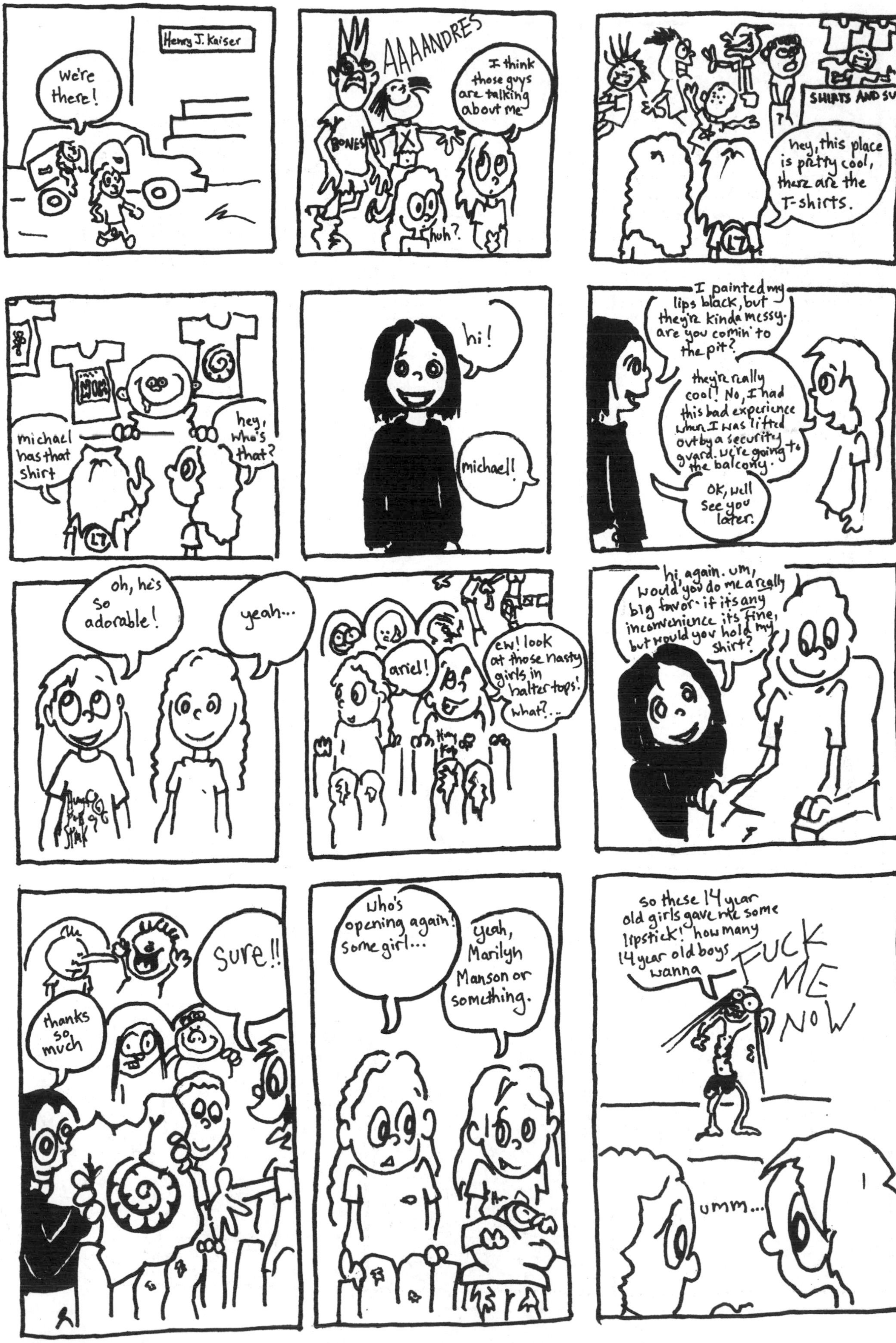
Henry J. Kaiser
We're there!
AAAANDRES
I think those guys are talking about me
huh?
SHIRTS AND SU
hey, this place is pretty cool, there are the T-shirts.
michael has that shirt
hey, who's that?
hi!
michael!
I painted my lips black, but they're kinda messy. are you comin' to the pit?
they're really cool! No, I had this bad experience when I was lifted out by a security guard. we're going to the balcony.
Ok, well see you later.
oh, he's so adorable!
yeah...
ariel!
ew! look at those nasty girls in halter tops!
what?...
hi, again. um, would you do me a really big favor. if its any inconvenience its fine, but would you hold my shirt?
sure!!
thanks so much
who's opening again?
some girl...
yeah, Marilyn Manson or something.
so these 14 year old girls gave me some lipstick! how many 14 year old boys wanna
FUCK ME NOW
umm...

the second act was even more traumatizing it was some kind of traveling freak show.

there was Bee Bee the Circus Queen

Knives!

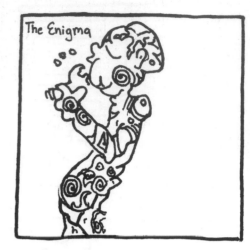

The Enigma

A guy who lifted things with his piercings...guy

and worst of all a guy who fit his entire body through a very small tennis racket.

he had to pull up his skin and other things to accomplish this.

Finally it was over. Caroline and I relaxed, ready for Trent

He opened with Mr. Self Destruct (well, pinion for the knowledgable fans) and it was really good

I AM THE VOICE INSIDE YOUR HEAD

When we waited for him to do Closer everyone put up their lighters I adjusted the flame on mine and it shot up menacingly.

"Hurt" was probably the best song because he brought down this screen that showed decaying animals.

When the concert was over my only regrets were that he didn't play "Burn" (from Natural Born Killers) or "Heresy", my favorite song.

no burn?

Everyone started pouring out of the building and Caroline and I just got swept up in the rush.

We waited outside for awhile and then my parents' trusty blue vista showed up and we scrambled in.

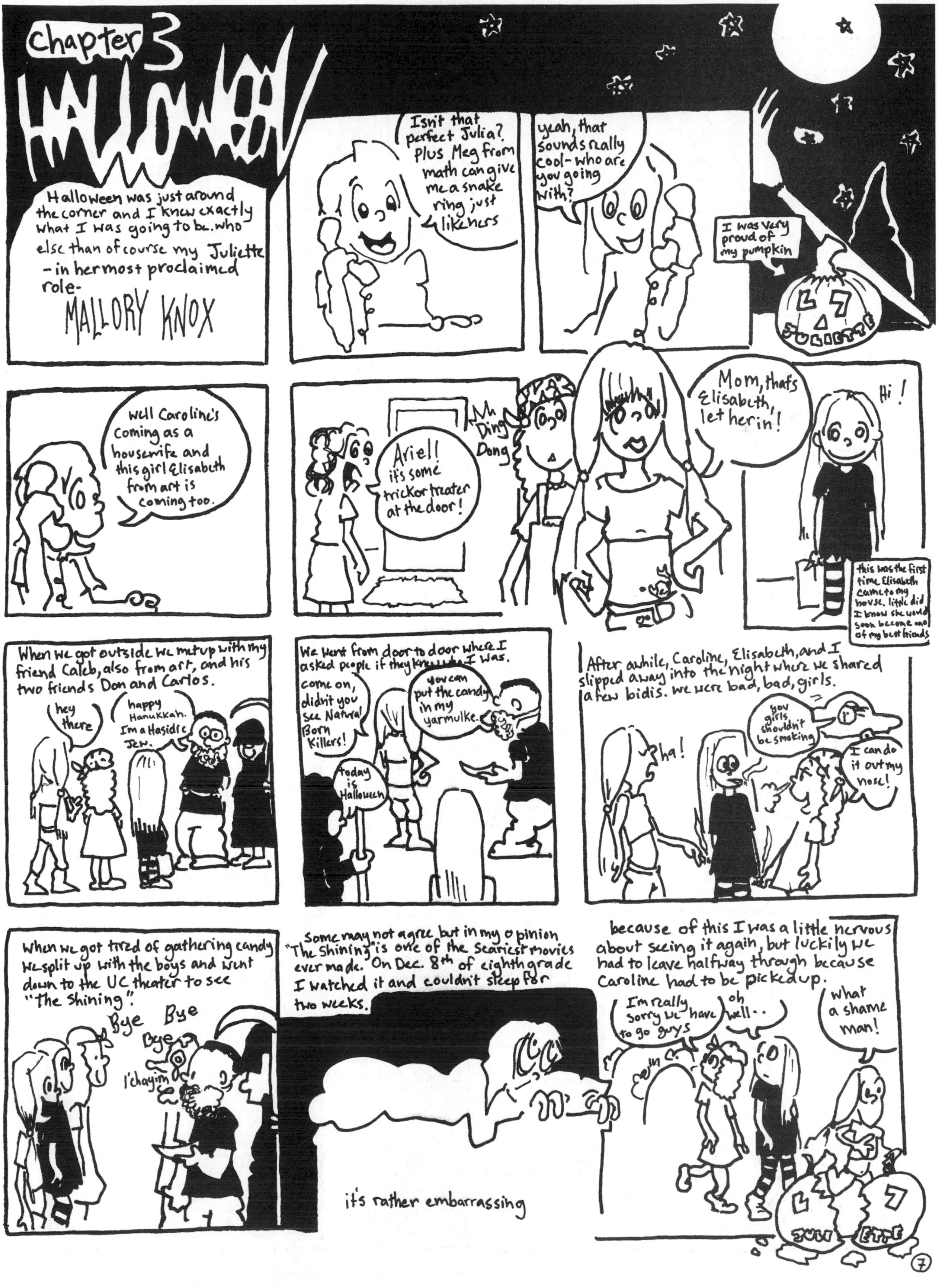

Chapter 3
HALLOWEEN
Halloween was just around the corner and I knew exactly what I was going to be. who else than of course my Juliette - in her most proclaimed role-
MALLORY KNOX
Isn't that perfect Julia? Plus Meg from math can give me a snake ring just like hers
yeah, that sounds really cool- who are you going with?
I was very proud of my pumpkin
JULIETTE
Well Caroline's coming as a housewife and this girl Elisabeth from art is coming too.
Ding Dong
Ariel! it's some trick or treater at the door!
Mom, that's Elisabeth, let her in!
Hi!
this was the first time Elisabeth came to my house. little did I know she would soon become one of my best friends
When we got outside we met up with my friend Caleb, also from art, and his two friends Don and Carlos.
hey there
happy Hanukkah. I'm a Hasidic Jew.
We went from door to door where I asked people if they kn... I was.
come on, didn't you see Natural Born Killers!
you can put the candy in my yarmulke.
today is Halloween
After awhile, Caroline, Elisabeth, and I slipped away into the night where we shared a few bidis. we were bad, bad, girls.
ha!
you girls shouldn't be smoking
I can do it out my nose!
When we got tired of gathering candy we split up with the boys and went down to the UC theater to see "The Shining".
Bye Bye
Bye
l'chayim
Some may not agree but in my opinion "The Shining" is one of the scariest movies ever made. On Dec. 8th of eighth grade I watched it and couldn't sleep for two weeks.
it's rather embarrassing
because of this I was a little nervous about seeing it again, but luckily we had to leave halfway through because Caroline had to be picked up.
I'm really sorry we have to go guys
oh well..
what a shame man!
JULI ETTE
7

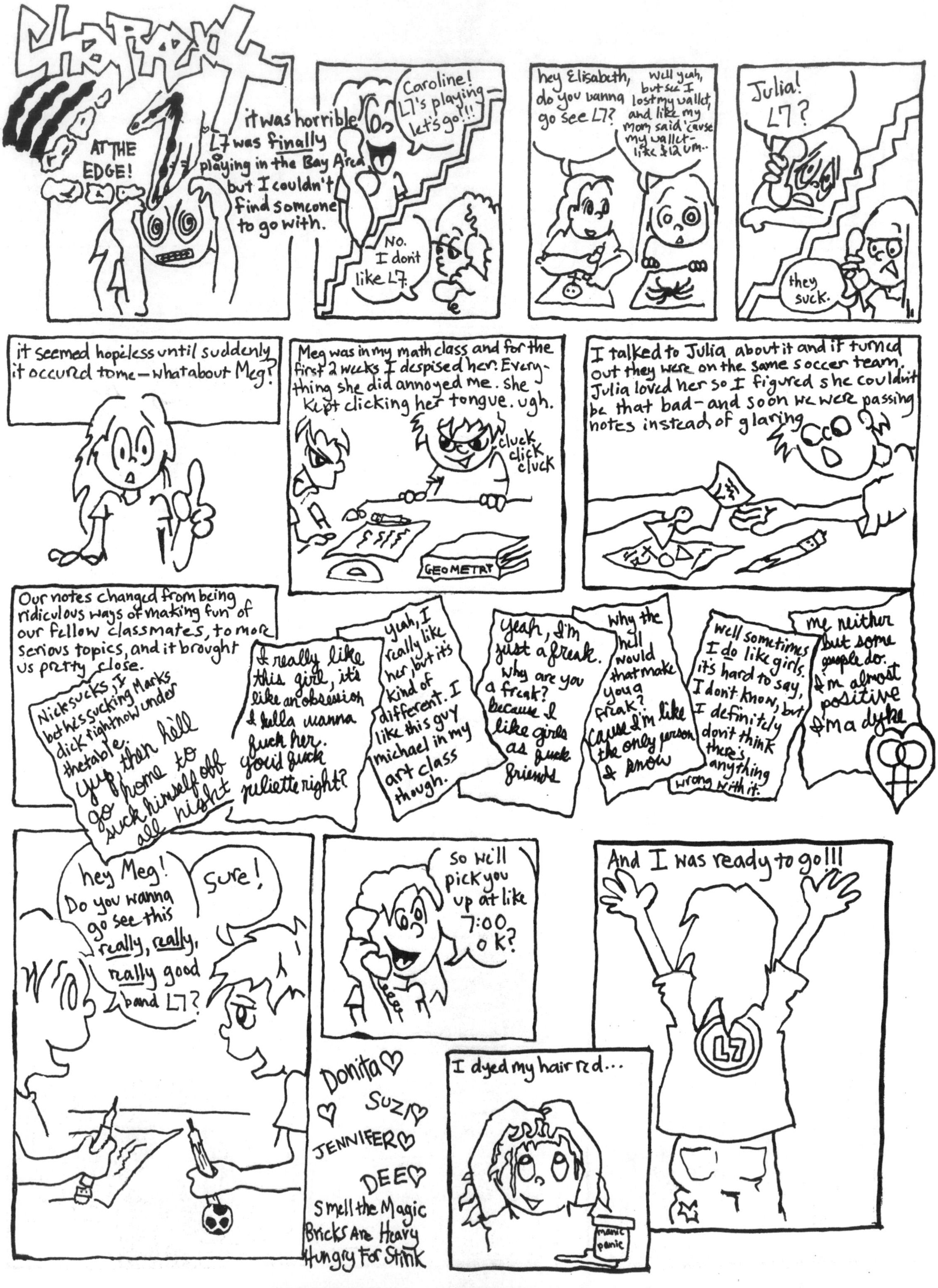

AT THE EDGE!
it was horrible. L7 was finally playing in the Bay Area but I couldn't find someone to go with.
Caroline! L7's playing— let's go!!!
No. I dont like L7.
hey Elisabeth, do you wanna go see L7?
Well yeah, but see I lost my wallet, and like my Mom said 'cause my wallet- like & i a um..
Julia! L7?
they suck.
it seemed hopeless until suddenly it occured to me—what about Meg?
Meg was in my math class and for the first 2 weeks I despised her. Everything she did annoyed me. she kept clicking her tongue. ugh.
cluck click cluck
GEOMETRY
I talked to Julia about it and it turned out they were on the same soccer team. Julia loved her so I figured she couldnt be that bad—and soon we were passing notes instead of glaring.
Our notes changed from being ridiculous ways of making fun of our fellow classmates, to more serious topics, and it brought us pretty close.
Nick sucks, I bet his sucking Marks dick right now under the table.
yup, then he'll go home to suck himself off all night
I really like this girl, it's like an obsession I hella wanna fuck her. you'd fuck juliette right?
yeah, I really like her, but it's kind of different. I like this guy michael in my art class though.
yeah, I'm just a freak.
Why are you a freak?
Because I like girls as fuck friends
why the hell would that make you a freak?
Cause I'm like the only person I know
well sometimes I do like girls. it's hard to say, I don't know, but I definitely don't think there's anything wrong with it.
me neither but some people do. I'm almost positive I'm a dyke
hey Meg! Do you wanna go see this really, really, really good band L7?
Sure!
so we'll pick you up at like 7:00 ok?
And I was ready to go!!!
L7
Donita♡
Suzi♡
JENNIFER♡
DEE♡
Smell the Magic
Bricks Are Heavy
Hungry For Stink
I dyed my hair red...
manic panic

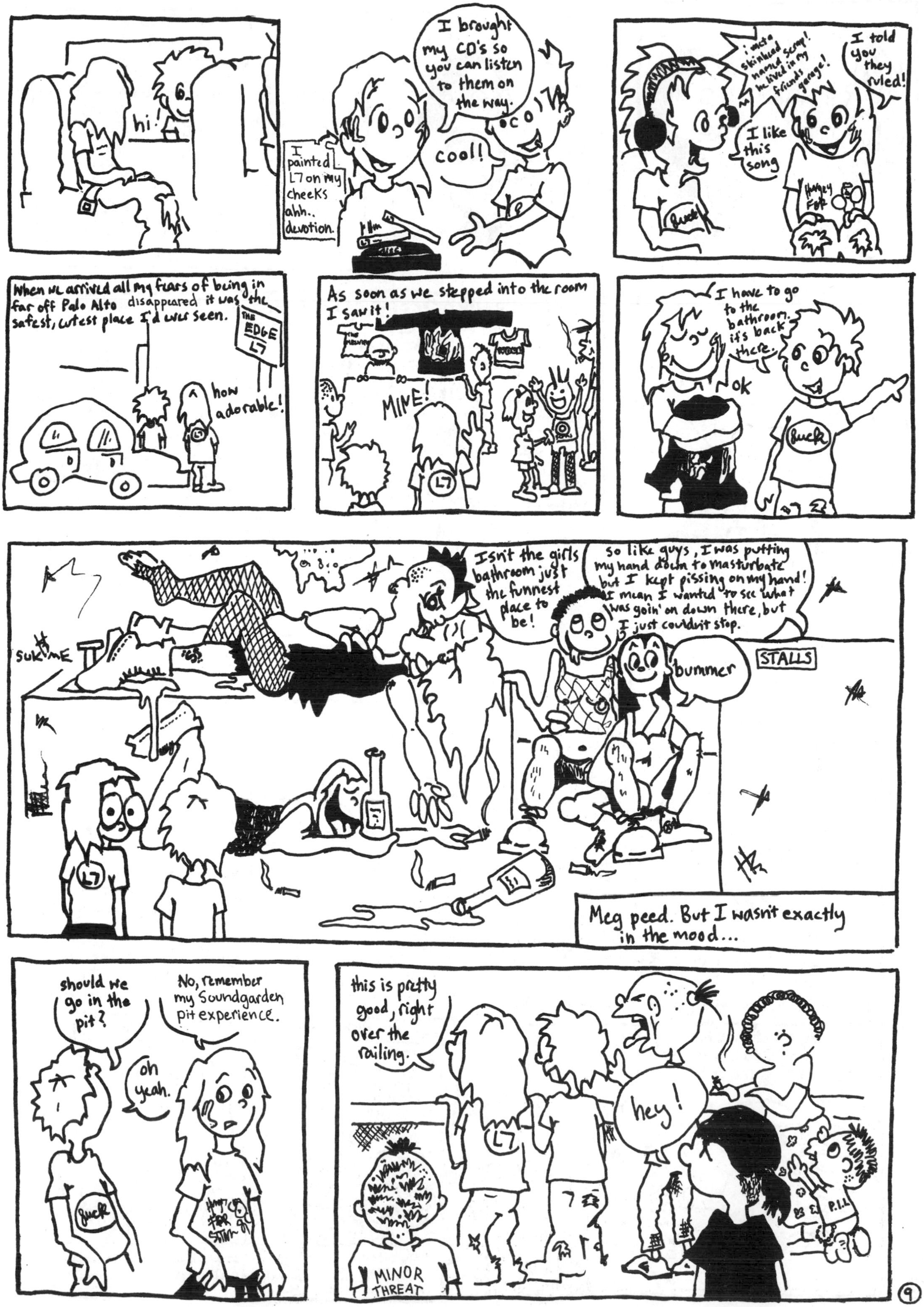
hi!
I brought my CD's so you can listen to them on the way.
I painted L7 on my cheeks ahh.. devotion.
cool!
i met a skinhead named scrap! he lived in my friends garage!
I told you they ruled!
I like this song
When we arrived all my fears of being in far off Palo Alto disappeared it was the safest, cutest place I'd ever seen.
THE EDGE L7
how adorable!
As soon as we stepped into the room I saw it!
MINE!
I have to go to the bathroom. it's back there.
ok
Isn't the girls bathroom just the funnest place to be!
so like guys, I was putting my hand down to masturbate but I kept pissing on my hand! I mean I wanted to see what was goin' on down there, but I just couldn't stop.
bummer
STALLS
SUK ME
L7
Meg peed. But I wasn't exactly in the mood...
should we go in the pit?
No, remember my Soundgarden pit experience.
oh yeah.
this is pretty good, right over the railing.
hey!
L7
MINOR THREAT

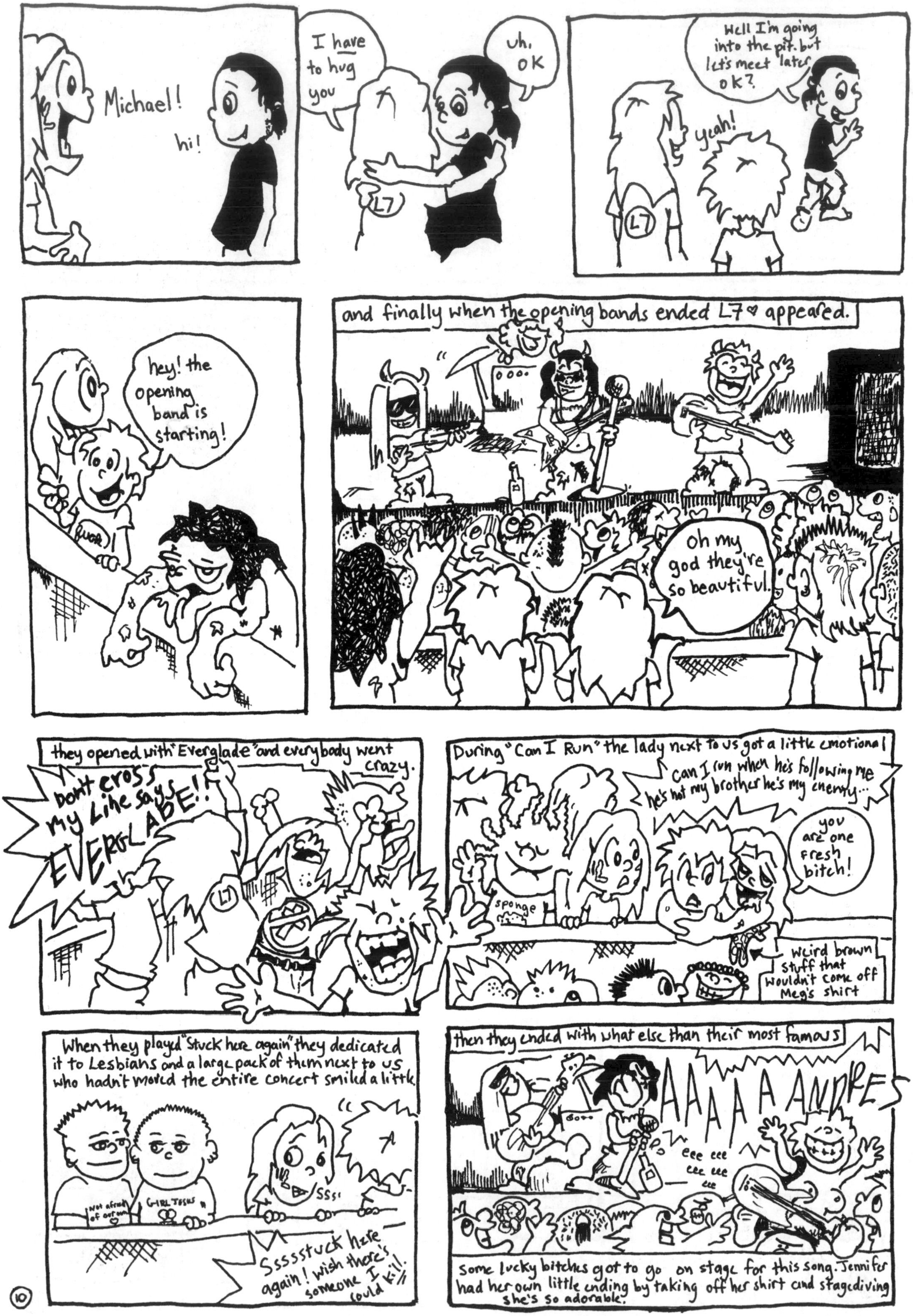

Michael!
hi!
I have to hug you
uh, OK
Well I'm going into the pit, but let's meet later OK?
yeah!
hey! the opening band is starting!
and finally when the opening bands ended L7♥ appeared.
oh my god they're so beautiful.
they opened with "Everglade" and everybody went crazy.
Don't cross my line says EVERGLADE!!
During "Can I Run" the lady next to us got a little emotional
Can I run when he's following me he's not my brother he's my enemy...
you are one fresh bitch!
sponge
weird brown stuff that wouldn't come off Meg's shirt
When they played "Stuck here again" they dedicated it to Lesbians and a large pack of them next to us who hadn't moved the entire concert smiled a little
Not afraid of our own
GIRL JESUS
Sss
Sssssstuck here again! wish there's someone I could kill
then they ended with what else than their most famous
AAAAAANDRES
eee eee eee eee eee
Some lucky bitches got to go on stage for this song. Jennifer had her own little ending by taking off her shirt and stagediving she's so adorable.

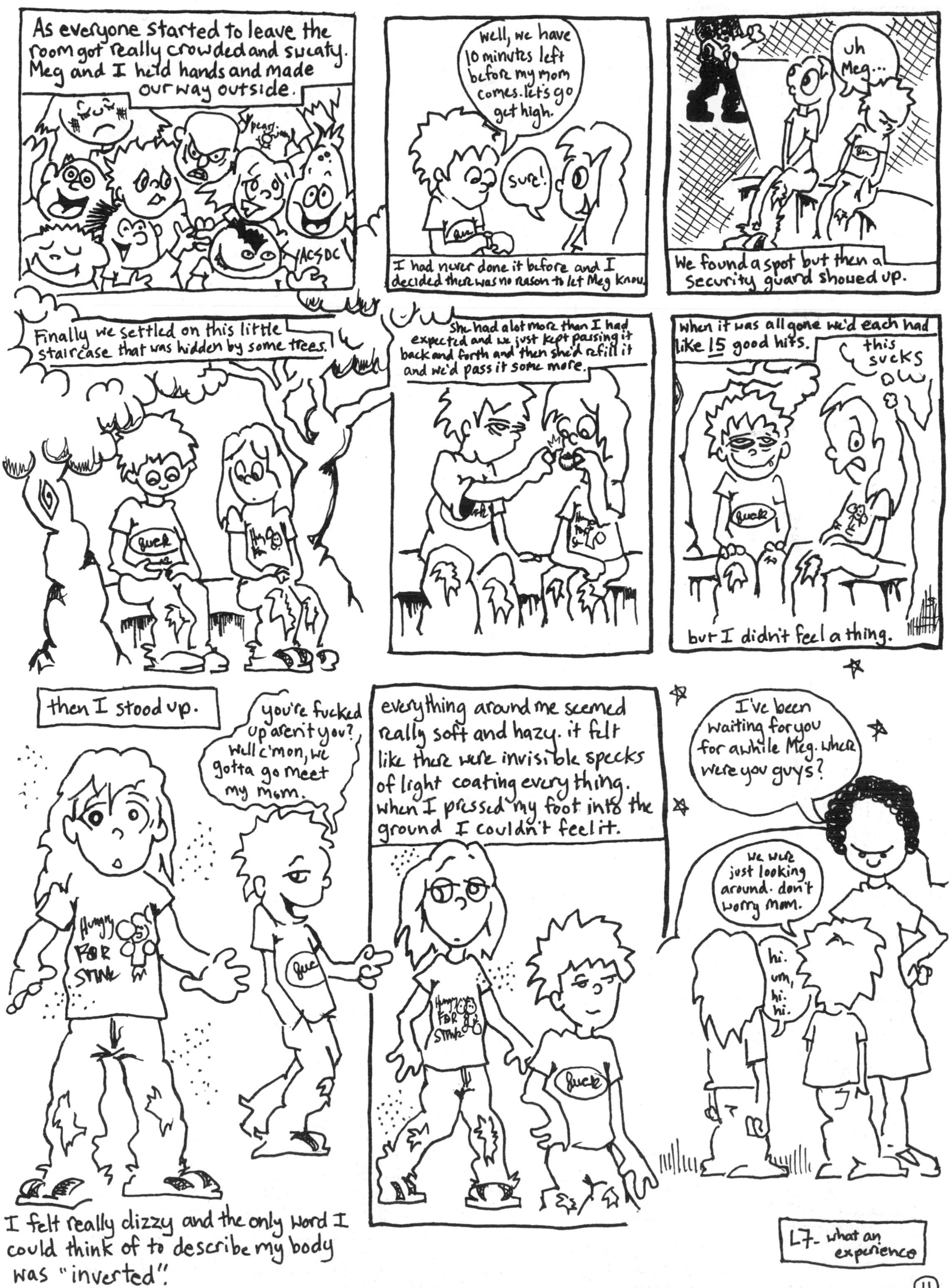

As everyone started to leave the room got really crowded and sweaty. Meg and I held hands and made our way outside.
pearl jam
AC/DC
Well, we have 10 minutes left before my mom comes. let's go get high.
sure!
I had never done it before and I decided there was no reason to let Meg know.
uh Meg...
We found a spot but then a security guard showed up.
Finally we settled on this little staircase that was hidden by some trees.
She had alot more than I had expected and we just kept passing it back and forth and then she'd refill it and we'd pass it some more.
when it was all gone we'd each had like 15 good hits.
this sucks
ow
but I didn't feel a thing.
then I stood up.
you're fucked up aren't you? well c'mon, we gotta go meet my mom.
Hungry FOR STINK
everything around me seemed really soft and hazy. it felt like there were invisible specks of light coating everything. when I pressed my foot into the ground I couldn't feel it.
I've been waiting for you for awhile Meg. where were you guys?
we were just looking around. don't worry mom.
hi. um, hi. hi.
I felt really dizzy and the only word I could think of to describe my body was "inverted".
L7- what an experience

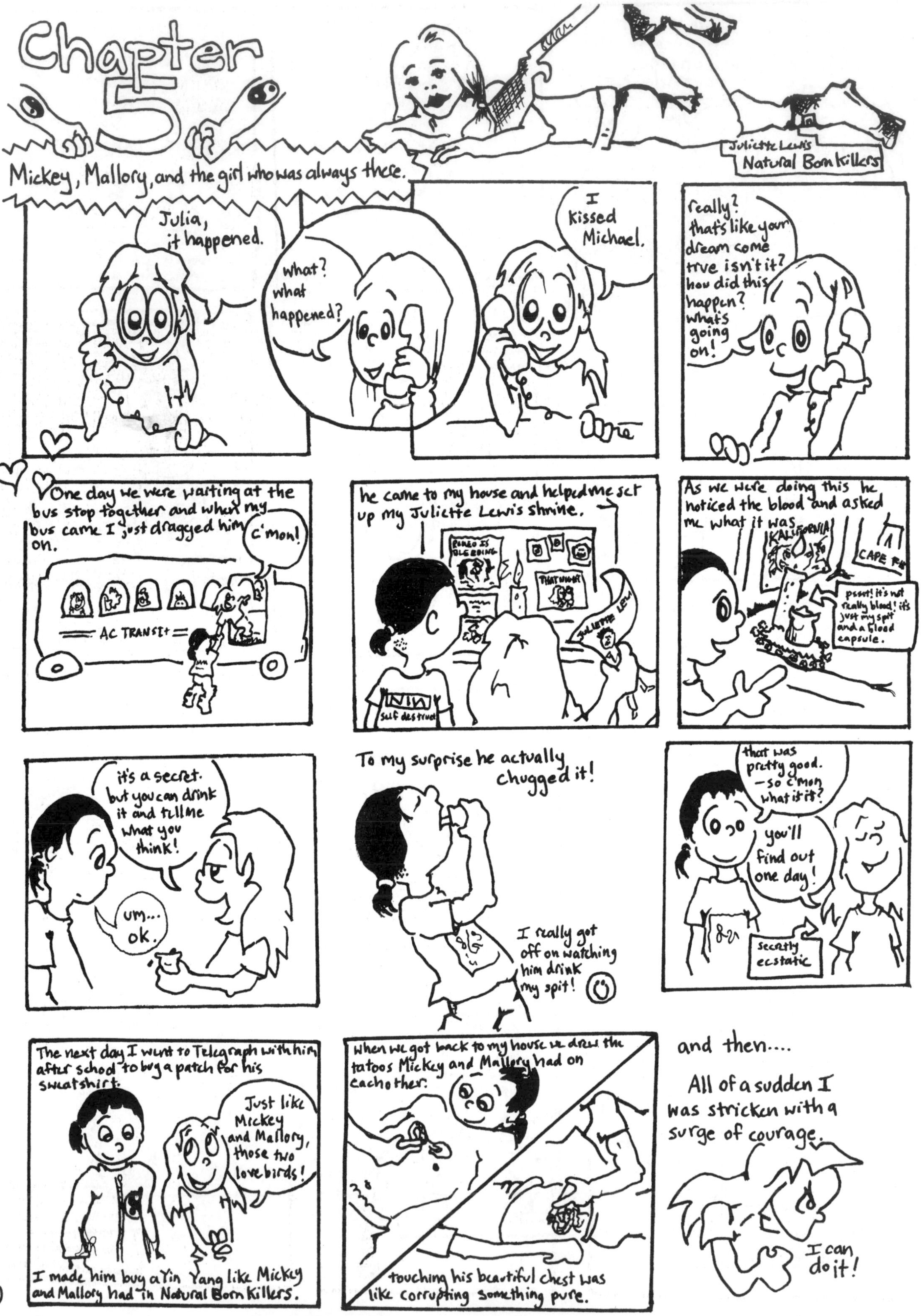

Chapter 5
Juliette Lewis
Natural Born Killers
Mickey, Mallory, and the girl who was always there.
Julia, it happened.
what? what happened?
I kissed Michael.
really? that's like your dream come true isn't it? how did this happen? what's going on!
One day we were waiting at the bus stop together and when my bus came I just dragged him on.
c'mon!
AC TRANSIT
he came to my house and helped me set up my Juliette Lewis shrine.
ROMEO IS BLEEDING
THAT NIGHT
JULIETTE LEWIS
NIN
self destruct
As we were doing this he noticed the blood and asked me what it was.
KALIFORNIA
psst! it's not really blood! it's just my spit and a blood capsule.
it's a secret. but you can drink it and tell me what you think!
um... ok.
To my surprise he actually chugged it!
I really got off on watching him drink my spit!
that was pretty good. —so c'mon what is it?
you'll find out one day!
secretly ecstatic
The next day I went to Telegraph with him after school to buy a patch for his sweatshirt.
Just like Mickey and Mallory, those two love birds!
I made him buy a Yin Yang like Mickey and Mallory had in Natural Born Killers.
When we got back to my house we drew the tatoos Mickey and Mallory had on each other.
touching his beautiful chest was like corrupting something pure.
and then....
All of a sudden I was stricken with a surge of courage.
I can do it!

'So what do you want me to do?'

Juliette Lewis line from Natural Born Killers.

oh, um, wait... I don't remember. what's next?

'Commone, what do you want me to do?'

something like 'squeeze my nipple and kiss me'?

right line!

'oh, you're so specific'

next line!

I HAVE NEVER BEEN SO HAPPY IN MY LIFE.

So from that day on I wrapped myself up in a world named Michael. and as it turned out he wasn't the only person living there.

there was also Margaret

One day she came to visit our art class.

I didn't know who she was but she kept staring at me.

I forgot how the conversation started but we ended up talking about what we were going to be when we grew up.

I'm going to be a stalker.

oh really? who are you going to stalk?

you.

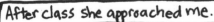

After class she approached me.

So I have to meet you.

um, ok.

you can cut 3rd night? let's go talk in the bathroom.

sure

you must think this is really weird. some strange junior girl you don't know saying she has to meet you.

oh, no I think it's really cool.

actually this was only half the truth. the other half was scared she was going to try to rape me in there.

⑬

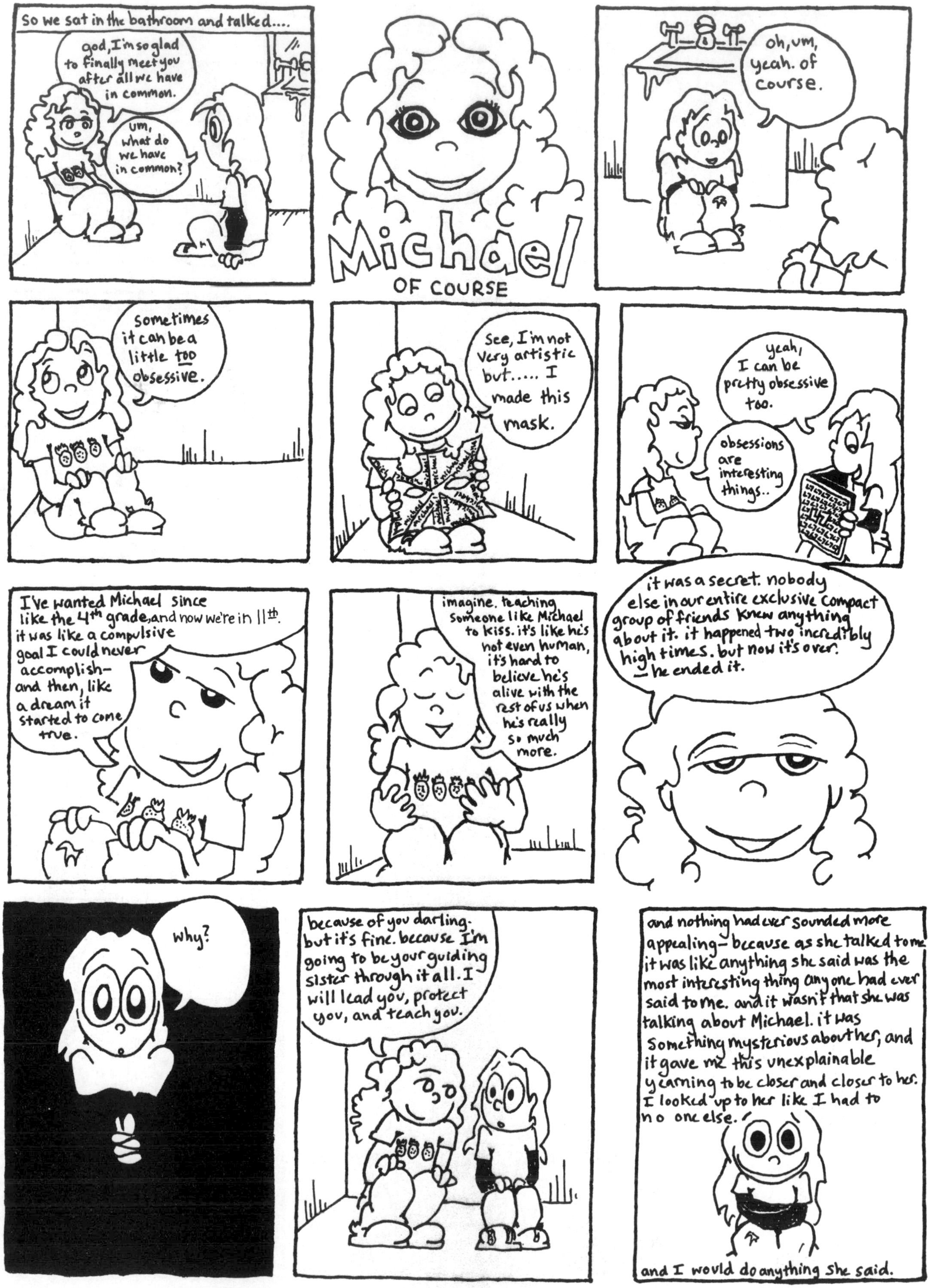

So we sat in the bathroom and talked....
god, I'm so glad to finally meet you after all we have in common.
um, what do we have in common?
Michael
OF COURSE
oh, um, yeah. of course.
Sometimes it can be a little too obsessive.
See, I'm not very artistic but..... I made this mask.
yeah, I can be pretty obsessive too.
obsessions are interesting things..
I've wanted Michael since like the 4th grade, and now we're in 11th. it was like a compulsive goal I could never accomplish- and then, like a dream it started to come true.
imagine. teaching someone like Michael to kiss. it's like he's not even human, it's hard to believe he's alive with the rest of us when he's really so much more.
it was a secret. nobody else in our entire exclusive compact group of friends knew anything about it. it happened two incredibly high times. but now it's over. —he ended it.
why?
because of you darling. but it's fine. because I'm going to be your guiding sister through it all. I will lead you, protect you, and teach you.
and nothing had ever sounded more appealing— because as she talked to me it was like anything she said was the most interesting thing anyone had ever said to me. and it wasn't that she was talking about Michael. it was something mysterious about her, and it gave me this unexplainable yearning to be closer and closer to her. I looked up to her like I had to no one else.
and I would do anything she said.

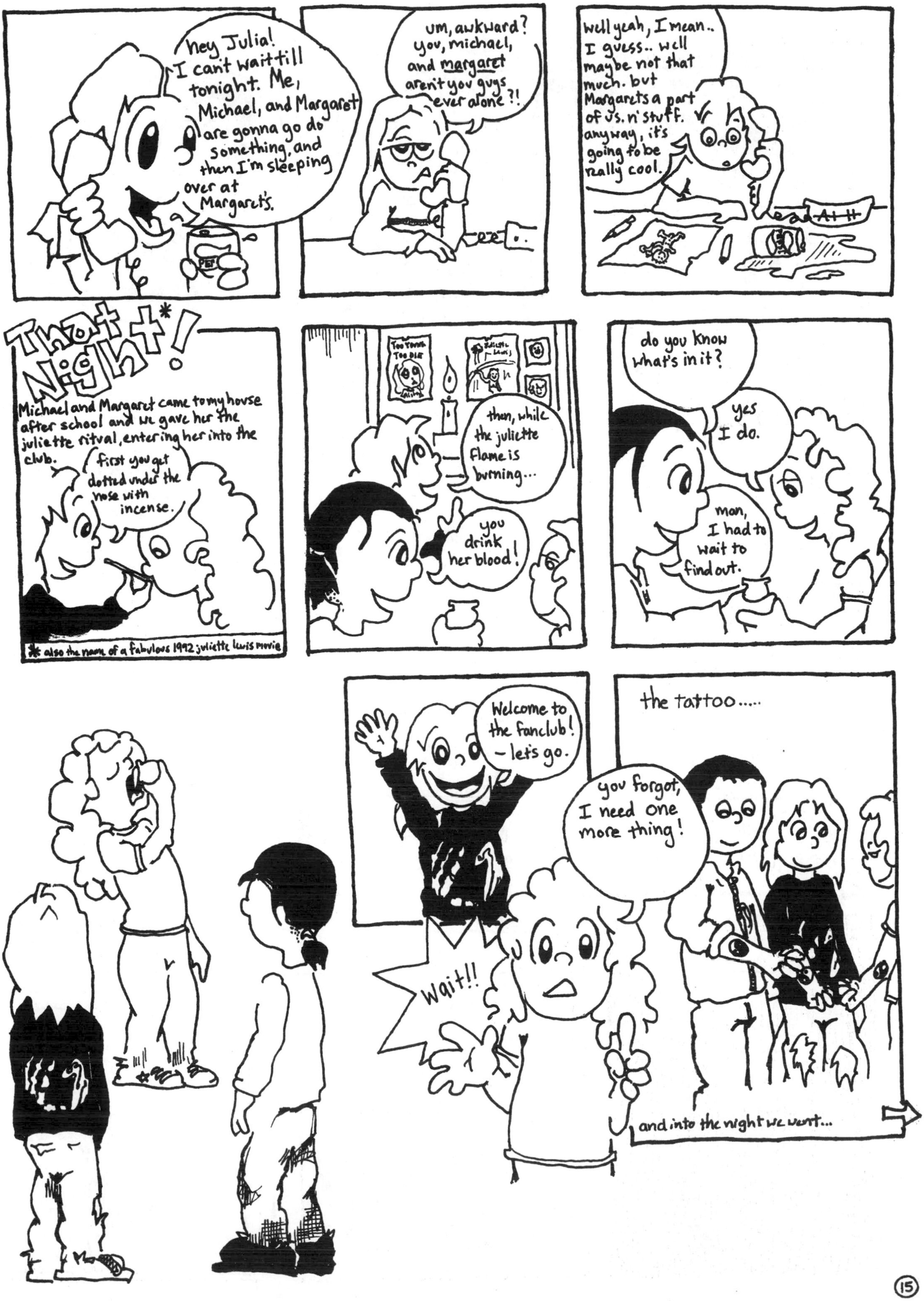
hey Julia! I cant wait till tonight. Me, Michael, and Margaret are gonna go do something, and then I'm sleeping over at Margaret's.
um, awkward? you, michael, and margaret aren't you guys ever alone?!
well yeah, I mean.. I guess.. well maybe not that much. but Margarets a part of us. n' stuff. anyway, it's going to be really cool.
That Night*!
Michael and Margaret came to my house after school and we gave her the juliette ritual, entering her into the club.
first you get dotted under the nose with incense.
* also the name of a fabulous 1992 juliette lewis movie
then, while the juliette flame is burning...
you drink her blood!
do you know what's in it?
yes I do.
man, I had to wait to find out.
Welcome to the fanclub! - let's go.
the tattoo.....
you forgot, I need one more thing!
wait!!
and into the night we went...

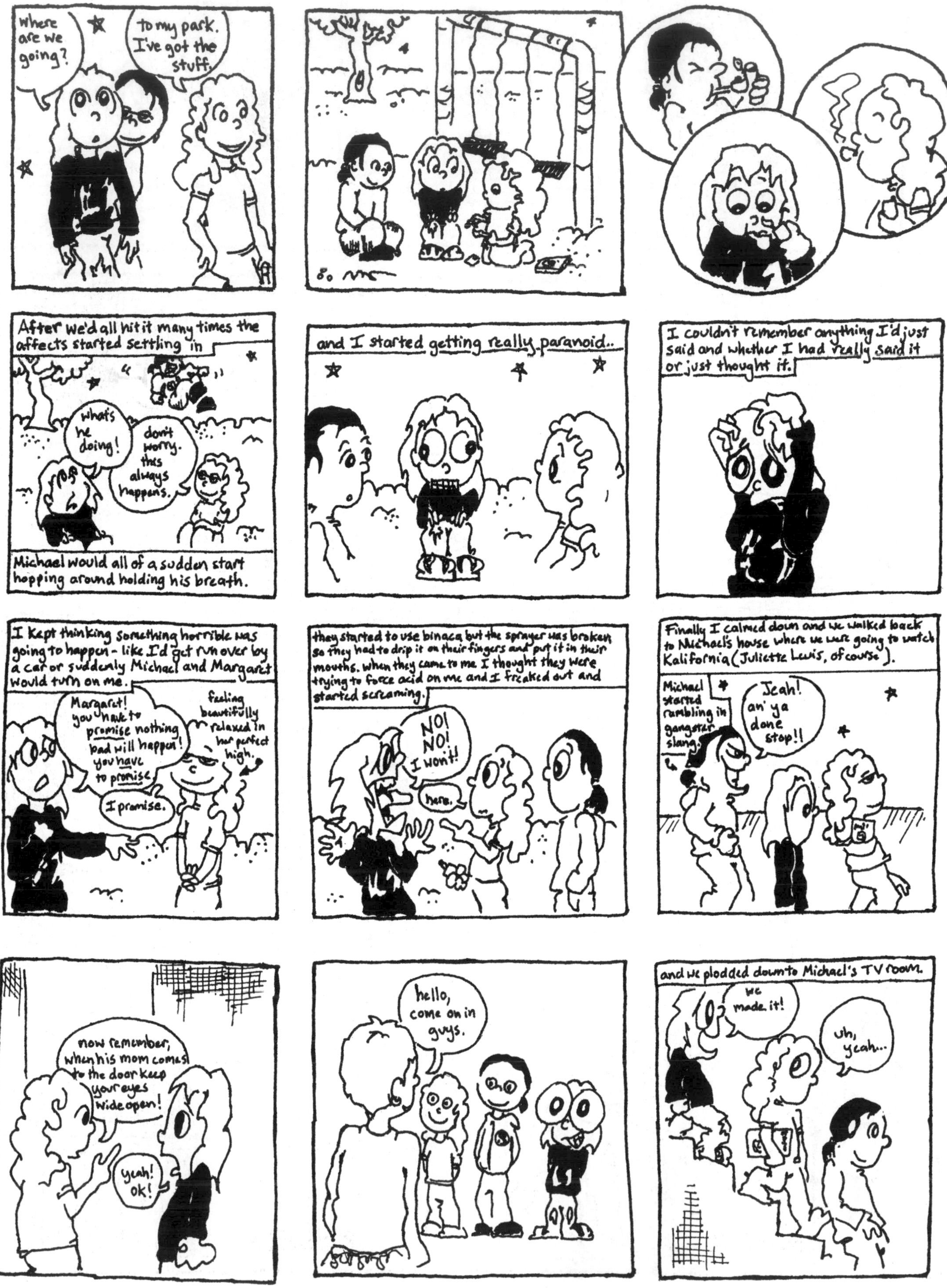
where are we going?
to my park. I've got the stuff.
After we'd all hit it many times the affects started settling in
what's he doing!
don't worry. this always happens.
Michael would all of a sudden start hopping around holding his breath.
and I started getting really paranoid..
I couldn't remember anything I'd just said and whether I had really said it or just thought it.
I kept thinking something horrible was going to happen - like I'd get run over by a car or suddenly Michael and Margaret would turn on me.
Margaret! you have to promise nothing bad will happen! you have to promise.
feeling beautifully relaxed in her perfect high.
I promise.
they started to use binaca but the sprayer was broken so they had to drip it on their fingers and put it in their mouths. when they came to me I thought they were trying to force acid on me and I freaked out and started screaming.
NO! NO! I won't!
here.
Finally I calmed down and we walked back to Michael's house where we were going to watch Kalifornia (Juliette Lewis, of course).
Michael started rambling in gangster slang.
Yeah! an' ya done stop!!
now remember, when his mom comes to the door keep your eyes wide open!
yeah! ok!
hello, come on in guys.
and we plodded down to Michael's TV room.
We made it!
uh, yeah...

For the beginning of the movie we all three sat on the couch....

but when Juliette Lewis came on it was obvious that wasn't going to work.

So Margaret moved down to the floor- and she did this so calmly, so maturely - I felt this painful love for her, so strong I wanted to cry.

I love you so much Margaret

oh, thank you.

and she sat there, making random comments on the movie, some of which I'd try to respond to, but other stuff was kinda going on...

y-yeah.

oh, that was cute what juliette said.

it was definitely the most intense night Michael and I ever had together.

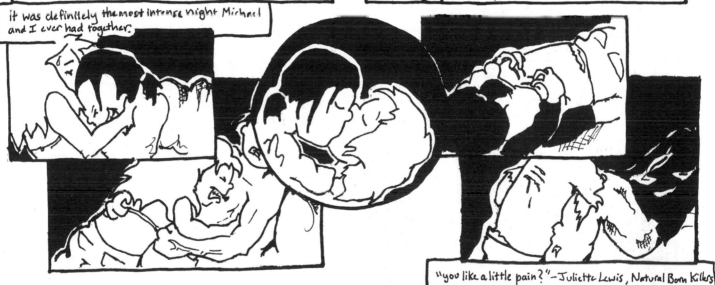

"you like a little pain?"- Juliette Lewis, Natural Born Killers

When the movie was over we all sorta got up and collected ourselves.

uh. yeah.

yeah, I really like it.

that was a really good movie.

Then some of the friends in Margaret and Michael's "group" called to say they were coming over.

Rick, Calvin, Tess, Angela, an' Rob are coming over.

great!

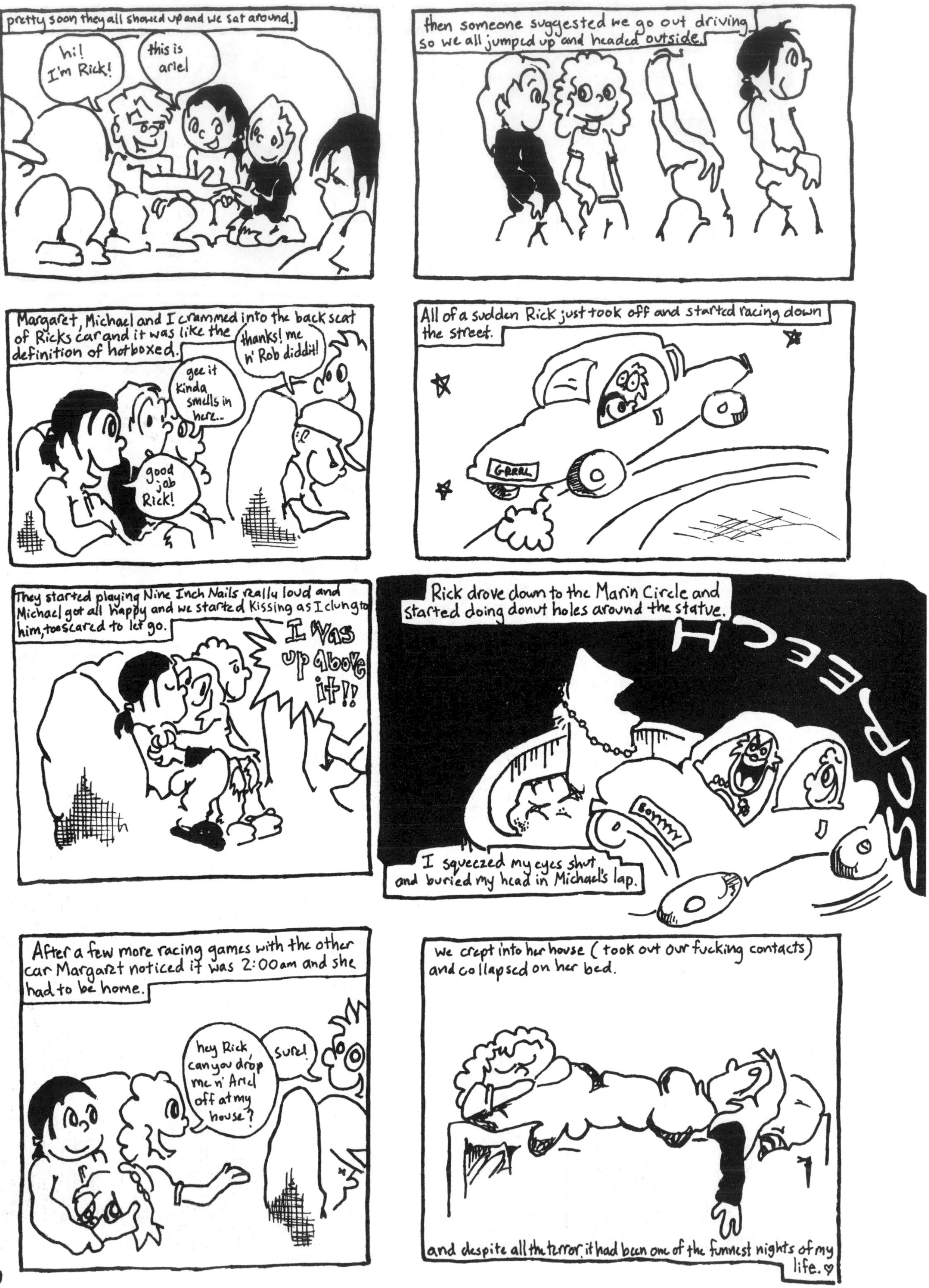

pretty soon they all showed up and we sat around.
hi! I'm Rick!
this is ariel
then someone suggested we go out driving so we all jumped up and headed outside.
Margaret, Michael and I crammed into the back seat of Ricks car and it was like the definition of hotboxed.
thanks! me n' Rob diddit!
gee it kinda smells in here..
good job Rick!
All of a sudden Rick just took off and started racing down the street.
GRRRL
They started playing Nine Inch Nails really loud and Michael got all happy and we started kissing as I clung to him, too scared to let go.
I was up above it!!
Rick drove down to the Marin Circle and started doing donut holes around the statue.
SCREECH
BOYYYY
I squeezed my eyes shut and buried my head in Michael's lap.
After a few more racing games with the other car Margaret noticed it was 2:00am and she had to be home.
hey Rick, can you drop me n' Ariel off at my house?
sure!
we crept into her house (took out our fucking contacts) and collapsed on her bed.
and despite all the terror, it had been one of the funnest nights of my life. ♡

Next Week

good! I need a fucking break

"rrring"

999

GEOMETRY

hi! so, like, what's happening? how's michael?

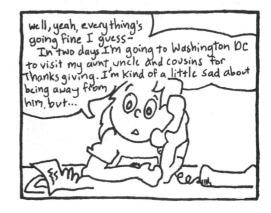

well, yeah, everything's going fine I guess— In two days I'm going to Washington DC to visit my aunt, uncle and cousins for Thanksgiving. I'm kind of a little sad about being away from him, but...

Oh, it's only a week! I wouldn't worry about it!

yeah, and I am looking forward to seeing my cousins Sam and Sarah. I'll just have a nice good-bye with him tomorrow.

sure, it's no big deal.

the next day at school.

Ariel, I don't really wanna go to ballet today. Can you do something after school?

Well, Michael's coming over but... but you can come too.

Elisabeth♡

I just couldn't say no to her sweet eager face.

yea! it's break!!

Woo hoo hurrah.

Elisabeth's coming too.

fine.

So it was pretty awkward. Elisabeth sat on the floor and painted in her sketchbook while Michael and I lay on the bed.

STARTS FRIDAY BRAD PITT JULIETTE

he didn't seem too happy.

When she left things got a little better, and he gave me something on my neck to remember him by.

I gave him one right above his nipple.

When we got outside we acted out one last Juliette movie scene.

hey now!

It was from "That Night" where she kisses this guy for the first time.

and that was good-bye.

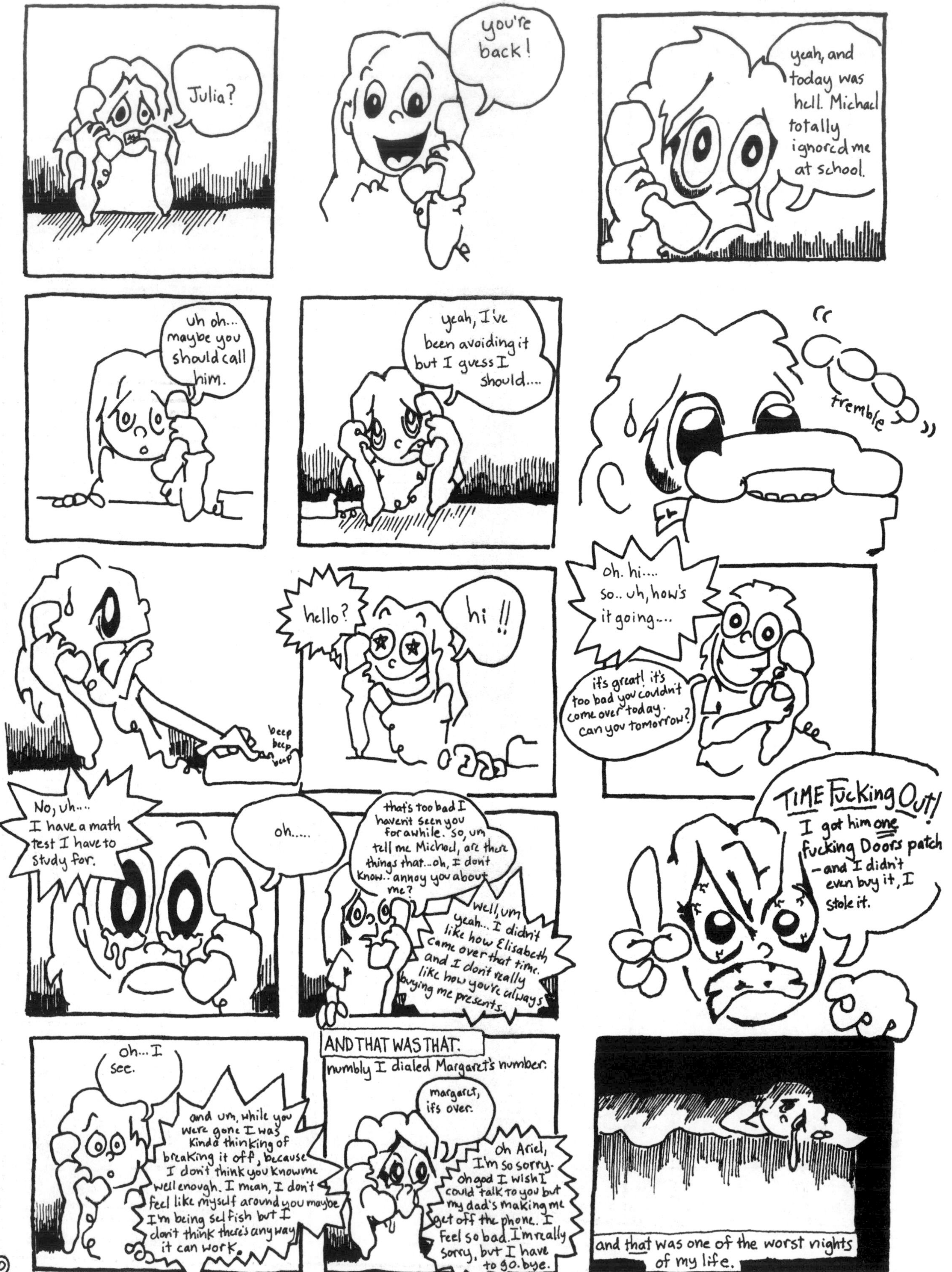

Julia?
you're back!
yeah, and today was hell. Michael totally ignored me at school.
uh oh... maybe you should call him.
yeah, I've been avoiding it but I guess I should....
tremble
beep beep beep
hello?
hi !!
oh. hi.... so.. uh, how's it going....
it's great! it's too bad you couldn't come over today. can you tomorrow?
No, uh.... I have a math test I have to study for.
oh.....
that's too bad I haven't seen you for awhile. so, um tell me Michael, are there things that...oh, I don't know.. annoy you about me?
well, um yeah... I didn't like how Elisabeth came over that time. and I don't really like how you're always buying me presents.
TIME Fucking Out! I got him one fucking Doors patch - and I didn't even buy it, I stole it.
oh... I see.
and um, while you were gone I was kinda thinking of breaking it off, because I don't think you know me well enough. I mean, I don't feel like myself around you maybe I'm being selfish but I don't think there's any way it can work.
AND THAT WAS THAT.
numbly I dialed Margaret's number.
margaret, it's over.
Oh Ariel, I'm so sorry. oh god I wish I could talk to you but my dad's making me get off the phone. I feel so bad. I'm really sorry, but I have to go. bye.
and that was one of the worst nights of my life.

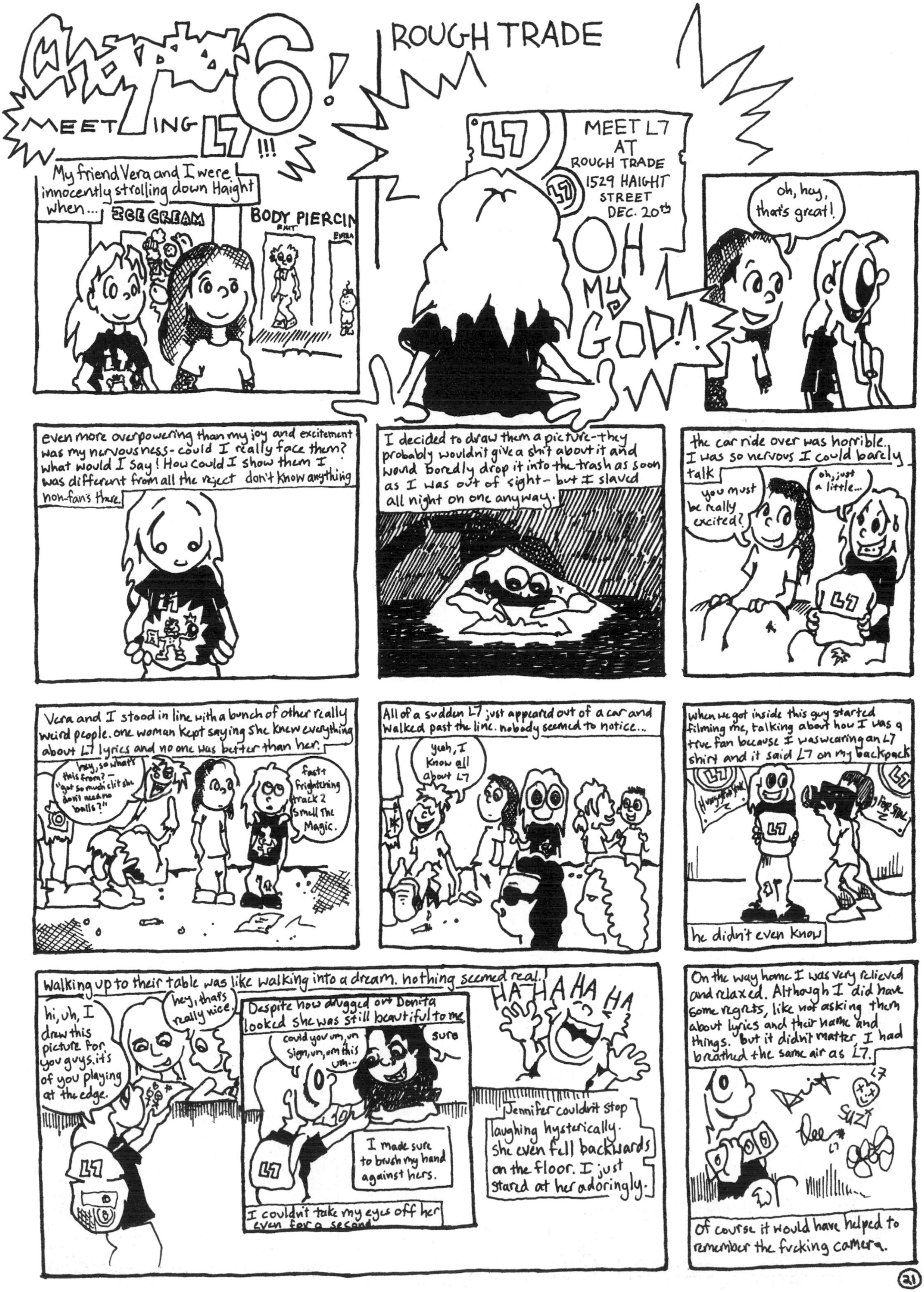
Chapter 6! MEETING L7 !!!
ROUGH TRADE
My friend Vera and I were innocently strolling down Haight when...
ICE CREAM
BODY PIERCIN
MEET L7 AT ROUGH TRADE 1529 HAIGHT STREET DEC. 20th
OH MY GOD!
oh, hey, that's great!
even more overpowering than my joy and excitement was my nervousness- could I really face them? what would I say! How could I show them I was different from all the reject don't know anything non-fan's there.
I decided to draw them a picture-they probably wouldn't give a shit about it and would boredly drop it into the trash as soon as I was out of sight- but I slaved all night on one anyway.
the car ride over was horrible. I was so nervous I could barely talk
you must be really excited?
oh, just a little...
Vera and I stood in line with a bunch of other really weird people. one woman kept saying she knew everything about L7 lyrics and no one was better than her.
hey, so what's this from? — "got so much clit she don't need no balls?"
fast+ frightening track 2 Smell The Magic.
All of a sudden L7 just appeared out of a car and walked past the line. nobody seemed to notice...
yeah, I know all about L7
when we got inside this guy started filming me, talking about how I was a true fan because I was wearing an L7 shirt and it said L7 on my backpack
he didn't even know
walking up to their table was like walking into a dream. nothing seemed real.
hi, uh, I drew this picture for you guys. it's of you playing at the edge.
hey, that's really nice.
Despite how drugged out Donita looked she was still beautiful to me.
could you um, un sign, un, um this um...
sure
I made sure to brush my hand against hers.
I couldn't take my eyes off her even for a second.
HA HA HA HA HA
Jennifer couldn't stop laughing hysterically. she even fell backwards on the floor. I just stared at her adoringly.
On the way home I was very relieved and relaxed. Although I did have some regrets, like not asking them about lyrics and their name and things. But it didn't matter. I had breathed the same air as L7.
Of course it would have helped to remember the fucking camera.

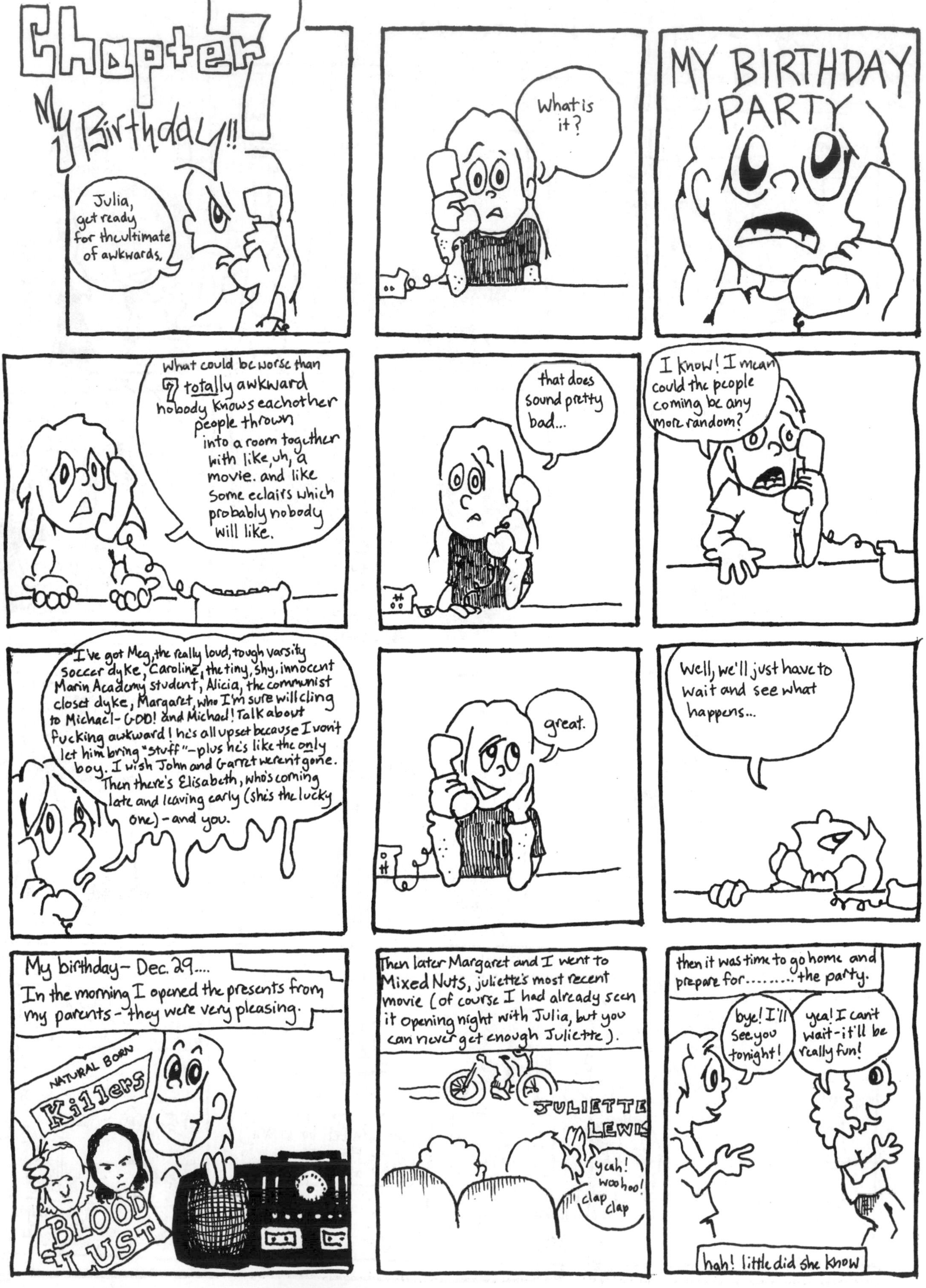

Chapter 7
My Birthday!!
Julia, get ready for the ultimate of awkwards.
What is it?
MY BIRTHDAY PARTY
What could be worse than 7 totally awkward nobody knows eachother people thrown into a room together with like, uh, a movie. and like some eclairs which probably nobody will like.
that does sound pretty bad...
I know! I mean could the people coming be any more random?
I've got Meg, the really loud, tough varsity soccer dyke, Caroline, the tiny, shy, innocent Marin Academy student, Alicia, the communist closet dyke, Margaret, who I'm sure will cling to Michael- GOD! and Michael! Talk about fucking awkward! he's all upset because I won't let him bring "stuff"- plus he's like the only boy. I wish John and Garret weren't gone. Then there's Elisabeth, who's coming late and leaving early (she's the lucky one) - and you.
great.
Well, we'll just have to wait and see what happens...
My birthday- Dec. 29.... In the morning I opened the presents from my parents - they were very pleasing.
NATURAL BORN Killers
BLOOD LUST
Then later Margaret and I went to Mixed Nuts, juliette's most recent movie (of course I had already seen it opening night with Julia, but you can never get enough Juliette).
JULIETTE LEWIS
yeah! woohoo! clap clap
then it was time to go home and prepare for......... the party.
bye! I'll see you tonight!
yea! I can't wait - it'll be really fun!
hah! little did she know

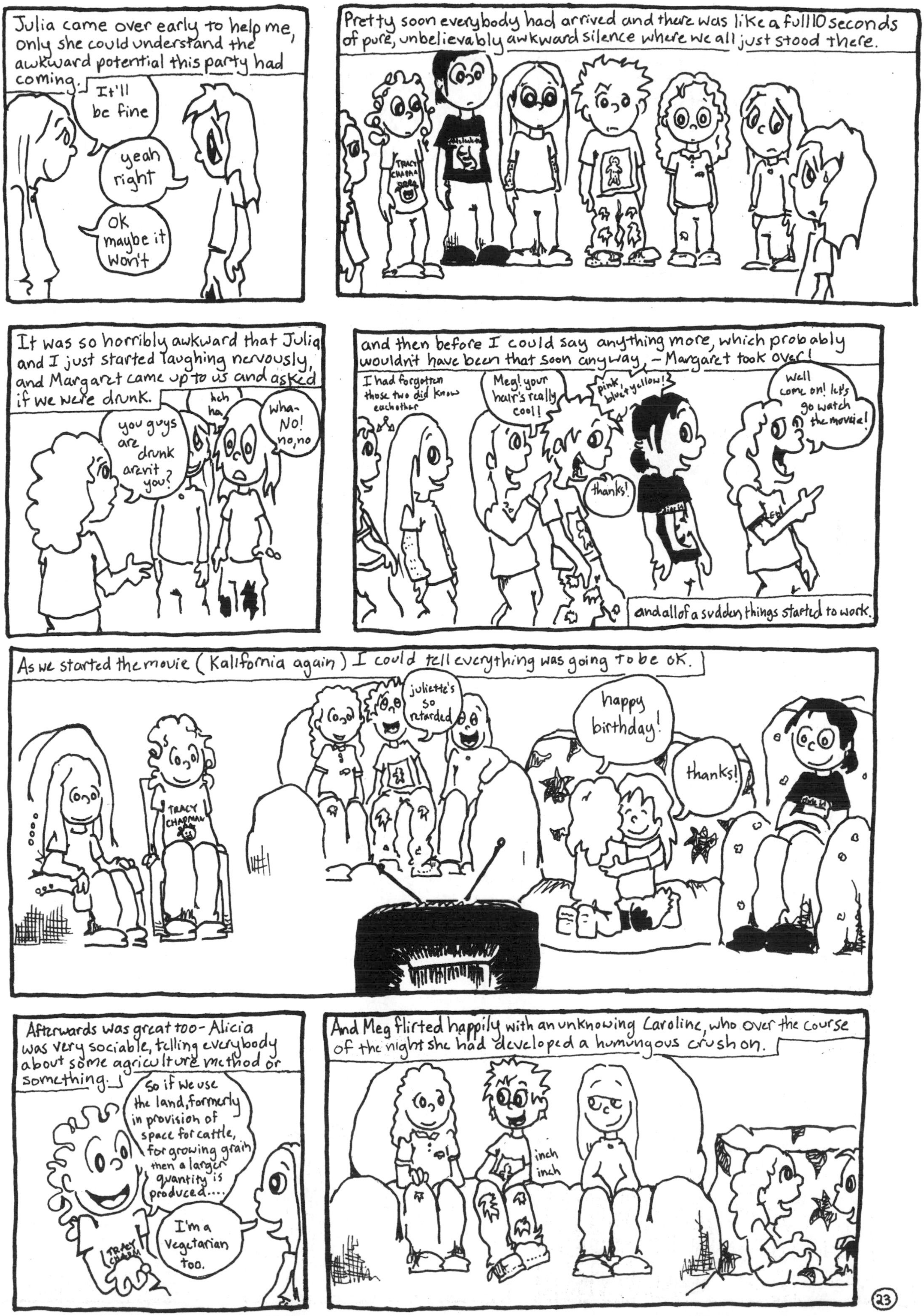

Julia came over early to help me, only she could understand the awkward potential this party had coming.
It'll be fine
yeah right
OK maybe it won't
Pretty soon everybody had arrived and there was like a full 10 seconds of pure, unbelievably awkward silence where we all just stood there.
TRACY CHAPMAN
It was so horribly awkward that Julia and I just started laughing nervously, and Margaret came up to us and asked if we were drunk.
you guys are drunk aren't you?
heh ha
wha- No! no, no
and then before I could say anything more, which probably wouldn't have been that soon anyway, - Margaret took over!
I had forgotten those two did know each other
Meg! your hair's really cool!
pink, blue, yellow!
thanks!
well come on! let's go watch the movie!
and all of a sudden things started to work.
As we started the movie (Kalifornia again) I could tell everything was going to be OK.
juliette's so retarded
happy birthday!
thanks!
TRACY CHAPMAN
Afterwards was great too- Alicia was very sociable, telling everybody about some agriculture method or something.
So if we use the land, formerly in provision of space for cattle, for growing grain then a larger quantity is produced....
I'm a vegetarian too.
TRACY CHAPM
And Meg flirted happily with an unknowing Caroline, who over the course of the night she had developed a humungous crush on.
inch inch

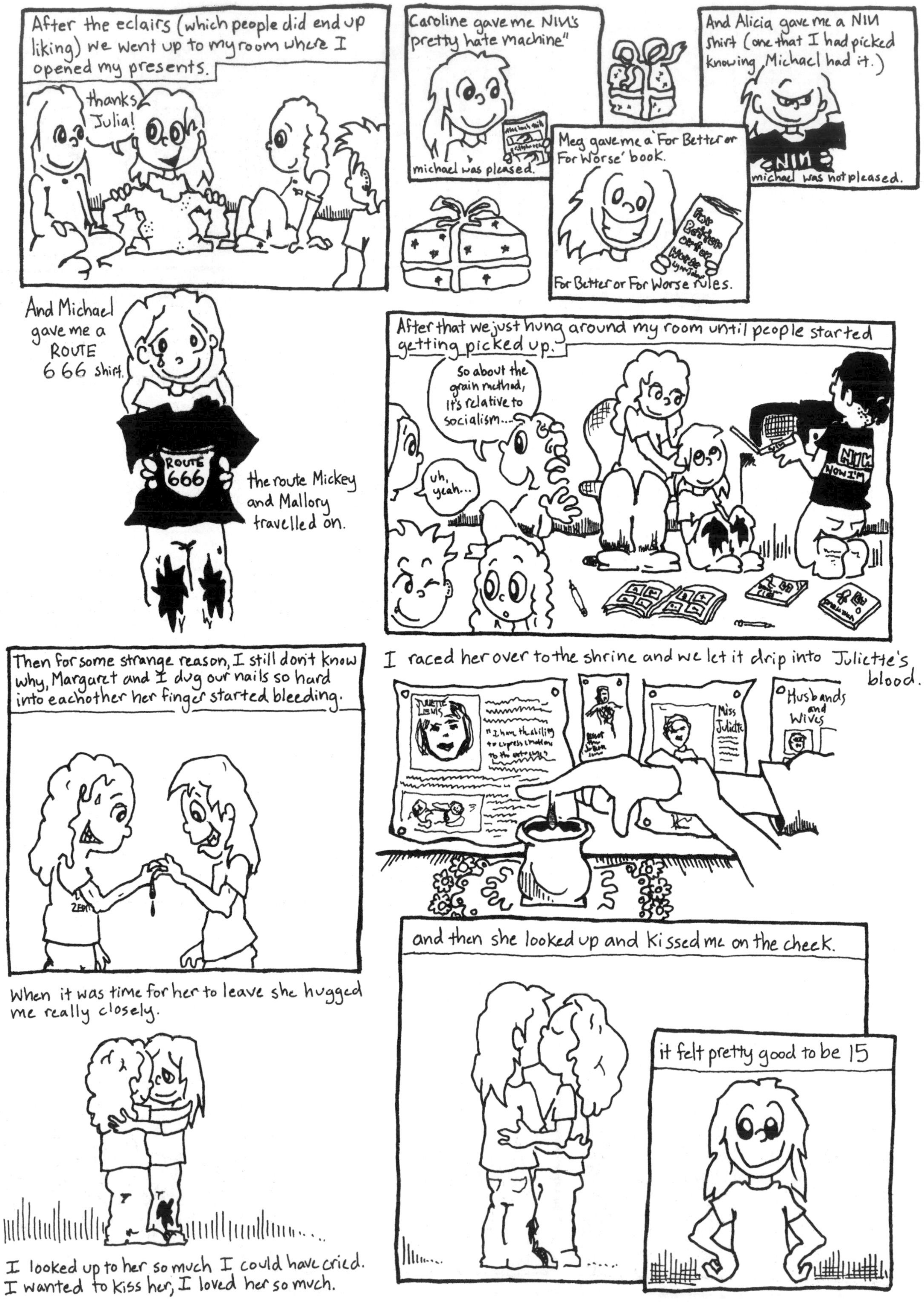

After the eclairs (which people did end up liking) we went up to my room where I opened my presents.
thanks Julia!
Caroline gave me NIN's pretty hate machine"
michael was pleased.
Meg gave me a 'For Better or For Worse' book.
For Better or For Worse
For Better or For Worse rules.
And Alicia gave me a NIN shirt (one that I had picked knowing Michael had it.)
NIN
michael was not pleased.
And Michael gave me a ROUTE 666 shirt.
ROUTE 666
the route Mickey and Mallory travelled on.
After that we just hung around my room until people started getting picked up.
So about the grain method, It's relative to socialism....
uh, yeah...
NIN NOW I'M
Then for some strange reason, I still don't know why, Margaret and I dug our nails so hard into eachother her finger started bleeding.
I raced her over to the shrine and we let it drip into Juliette's blood.
JULIETTE LEWIS
"I have the ability to express emotion to the extreme"
Miss Juliette
Husbands and Wives
When it was time for her to leave she hugged me really closely.
I looked up to her so much I could have cried. I wanted to kiss her, I loved her so much.
and then she looked up and kissed me on the cheek.
it felt pretty good to be 15

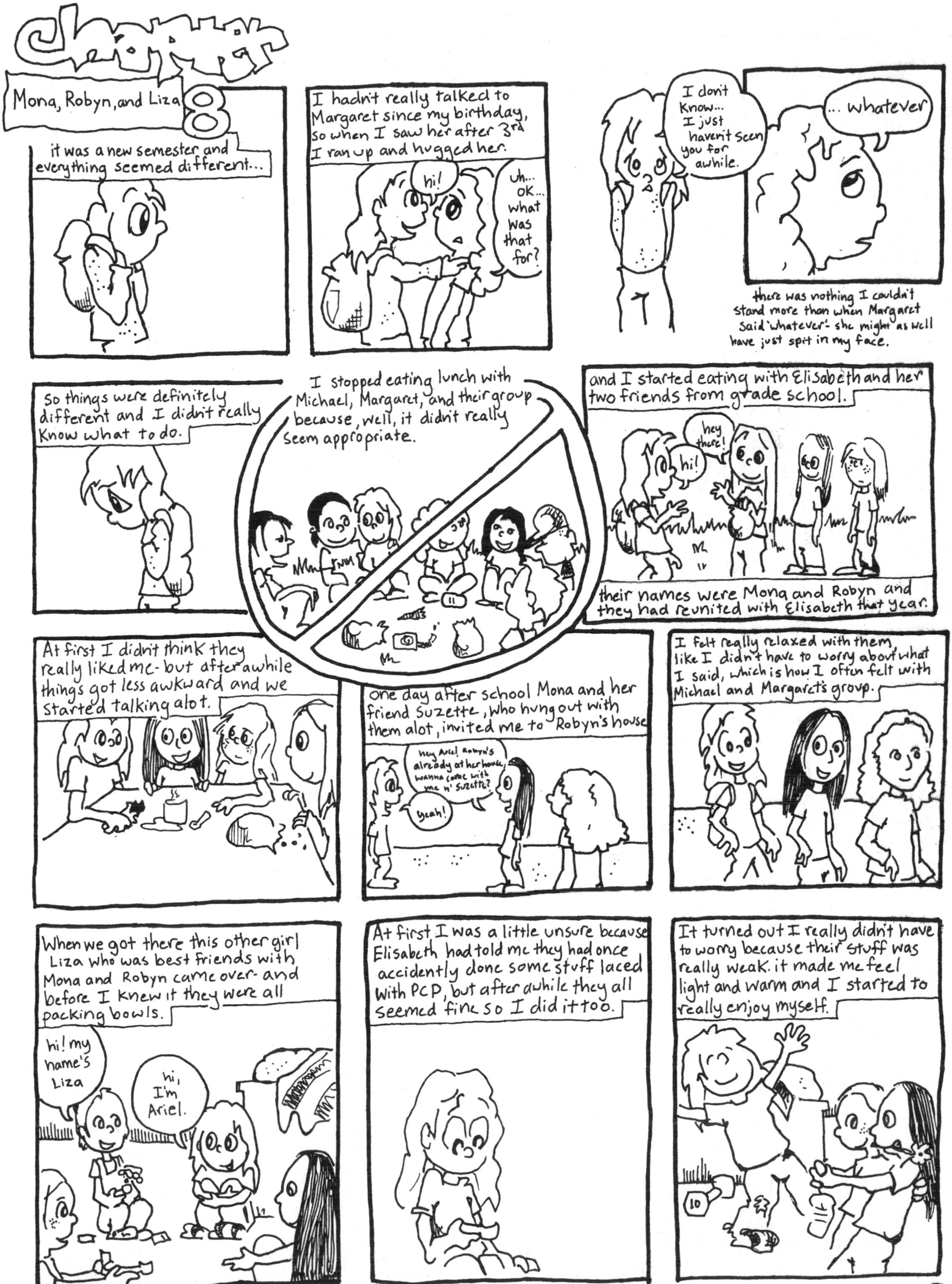
chapter
Mona, Robyn, and Liza
8
it was a new semester and everything seemed different...
I hadn't really talked to Margaret since my birthday, so when I saw her after 3rd I ran up and hugged her.
hi!
uh... OK... what was that for?
I don't know... I just haven't seen you for awhile.
... whatever
there was nothing I couldn't stand more than when Margaret said 'whatever'- she might as well have just spit in my face.
So things were definitely different and I didn't really know what to do.
I stopped eating lunch with Michael, Margaret, and their group because, well, it didn't really seem appropriate.
and I started eating with Elisabeth and her two friends from grade school.
hey there!
hi!
their names were Mona and Robyn and they had reunited with Elisabeth that year.
At first I didn't think they really liked me- but after awhile things got less awkward and we started talking alot.
one day after school Mona and her friend Suzette, who hung out with them alot, invited me to Robyn's house
hey Ariel! Robyn's already at her house, wanna come with me n' Suzette?
yeah!
I felt really relaxed with them, like I didn't have to worry about what I said, which is how I often felt with Michael and Margaret's group.
When we got there this other girl Liza who was best friends with Mona and Robyn came over- and before I knew it they were all packing bowls.
hi! my name's Liza
hi, I'm Ariel.
At first I was a little unsure because Elisabeth had told me they had once accidently done some stuff laced with PCP, but after awhile they all seemed fine so I did it too.
It turned out I really didn't have to worry because their stuff was really weak. it made me feel light and warm and I started to really enjoy myself.

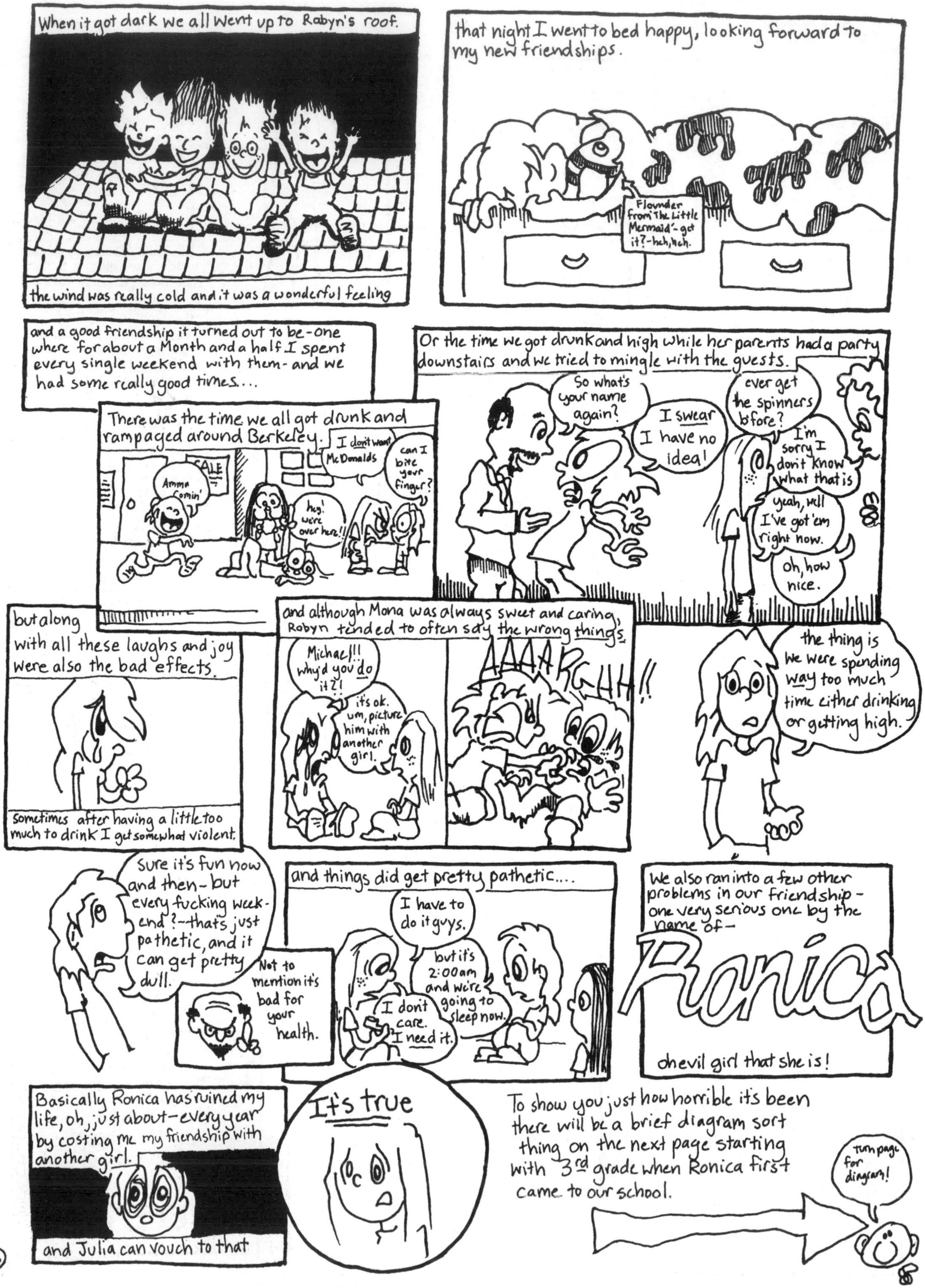

When it got dark we all went up to Robyn's roof.
the wind was really cold and it was a wonderful feeling
that night I went to bed happy, looking forward to my new friendships.
Flounder from The Little Mermaid'- get it?-heh, heh.
and a good friendship it turned out to be- one where for about a Month and a half I spent every single weekend with them- and we had some really good times...
There was the time we all got drunk and rampaged around Berkeley.
I don't want McDonalds
can I bite your finger?
SALE
Amma comin'
hey! we're over here!!
Or the time we got drunk and high while her parents had a party downstairs and we tried to mingle with the guests.
So what's your name again?
I swear I have no idea!
ever get the spinners b'fore?
I'm sorry I don't know what that is
yeah, well I've got 'em right now.
oh, how nice.
but along with all these laughs and joy were also the bad effects.
sometimes after having a little too much to drink I get somewhat violent.
and although Mona was always sweet and caring, Robyn tended to often say the wrong things,
Michael!! why'd you do it?!
it's ok. um, picture him with another girl.
AAAARGHH!!
the thing is we were spending way too much time either drinking or getting high.
Sure it's fun now and then- but every fucking week-end?- that's just pathetic, and it can get pretty dull.
Not to mention it's bad for your health.
and things did get pretty pathetic....
I have to do it guys.
but it's 2:00am and we're going to sleep now.
I don't care. I need it.
We also ran into a few other problems in our friendship- one very serious one by the name of-
Ronica
oh evil girl that she is!
Basically Ronica has ruined my life, oh, just about- every year by costing me my friendship with another girl.
and Julia can vouch to that
It's true
To show you just how horrible it's been there will be a brief diagram sort thing on the next page starting with 3rd grade when Ronica first came to our school.
Turn page for diagram!

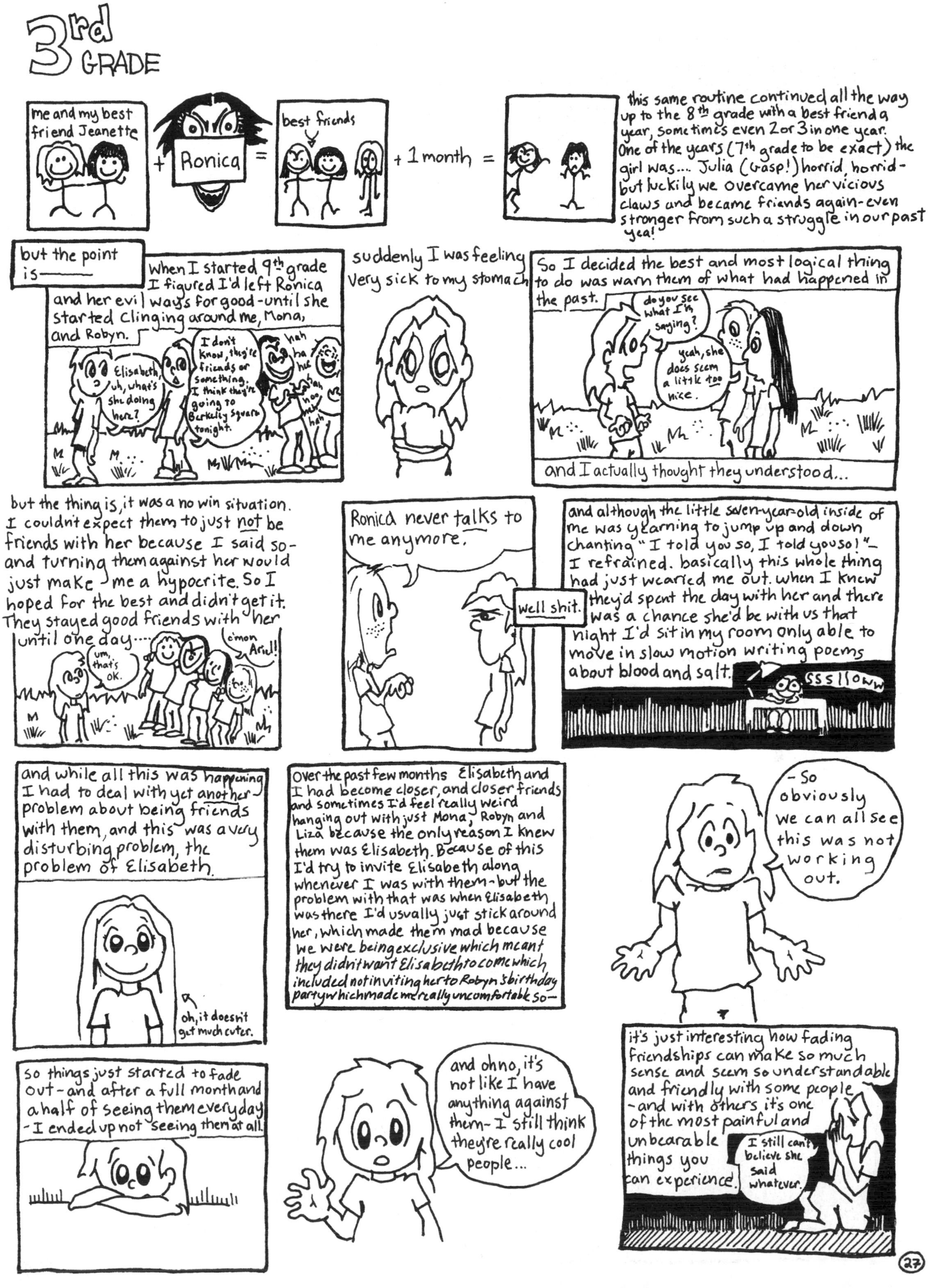

3rd GRADE
me and my best friend Jeanette
Ronica
best friends
+ 1 month =
this same routine continued all the way up to the 8th grade with a best friend a year, sometimes even 2 or 3 in one year. One of the years (7th grade to be exact) the girl was.... Julia (Gasp!) horrid, horrid - but luckily we overcame her vicious claws and became friends again - even stronger from such a struggle in our past year!
but the point is———
When I started 9th grade I figured I'd left Ronica and her evil ways for good - until she started clinging around me, Mona, and Robyn.
Elisabeth, uh, what's she doing here?
I don't know, they're friends or something. I think they're going to Berkeley Square tonight.
suddenly I was feeling very sick to my stomach
So I decided the best and most logical thing to do was warn them of what had happened in the past.
do you see what I'm saying?
yeah, she does seem a little too nice.
and I actually thought they understood...
but the thing is, it was a no win situation. I couldn't expect them to just not be friends with her because I said so - and turning them against her would just make me a hypocrite. So I hoped for the best and didn't get it. They stayed good friends with her until one day....
um, that's OK.
c'mon Ariel!
Ronica never talks to me anymore.
well shit.
and although the little seven-year-old inside of me was yearning to jump up and down chanting "I told you so, I told you so!" - I refrained. basically this whole thing had just wearied me out. when I knew they'd spent the day with her and there was a chance she'd be with us that night I'd sit in my room only able to move in slow motion writing poems about blood and salt.
ssslloww
and while all this was happening I had to deal with yet another problem about being friends with them, and this was a very disturbing problem, the problem of Elisabeth.
oh, it doesn't get much cuter.
Over the past few months Elisabeth and I had become closer, and closer friends and sometimes I'd feel really weird hanging out with just Mona, Robyn and Liza because the only reason I knew them was Elisabeth. Because of this I'd try to invite Elisabeth along whenever I was with them - but the problem with that was when Elisabeth was there I'd usually just stick around her, which made them mad because we were being exclusive which meant they didn't want Elisabeth to come which included not inviting her to Robyn's birthday party which made me really uncomfortable so-
- So obviously we can all see this was not working out.
so things just started to fade out - and after a full month and a half of seeing them everyday - I ended up not seeing them at all.
and oh no, it's not like I have anything against them - I still think they're really cool people...
it's just interesting how fading friendships can make so much sense and seem so understandable and friendly with some people - and with others it's one of the most painful and unbearable things you can experience.
I still can't believe she said whatever.

chapter 4

Eventually, due to Meg and me talking too much, I was moved to the back of the math class.

I hated it back there because I wasn't even part of the group next to me. I had my own little desk pushed off to the side - plus there was this weird annoying short sophomore guy who wouldn't quit talking to me.

His name was Mavis and like me he was shoved to the back of class for talking - and while at first he was loud and obnoxious after awhile I just couldn't help laughing at his jokes and I started talking to him even more than I had to Meg.

that song drives me INSANE! I'm going to their fucking concert- bringing a gun and when he comes on I'll blow his fucking HEAD OFF!!! there's your BANG BANG!!!

you bang bang bang bang bang bang bang blam!!

ALICE IN

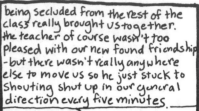

being secluded from the rest of the class really brought us together. the teacher of course wasn't too pleased with our new found friendship - but there wasn't really anywhere else to move us so he just stuck to shouting shut up in our general direction every five minutes.

WOW!! so you're an artist! that's really cool!!

thanks!

he was really enthusiastic about everything. it was exhausting but I loved it.

So what are you doing this weekend?

Well tonight Elisabeth and I are going to watch a movie.

Cool! I'm probably doing something with my friend Zach- he likes to get really drunk so I just watch him pass out.

uh cool....

yeah, so it sounds ok but I also kinda wanna watch this movie with you guys

yeah, that would be good, I'll talk to Elisabeth about it.

So Elisabeth, is it ok if this Mavis guy comes tonight.

isn't he that juggler?

yeah! isn't he cute!

sure.

So does he like you or something?

I don't know maybe, yeah I think maybe.

Well, do you like him?

I don't know!!! I don't know... I mean, this is really stupid- but I still can't get over Michael.

Michael's retarded.

I know, I know...

later that evening...

he's here!

Ding! Dong!

um, I'm Elisabeth.

We're going to watch Kalifornia!

hey! I'm Mavis!! cool! I've never seen that!

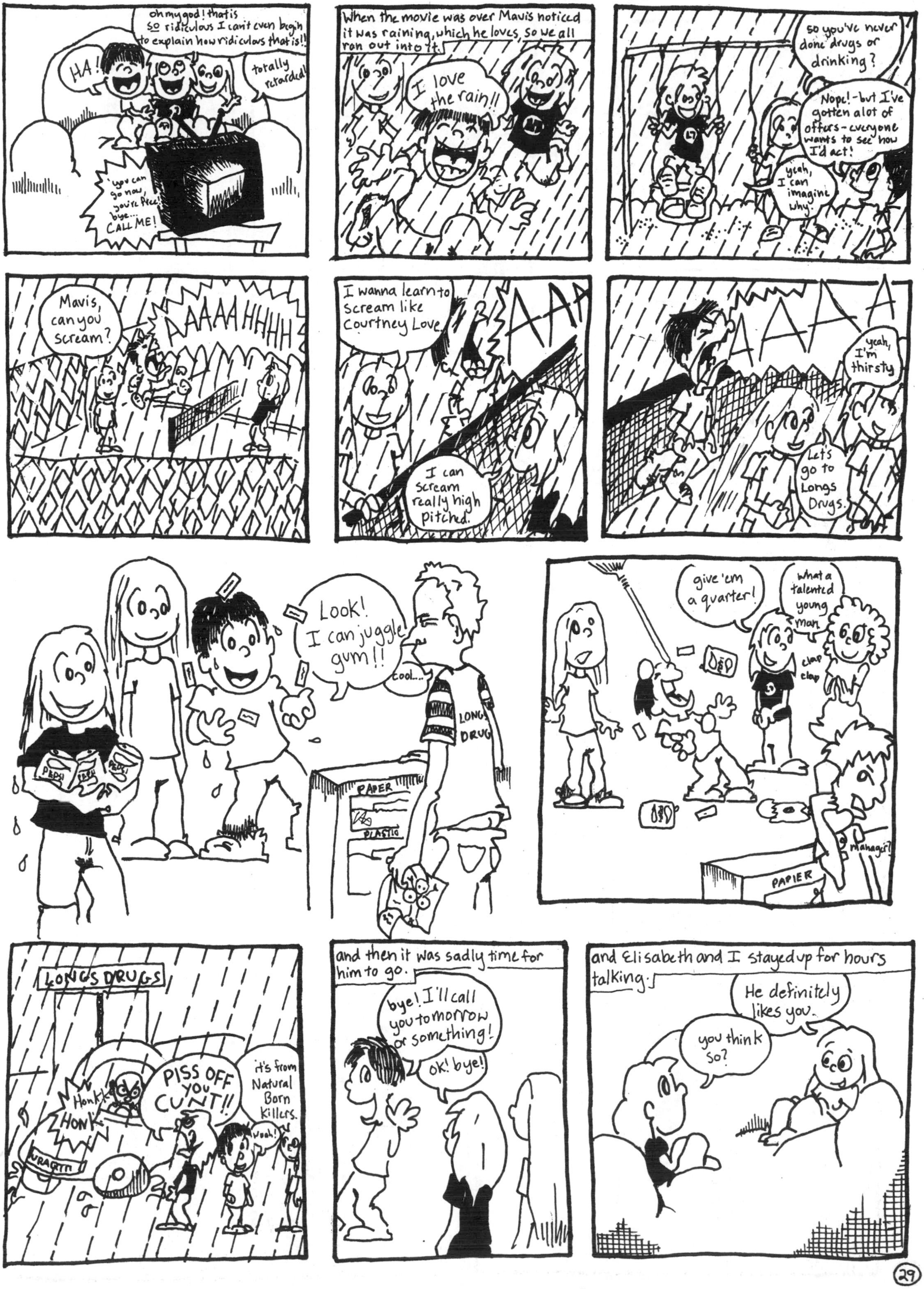
oh my god! that is SO ridiculous I can't even begin to explain how ridiculous that is!!
HA!
totally retarded!
"you can go now, you're free! bye... CALL ME!
When the movie was over Mavis noticed it was raining, which he loves, so we all ran out into it.
I love the rain!!
so you've never done drugs or drinking?
Nope!-but I've gotten alot of offers-everyone wants to see how I'd act!
yeah, I can imagine why.
Mavis, can you scream?
AAAAAHHHH
I wanna learn to scream like Courtney Love.
AAA
I can scream really high pitched.
AAAA
yeah, I'm thirsty
Let's go to Longs Drugs.
Look! I can juggle gum!!
cool...
PEPSI
LONGS DRUG
PAPER
PLASTIC
give 'em a quarter!
what a talented young man
clap clap
PAPIER
manager
LONGS DRUGS
HONK HONK
PISS OFF YOU CUNT!!
it's from Natural Born Killers.
woah!
and then it was sadly time for him to go.
bye! I'll call you tomorrow or something!
ok! bye!
and Elisabeth and I stayed up for hours talking.
He definitely likes you.
you think so?

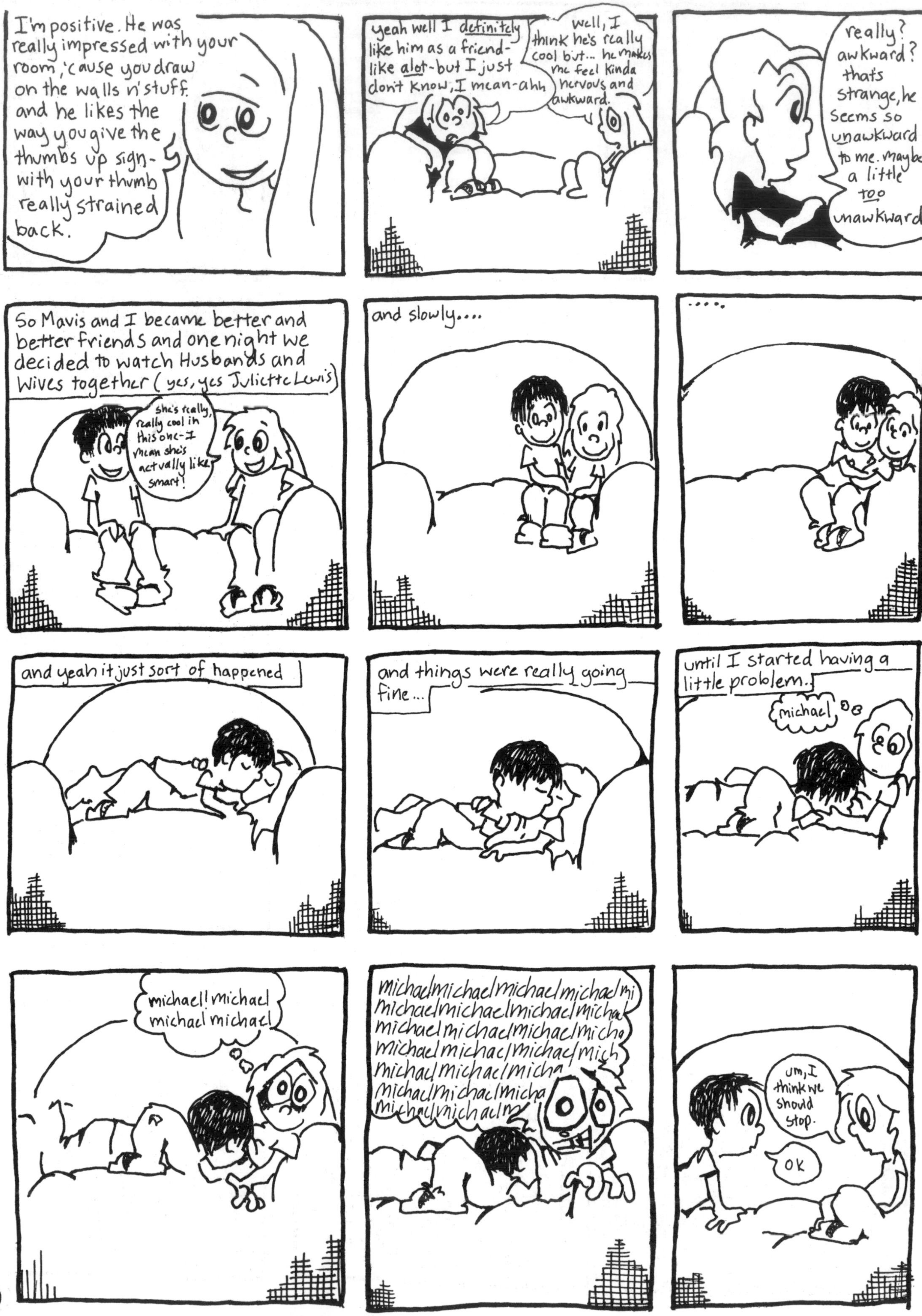
I'm positive. He was really impressed with your room, 'cause you draw on the walls n' stuff. and he likes the way you give the thumbs up sign- with your thumb really strained back.
yeah well I definitely like him as a friend- like alot- but I just don't know, I mean-ahh
well, I think he's really cool but... he makes me feel kinda nervous and awkward.
really? awkward? thats strange, he seems so unawkward to me. maybe a little too unawkward.
So Mavis and I became better and better friends and one night we decided to watch Husbands and Wives together (yes, yes Juliette Lewis)
she's really, really cool in this one- I mean she's actually like smart!
and slowly....
....
and yeah it just sort of happened
and things were really going fine...
until I started having a little problem.
michael
michael! michael michael michael
michaelmichaelmichaelmichaelmi michaelmichaelmichaelmichael michaelmichaelmichaelmicha michaelmichaelmichaelmich michaelmichaelmicha michaelmichaelmicha michaelmichaelm
um, I think we should stop.
ok

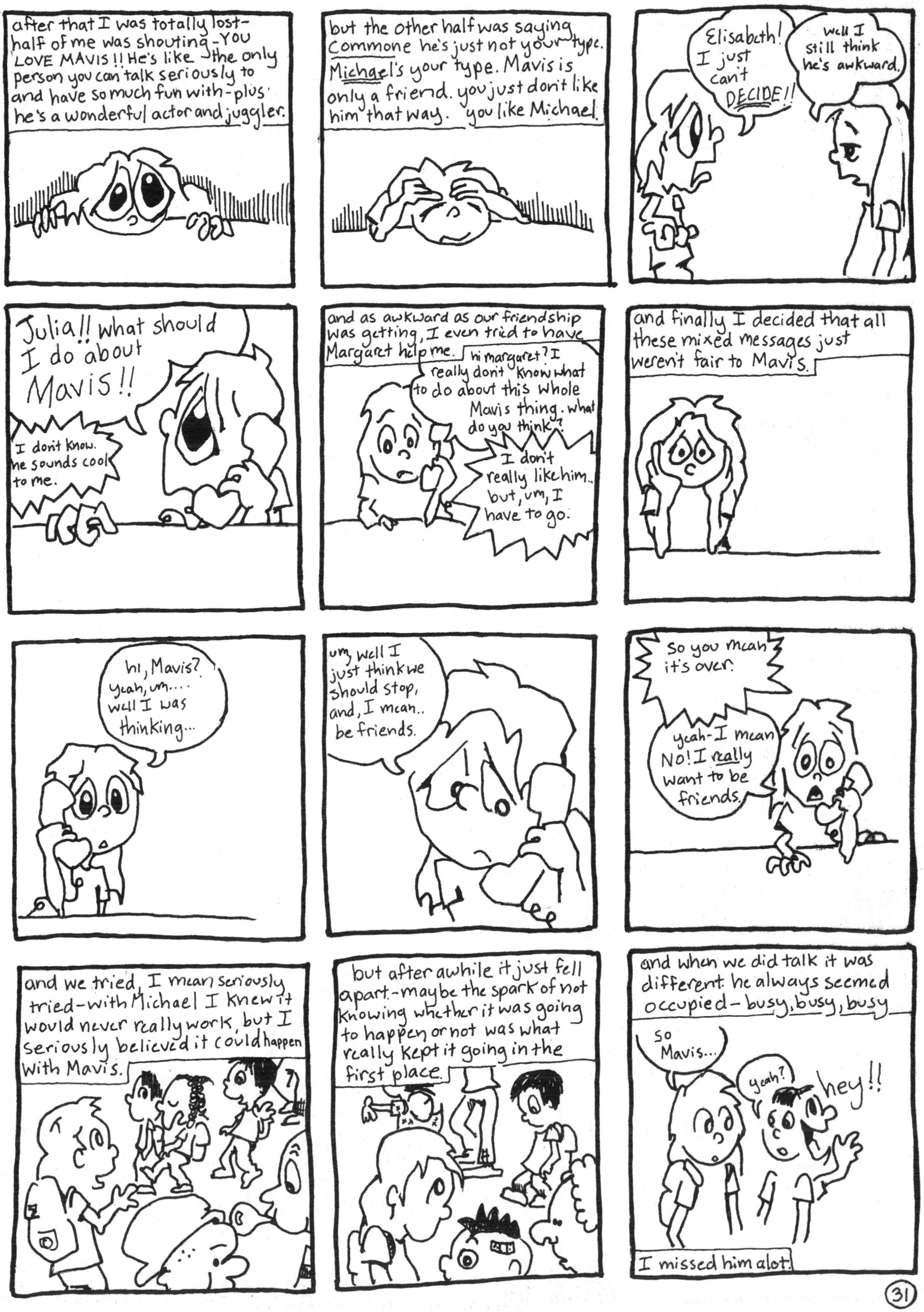
after that I was totally lost-half of me was shouting-YOU LOVE MAVIS!! He's like the only person you can talk seriously to and have so much fun with-plus he's a wonderful actor and juggler.
but the other half was saying Commone he's just not your type. Michael's your type. Mavis is only a friend. you just don't like him that way. you like Michael.
Elisabeth! I just can't DECIDE!!
well I still think he's awkward.
Julia!! what should I do about Mavis!!
I don't know. he sounds cool to me.
and as awkward as our friendship was getting, I even tried to have Margaret help me.
hi margaret? I really don't know what to do about this whole Mavis thing. what do you think?
I don't really like him.. but, um, I have to go.
and finally I decided that all these mixed messages just weren't fair to Mavis.
hi, Mavis? yeah, um.... well I was thinking...
um, well I just think we should stop, and, I mean.. be friends.
so you mean it's over.
yeah-I mean No! I really want to be friends.
and we tried, I mean seriously tried-with Michael I knew it would never really work, but I seriously believed it could happen with Mavis.
but after awhile it just fell apart-maybe the spark of not knowing whether it was going to happen or not was what really kept it going in the first place.
and when we did talk it was different. he always seemed occupied-busy, busy, busy
So Mavis...
yeah?
hey!!
I missed him alot.

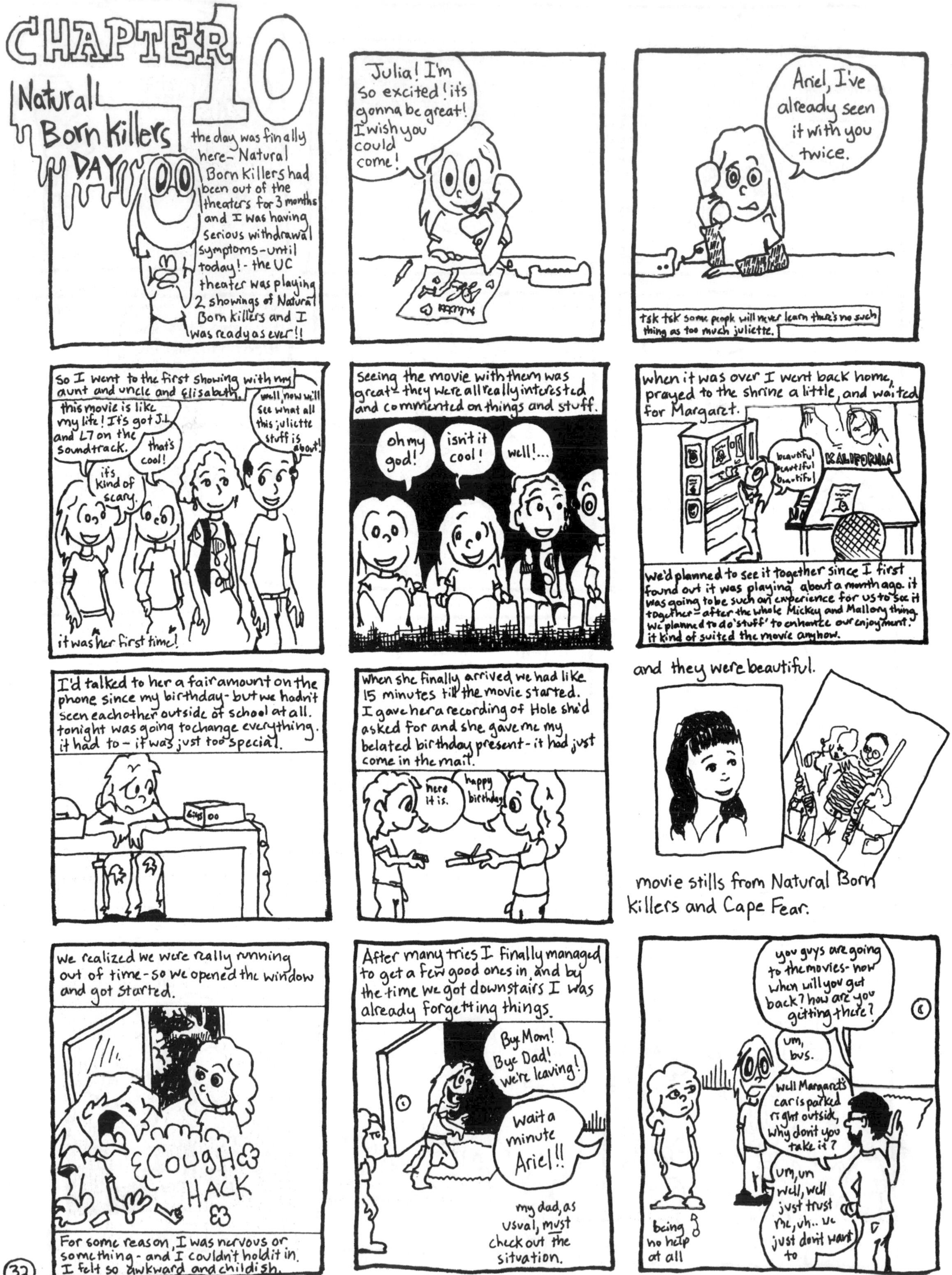
CHAPTER 10
Natural Born Killers DAY
the day was finally here- Natural Born Killers had been out of the theaters for 3 months and I was having serious withdrawal symptoms-until today!- the UC theater was playing 2 showings of Natural Born killers and I was ready as ever!!
Julia! I'm so excited! it's gonna be great! I wish you could come!
Ariel, I've already seen it with you twice.
tsk tsk some people will never learn there's no such thing as too much juliette.
So I went to the first showing with my aunt and uncle and Elisabeth.
this movie is like my life! It's got J.L. and L7 on the soundtrack.
that's cool!
it's kind of scary.
well, now we'll see what all this juliette stuff is about!
it was her first time!
Seeing the movie with them was great- they were all really interested and commented on things and stuff.
oh my god!
isn't it cool!
well!...
when it was over I went back home, prayed to the shrine a little, and waited for Margaret.
beautiful beautiful beautiful
KALIFORNIA
we'd planned to see it together since I first found out it was playing about a month ago. it was going to be such an experience for us to see it together- after the whole Mickey and Mallory thing. we planned to do 'stuff' to enhance our enjoyment. it kind of suited the movie anyhow.
I'd talked to her a fair amount on the phone since my birthday- but we hadn't seen eachother outside of school at all. tonight was going to change everything. it had to- it was just too special.
When she finally arrived we had like 15 minutes till the movie started. I gave her a recording of Hole she'd asked for and she gave me my belated birthday present- it had just come in the mail.
here it is.
happy birthday
and they were beautiful.
movie stills from Natural Born killers and Cape Fear.
We realized we were really running out of time- so we opened the window and got started.
COUGH
HACK
For some reason, I was nervous or something- and I couldn't hold it in. I felt so awkward and childish.
After many tries I finally managed to get a few good ones in, and by the time we got downstairs I was already forgetting things.
Bye Mom! Bye Dad! We're leaving!
wait a minute Ariel!!
my dad, as usual, must check out the situation.
you guys are going to the movies- now when will you get back? how are you getting there?
um, bus.
well Margaret's car is parked right outside, why don't you take it?
um, un well, well just trust me, uh.. we just don't want to
being no help at all

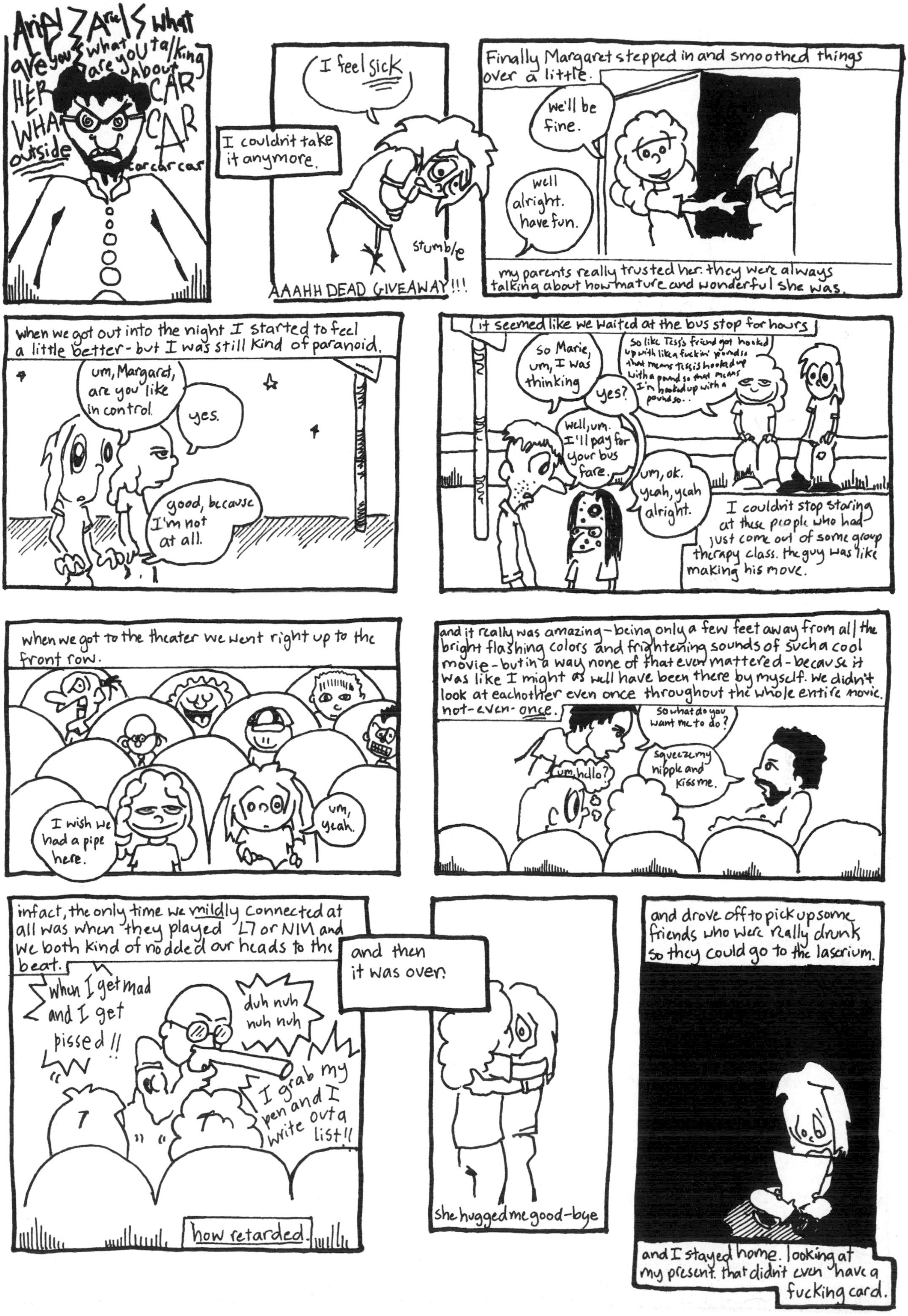

Ariel Ariel what are you what are you talking about
HER CAR WHAT outside CAR carcarcar
I feel sick
I couldn't take it anymore.
stumble
AAAHH DEAD GIVEAWAY!!!
Finally Margaret stepped in and smoothed things over a little.
We'll be fine.
well alright. have fun.
my parents really trusted her. they were always talking about how mature and wonderful she was.
when we got out into the night I started to feel a little better - but I was still kind of paranoid.
um, Margaret, are you like in control.
yes.
good, because I'm not at all.
it seemed like we waited at the bus stop for hours
So Marie, um, I was thinking
yes?
Well, um. I'll pay for your bus fare.
um, ok. yeah, yeah alright.
So like Tess's friend got hooked up with like a fuckin' pound so that means Tess is hooked up with a pound so that means I'm hooked up with a pound so..
I couldn't stop staring at these people who had just come out of some group therapy class. the guy was like making his move.
when we got to the theater we went right up to the front row.
I wish we had a pipe here.
um, yeah.
and it really was amazing - being only a few feet away from all the bright flashing colors and frightening sounds of such a cool movie - but in a way none of that even mattered - because it was like I might as well have been there by myself. We didn't look at eachother even once throughout the whole entire movie. not-even-once.
So what do you want me to do?
um, hello?
Squeeze my nipple and kiss me.
infact, the only time we mildly connected at all was when they played L7 or NIN and we both kind of nodded our heads to the beat.
When I get mad and I get pissed!!
duh nuh nuh nuh
I grab my pen and I write out a list!!
how retarded.
and then it was over.
she hugged me good-bye
and drove off to pick up some friends who were really drunk so they could go to the laserium.
and I stayed home. looking at my present. that didn't even have a fucking card.

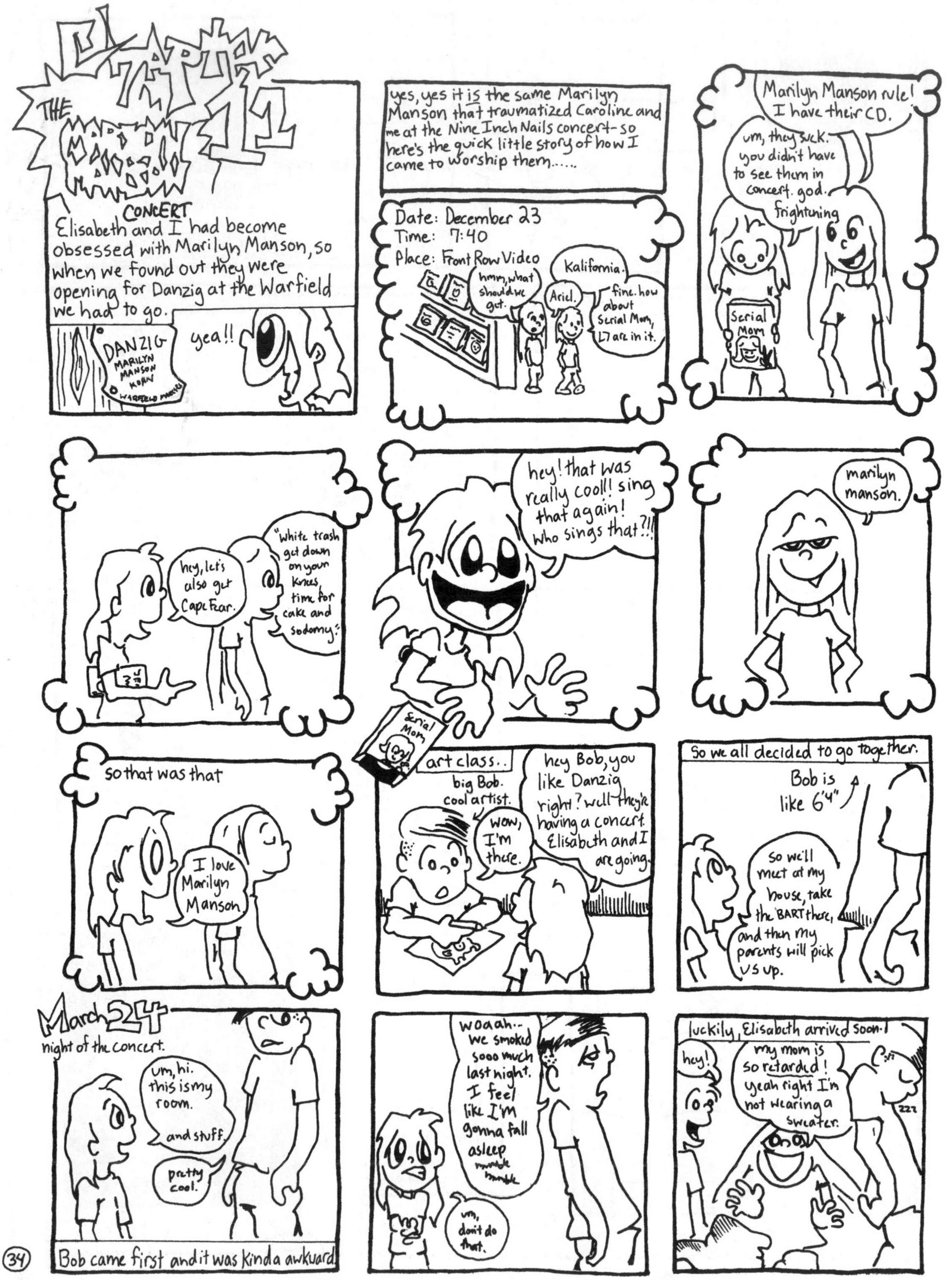
Chapter 11
THE CONCERT
Elisabeth and I had become obsessed with Marilyn Manson, so when we found out they were opening for Danzig at the Warfield we had to go.
DANZIG
MARILYN MANSON
KORN
WARFIELD
yea!!
yes, yes it is the same Marilyn Manson that traumatized Caroline and me at the Nine Inch Nails concert—so here's the quick little story of how I came to worship them……
Date: December 23
Time: 7:40
Place: Front Row Video
hmm, what should we get.
Kalifornia.
Ariel.
fine. how about Serial Mom, L7 are in it.
Marilyn Manson rule! I have their CD.
um, they suck. you didn't have to see them in concert. god. frightening
Serial Mom
hey, let's also get Cape Fear.
"White trash get down on your knees, time for cake and sodomy"
hey! that was really cool!! sing that again! Who sings that?!!
Serial Mom
marilyn manson.
so that was that
I love Marilyn Manson.
art class..
big Bob. cool artist.
hey Bob, you like Danzig right? well they're having a concert. Elisabeth and I are going.
wow, I'm there.
So we all decided to go together.
Bob is like 6'4"
so we'll meet at my house, take the BART there, and then my parents will pick us up.
March 24
night of the concert.
um, hi. this is my room.
and stuff.
pretty cool.
Bob came first and it was kinda awkward
woaah.. we smoked sooo much last night. I feel like I'm gonna fall asleep
mumble mumble
um, don't do that.
luckily, Elisabeth arrived soon.
hey!
my mom is so retarded! yeah right I'm not wearing a sweater.
zzz

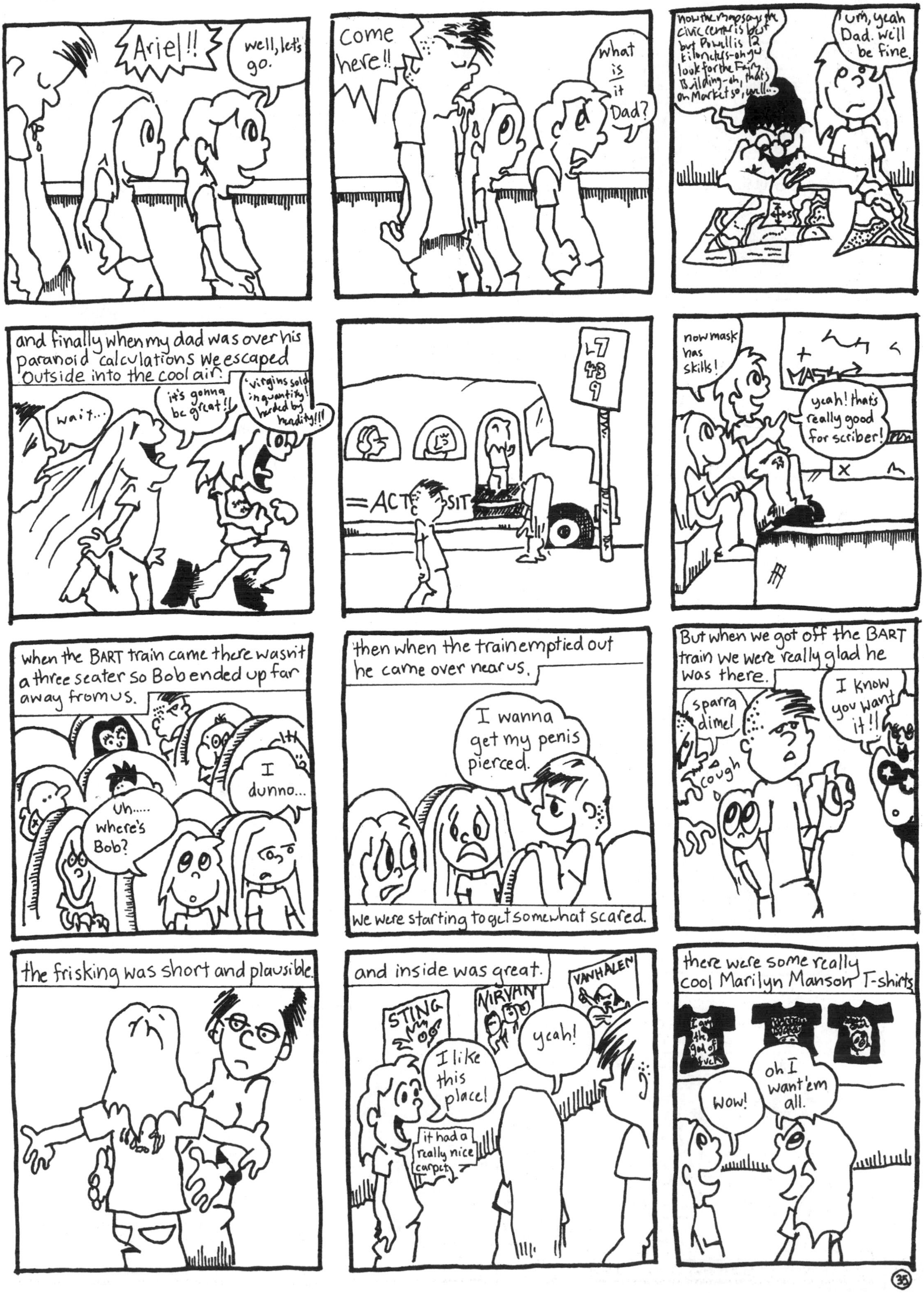
Ariel!!
well, let's go.
Come here!!
what is it Dad?
now the map says the civic center is but but Powell is 12 kilometers-oh you look for the Fairy Building-oh, that's on Market so, well...
um, yeah Dad. will be fine.
and finally when my dad was over his paranoid calculations we escaped outside into the cool air.
wait...
it's gonna be great!!
'virgins sold in quantity! herded by hardity!!!
L7
43
9
=ACT
SIT
now mask has skills!
yeah! that's really good for scriber!
when the BART train came there wasn't a three seater so Bob ended up far away from us.
I dunno...
uh..... where's Bob?
then when the train emptied out he came over near us.
I wanna get my penis pierced.
we were starting to get somewhat scared.
But when we got off the BART train we were really glad he was there.
sparra dime!
cough
I know you want it!!
the frisking was short and plausible.
and inside was great.
STING
NIRVAN
VANHALEN
I like this place!
yeah!
it had a really nice carpet.
there were some really cool Marilyn Manson T-shirts
Wow!
oh I want'em all.

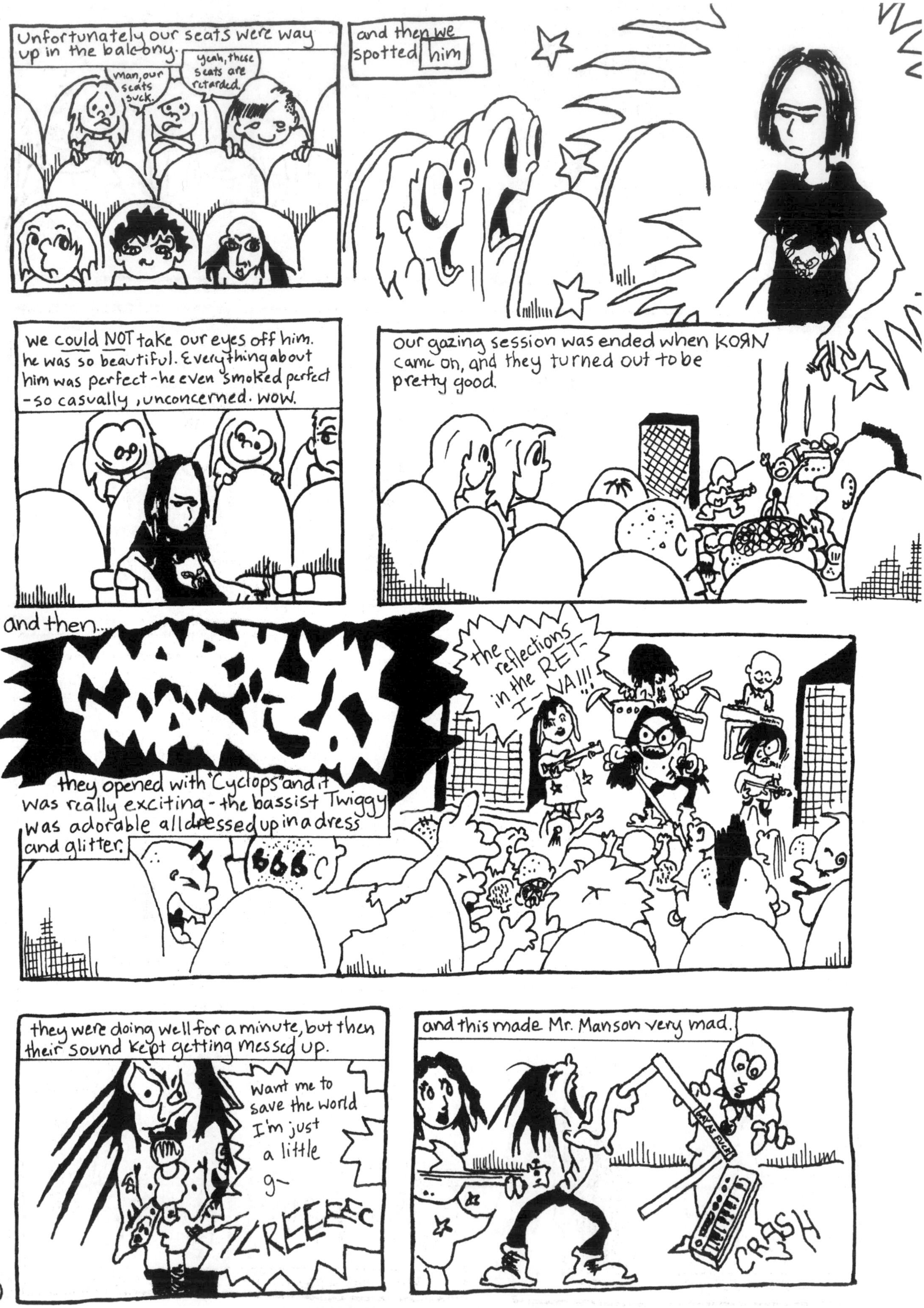

Unfortunately our seats were way up in the balcony.
man, our seats suck.
yeah, these seats are retarded.
and then we spotted him
we could NOT take our eyes off him. he was so beautiful. Everything about him was perfect - he even smoked perfect - so casually, unconcerned. WOW.
our gazing session was ended when KORN came on, and they turned out to be pretty good.
and then...
MARILYN MANSON
the reflections in the RET-I-NA!!!
they opened with "Cyclops" and it was really exciting - the bassist Twiggy was adorable all dressed up in a dress and glitter.
666
they were doing well for a minute, but then their sound kept getting messed up.
Want me to save the world I'm just a little g-
ZZREEEEEC
and this made Mr. Manson very mad.
CRASH

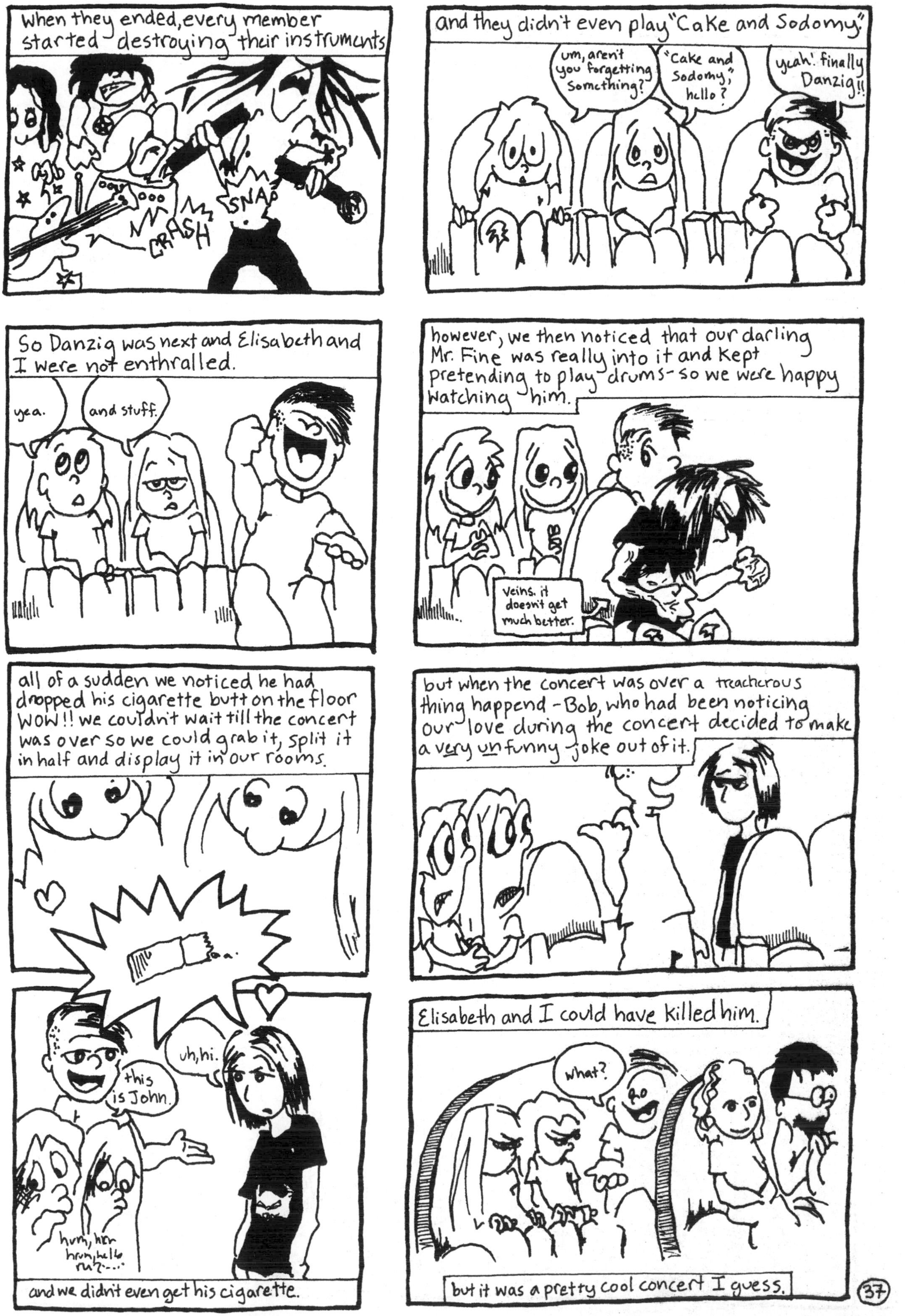
When they ended, every member started destroying their instruments
SNAP
CRASH
and they didn't even play "Cake and Sodomy."
um, aren't you forgetting something?
"Cake and Sodomy," hello?
yeah! finally Danzig!!
So Danzig was next and Elisabeth and I were not enthralled.
yea.
and stuff.
however, we then noticed that our darling Mr. Fine was really into it and kept pretending to play drums- so we were happy watching him.
veins. it doesn't get much better.
all of a sudden we noticed he had dropped his cigarette butt on the floor WOW!! we couldn't wait till the concert was over so we could grab it, split it in half and display it in our rooms.
but when the concert was over a treacherous thing happend - Bob, who had been noticing our love during the concert decided to make a very unfunny joke out of it.
this is John.
uh, hi.
and we didn't even get his cigarette.
Elisabeth and I could have killed him.
what?
but it was a pretty cool concert I guess.

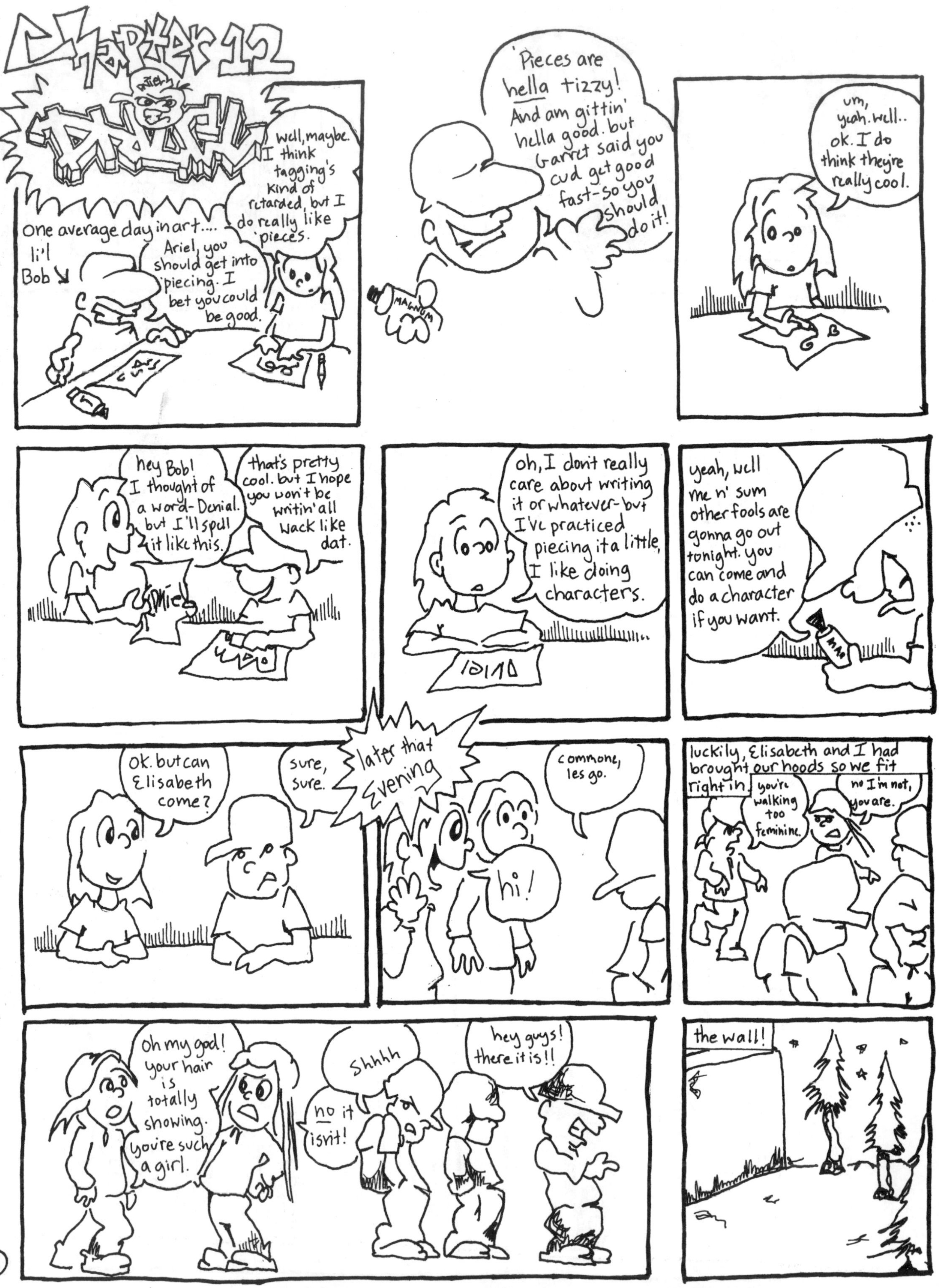

Chapter 12
Denial
One average day in art....
li'l Bob
Ariel, you should get into piecing. I bet you could be good.
well, maybe. I think tagging's kind of retarded, but I do really like pieces.
Pieces are hella tizzy! And am gittin' hella good. but Garret said you cud get good fast-so you should do it!
MAGNUM
um, yeah. well.. ok. I do think they're really cool.
hey Bob! I thought of a word-Denial. but I'll spell it like this.
that's pretty cool. but I hope you won't be writin' all wack like dat.
oh, I don't really care about writing it or whatever-but I've practiced piecing it a little, I like doing characters.
yeah, well me n' sum other fools are gonna go out tonight. you can come and do a character if you want.
ok. but can Elisabeth come?
sure, sure.
later that Evening
commone, les go.
hi!
luckily, Elisabeth and I had brought our hoods so we fit right in.
you're walking too feminine.
no I'm not, you are.
Oh my god! your hair is totally showing. You're such a girl.
no it isn't!
Shhhh
hey guys! there it is!!
the wall!

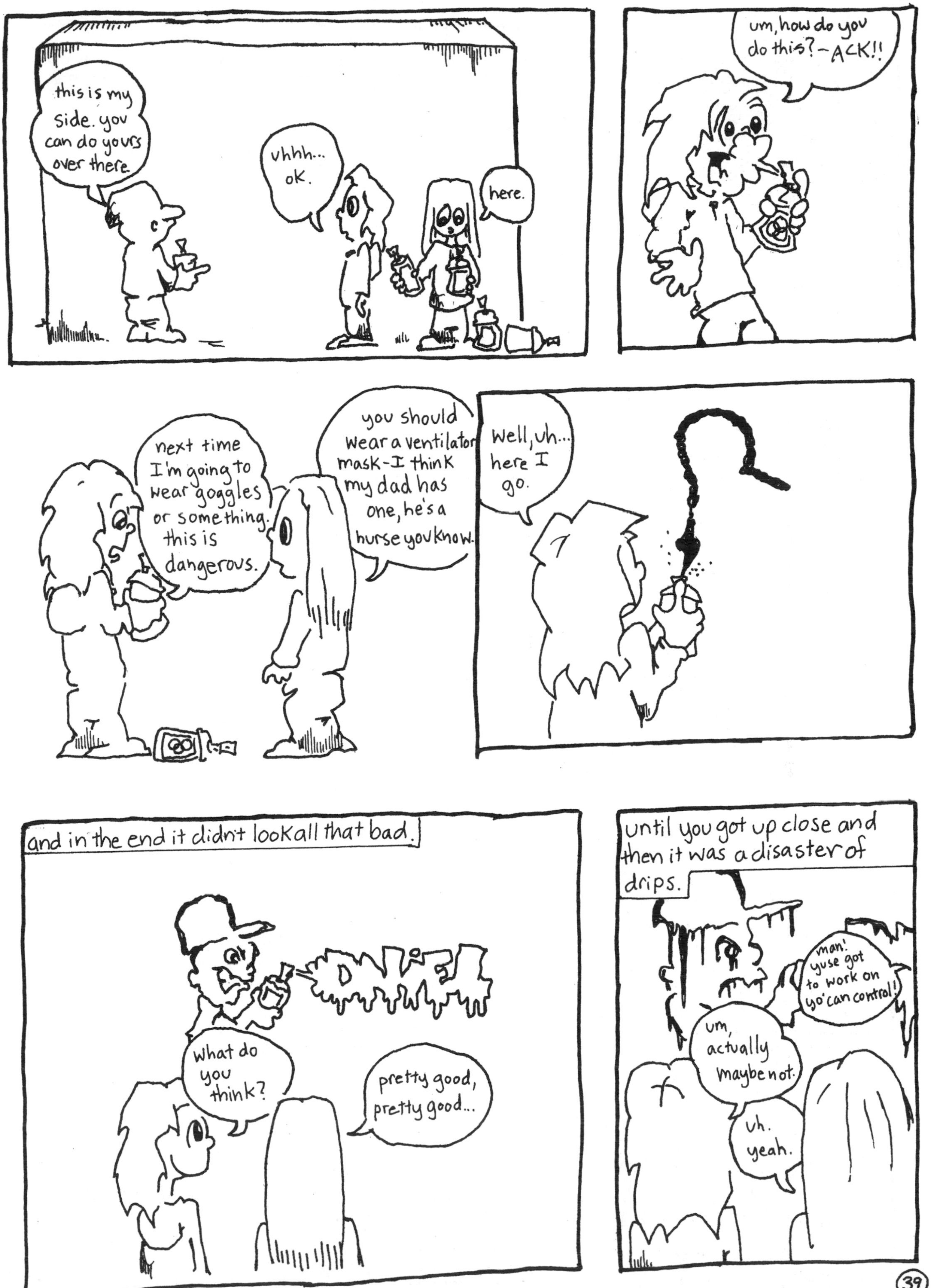
this is my side. you can do yours over there
uhhh... ok.
here.
um, how do you do this? -ACK!!
next time I'm going to wear goggles or something. this is dangerous.
you should wear a ventilator mask - I think my dad has one, he's a nurse you know.
Well, uh... here I go.
and in the end it didn't look all that bad.
What do you think?
pretty good, pretty good...
until you got up close and then it was a disaster of drips.
man! yuse got to work on yo' can control!
um, actually maybe not.
uh. yeah.

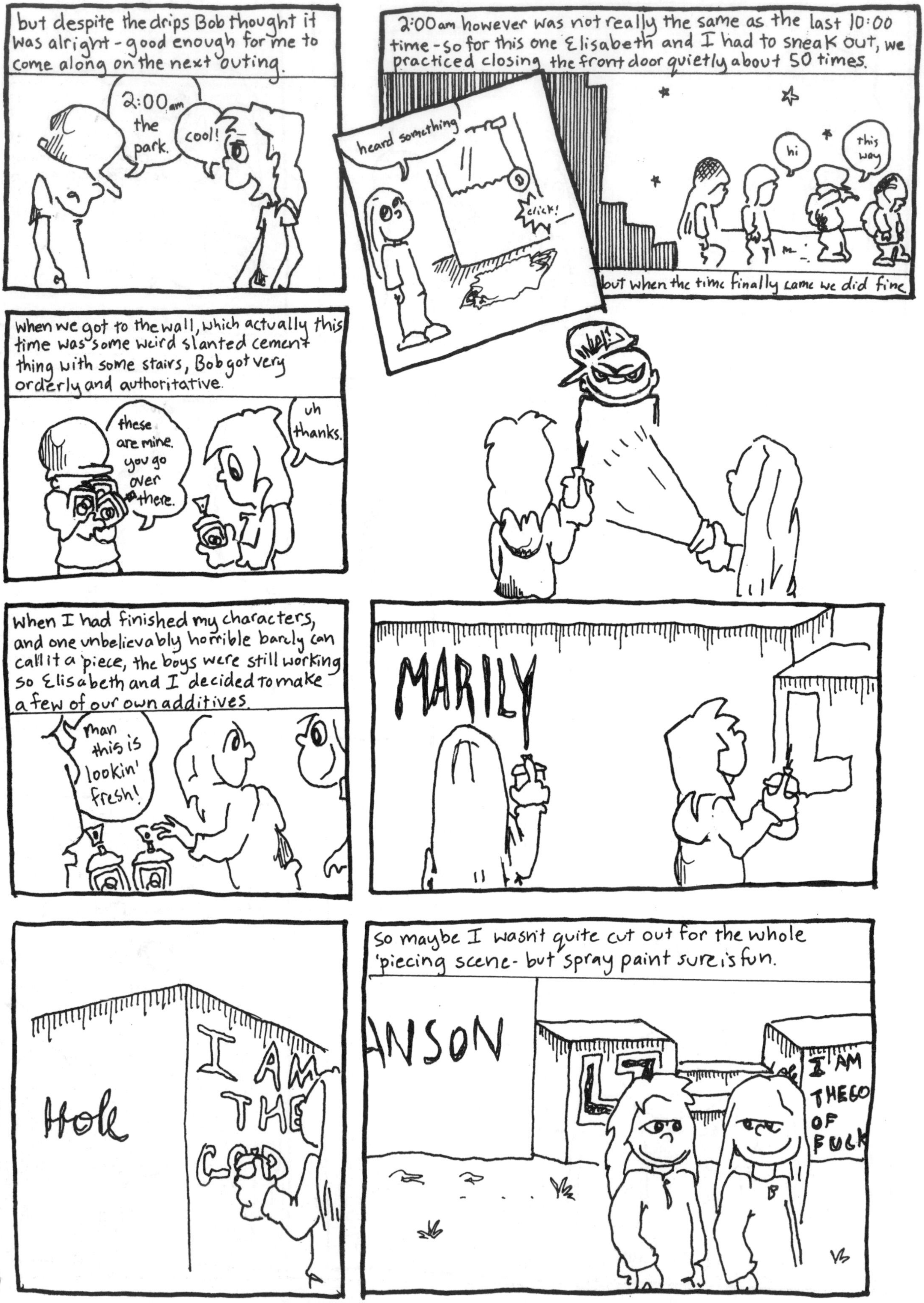
but despite the drips Bob thought it was alright - good enough for me to come along on the next outing.
2:00am the park.
cool!
2:00am however was not really the same as the last 10:00 time - so for this one Elisabeth and I had to sneak out, we practiced closing the front door quietly about 50 times.
heard something
click!
hi
this way
but when the time finally came we did fine.
When we got to the wall, which actually this time was some weird slanted cement thing with some stairs, Bob got very orderly and authoritative.
these are mine. you go over there.
uh thanks.
When I had finished my characters, and one unbelievably horrible barely can call it a piece, the boys were still working so Elisabeth and I decided to make a few of our own additives.
man this is lookin' fresh!
MARILY
Hole
I AM THE GOD
So maybe I wasn't quite cut out for the whole 'piecing scene- but spray paint sure is fun.
ANSON
I AM THE GO OF FUCK

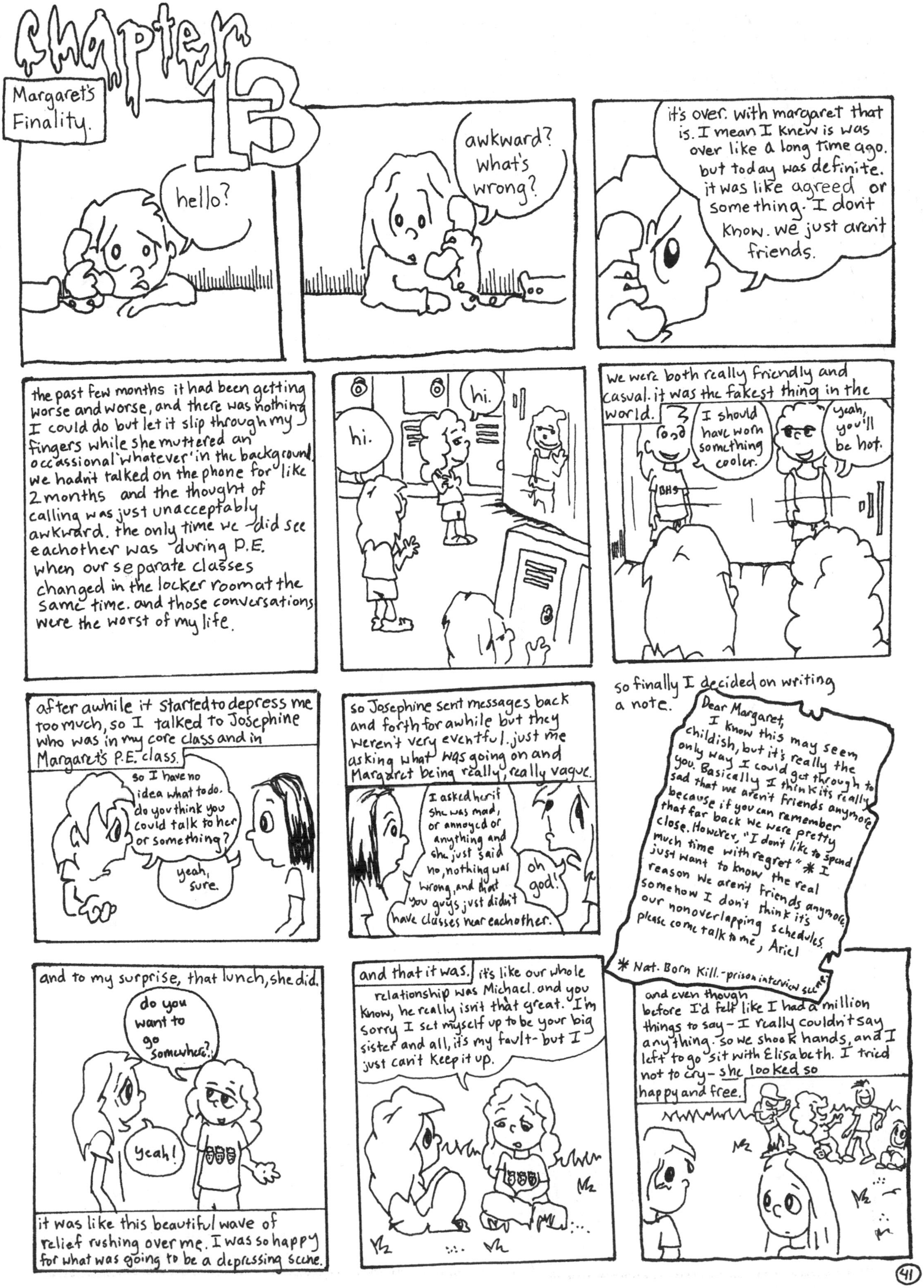

chapter 13
Margaret's Finality.
hello?
awkward? what's wrong?
it's over. with margaret that is. I mean I knew is was over like a long time ago. but today was definite. it was like agreed or something. I don't know. we just aren't friends.
the past few months it had been getting worse and worse, and there was nothing I could do but let it slip through my fingers while she muttered an occassional 'whatever' in the background. we hadn't talked on the phone for like 2 months and the thought of calling was just unacceptably awkward. the only time we did see eachother was during P.E. when our separate classes changed in the locker room at the same time. and those conversations were the worst of my life.
hi.
hi.
we were both really friendly and casual. it was the fakest thing in the world.
I should have worn something cooler.
yeah, you'll be hot.
BHS
after awhile it started to depress me too much, so I talked to Josephine who was in my core class and in Margaret's P.E. class.
so I have no idea what to do. do you think you could talk to her or something?
yeah, sure.
so Josephine sent messages back and forth for awhile but they weren't very eventful. just me asking what was going on and Margaret being really, really vague.
I asked her if she was mad, or annoyed or anything and she just said no, nothing was wrong, and that you guys just didn't have classes near eachother.
oh god!
so finally I decided on writing a note.
Dear Margaret,
I know this may seem childish, but it's really the only way I could get through to you. Basically I think it's really sad that we aren't friends anymore because if you can remember that far back we were pretty close. However, "I dont like to spend much time with regret" * I just want to know the real reason we aren't friends anymore. somehow I don't think it's our nonoverlapping schedules. please come talk to me, Ariel
* Nat. Born Kill. - prison interview scene
and to my surprise, that lunch, she did.
do you want to go somewhere?
yeah!
it was like this beautiful wave of relief rushing over me. I was so happy for what was going to be a depressing scene.
and that it was.
it's like our whole relationship was Michael. and you know, he really isn't that great. I'm sorry I set myself up to be your big sister and all, it's my fault - but I just can't keep it up.
and even though before I'd felt like I had a million things to say - I really couldn't say anything. so we shook hands, and I left to go sit with Elisabeth. I tried not to cry - she looked so happy and free.

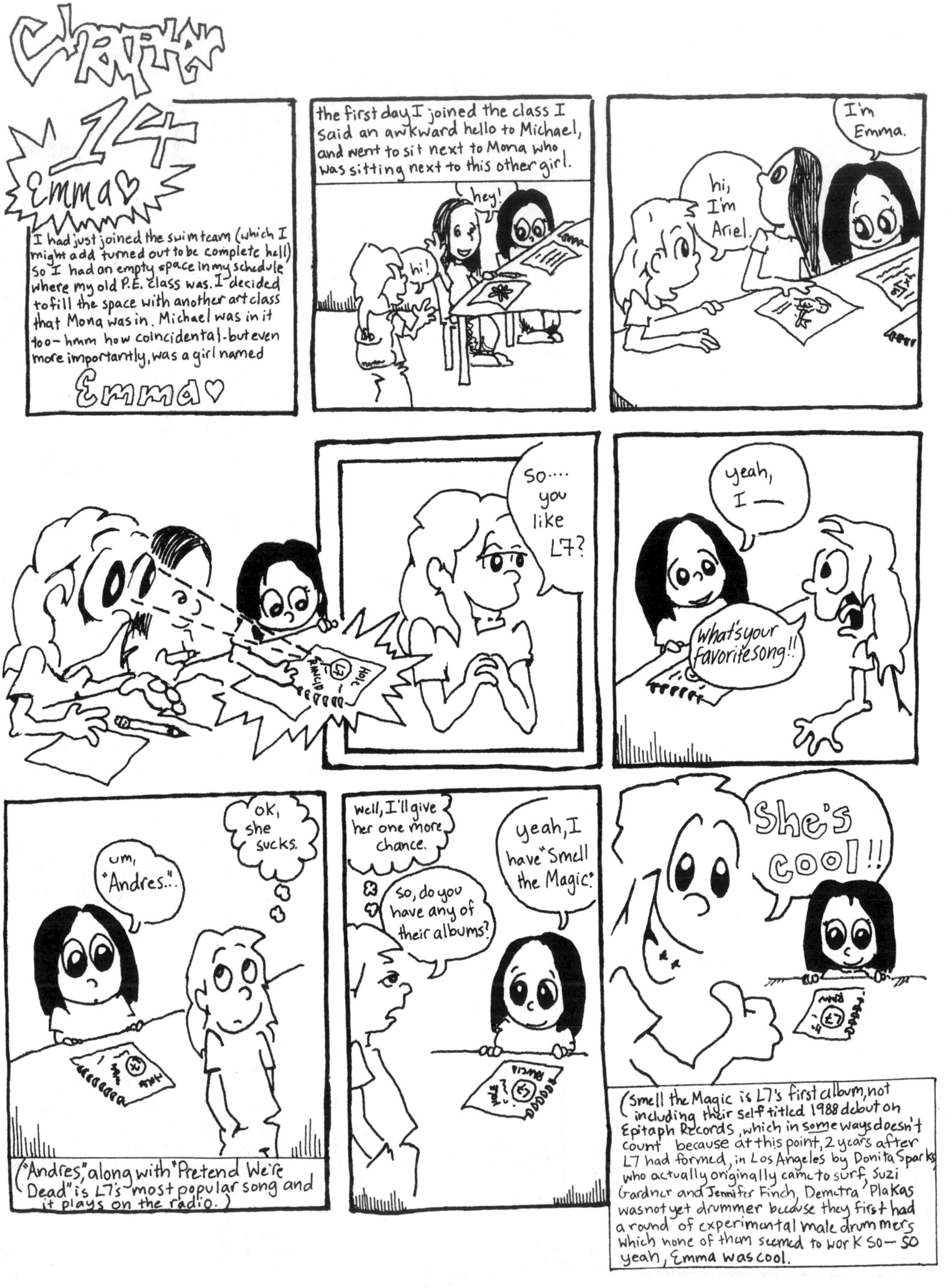

Chapter 14
Emma♡
I had just joined the swim team (which I might add turned out to be complete hell) so I had an empty space in my schedule where my old P.E. class was. I decided to fill the space with another art class that Mona was in. Michael was in it too- hmm how coincidental- but even more importantly, was a girl named
Emma♡
the first day I joined the class I said an awkward hello to Michael, and went to sit next to Mona who was sitting next to this other girl.
hey!
hi!
I'm Emma.
hi, I'm Ariel.
So.... you like L7?
yeah, I —
what's your favorite song!!
um, "Andres."
ok, she sucks.
("Andres," along with "Pretend We're Dead" is L7's most popular song and it plays on the radio.)
well, I'll give her one more chance.
So, do you have any of their albums?
yeah, I have "Smell the Magic"
She's cool!!
(Smell the Magic is L7's first album, not including their self titled 1988 debut on Epitaph Records, which in some ways doesn't count because at this point, 2 years after L7 had formed, in Los Angeles by Donita Sparks who actually originally came to surf, Suzi Gardner and Jennifer Finch, Demetra Plakas was not yet drummer because they first had a round of experimental male drummers which none of them seemed to work so— so yeah, Emma was cool.

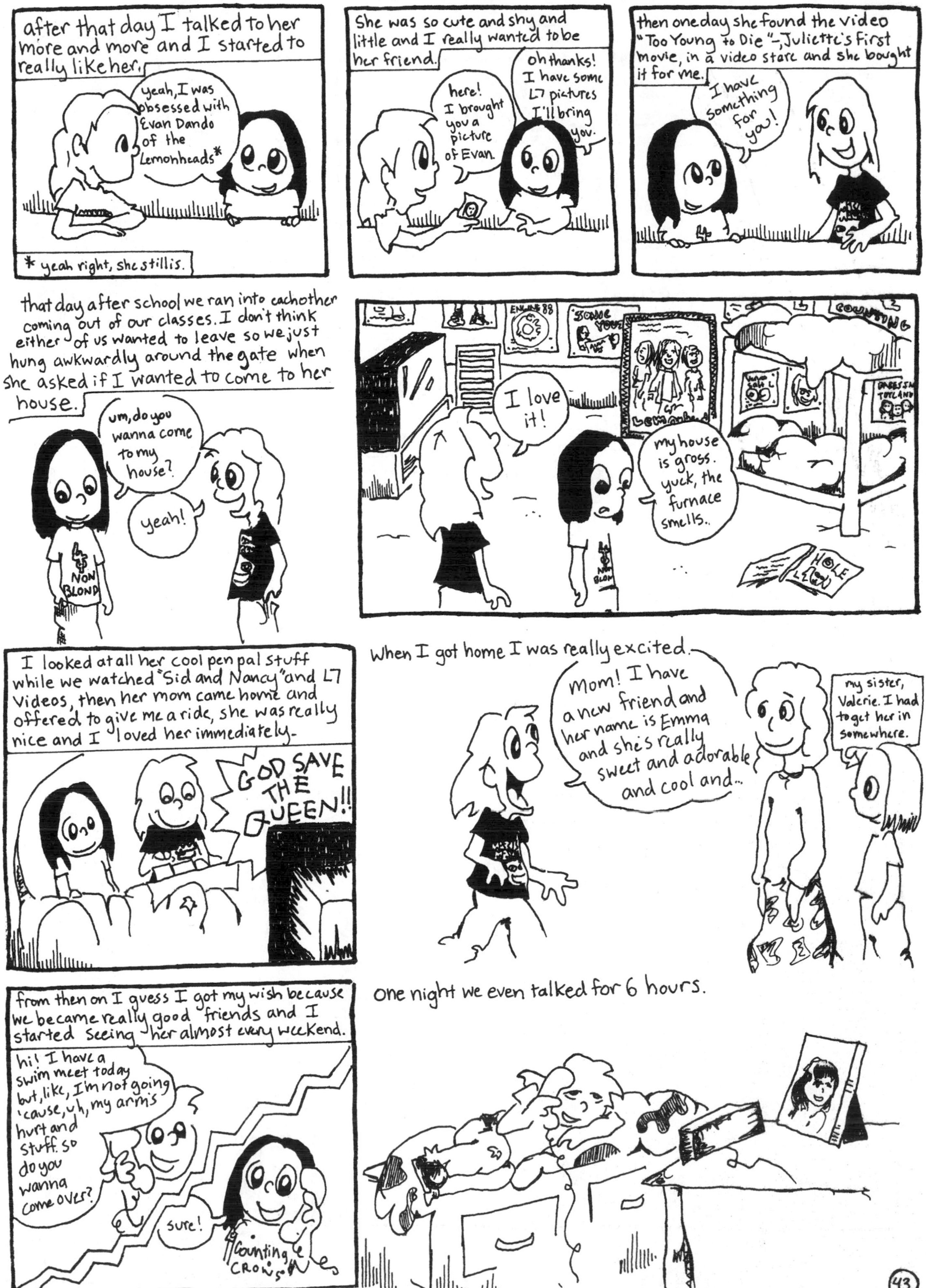

after that day I talked to her more and more and I started to really like her.
yeah, I was obsessed with Evan Dando of the Lemonheads*
* yeah right, she still is.
She was so cute and shy and little and I really wanted to be her friend.
here! I brought you a picture of Evan.
oh thanks! I have some L7 pictures I'll bring you.
then one day she found the video "Too Young to Die"—Juliette's First movie, in a video store and she bought it for me.
I have something for you!
that day after school we ran into eachother coming out of our classes. I don't think either of us wanted to leave so we just hung awkwardly around the gate when she asked if I wanted to come to her house.
um, do you wanna come to my house?
yeah!
I love it!
my house is gross. yuck, the furnace smells.
I looked at all her cool pen pal stuff while we watched "Sid and Nancy" and L7 videos, then her mom came home and offered to give me a ride, she was really nice and I loved her immediately.
GOD SAVE THE QUEEN!!
When I got home I was really excited.
Mom! I have a new friend and her name is Emma and she's really sweet and adorable and cool and...
my sister, Valerie. I had to get her in somewhere.
from then on I guess I got my wish because we became really good friends and I started seeing her almost every weekend.
hi! I have a swim meet today but, like, I'm not going 'cause, uh, my arm's hurt and stuff. so do you wanna come over?
sure!
Counting Crows
one night we even talked for 6 hours.

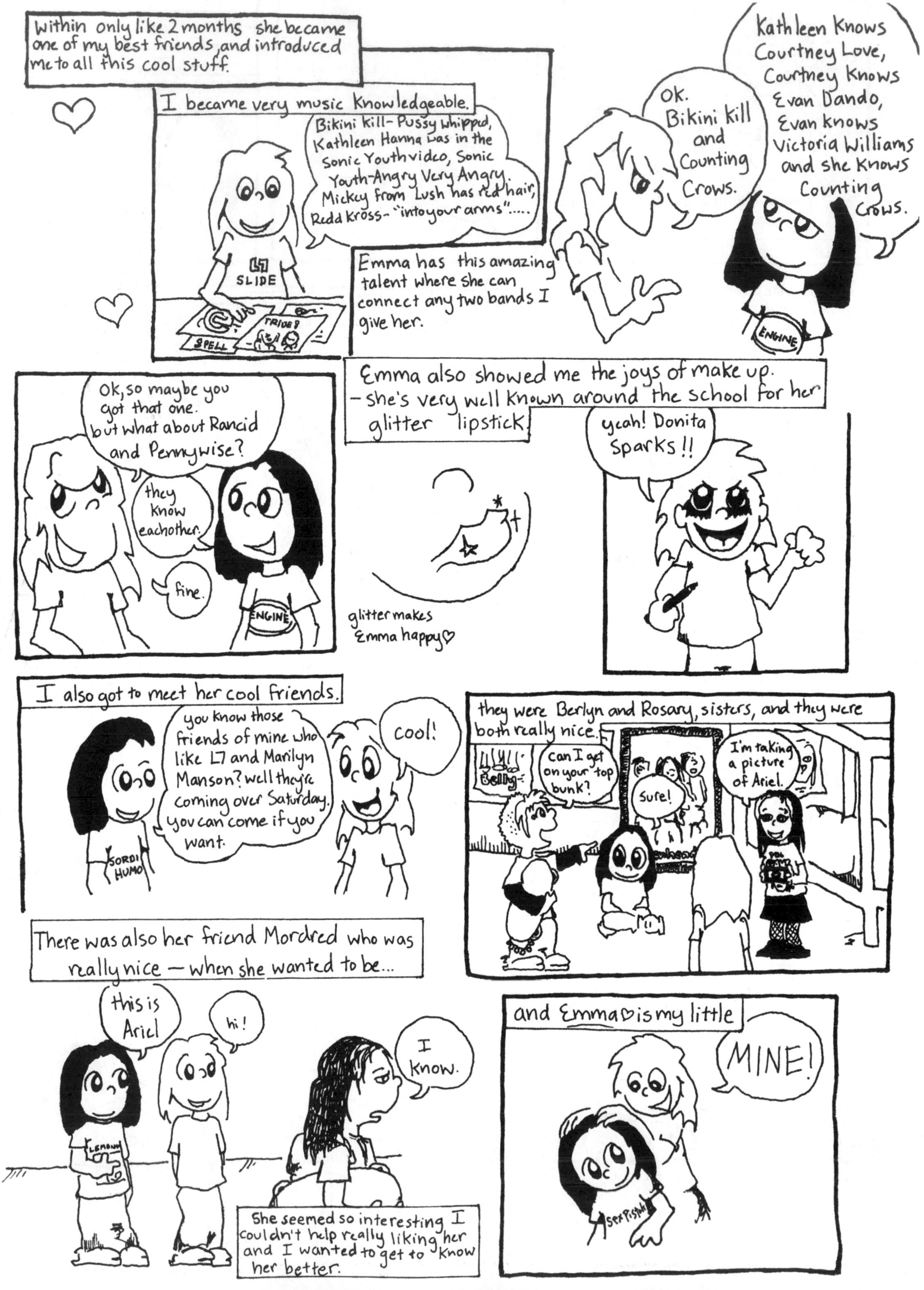

within only like 2 months she became one of my best friends, and introduced me to all this cool stuff.
I became very music knowledgeable.
Bikini kill- Pussy whipped, Kathleen Hanna was in the Sonic Youth video, Sonic Youth-Angry Very Angry. Mickey from Lush has red hair, Redd Kross- "into your arms".....
L7
SLIDE
SPELL
TRIBE?
Emma has this amazing talent where she can connect any two bands I give her.
Ok. Bikini Kill and Counting Crows.
Kathleen Knows Courtney Love, Courtney Knows Evan Dando, Evan knows Victoria Williams and she knows Counting Crows.
ENGINE
Ok, so maybe you got that one. but what about Rancid and Pennywise?
they know eachother.
fine.
ENGINE
Emma also showed me the joys of make up. - she's very well known around the school for her glitter lipstick.
glitter makes Emma happy♡
yeah! Donita Sparks!!
I also got to meet her cool friends.
you know those friends of mine who like L7 and Marilyn Manson? well they're coming over Saturday. you can come if you want.
cool!
SORDI HUMO
they were Berlyn and Rosary, sisters, and they were both really nice.
Can I get on your top bunk?
Sure!
I'm taking a picture of Ariel.
There was also her friend Mordred who was really nice — when she wanted to be...
this is Ariel
hi!
I know.
She seemed so interesting I couldn't help really liking her and I wanted to get to know her better.
and Emma♡is my little
MINE!
SEX PISTOLS

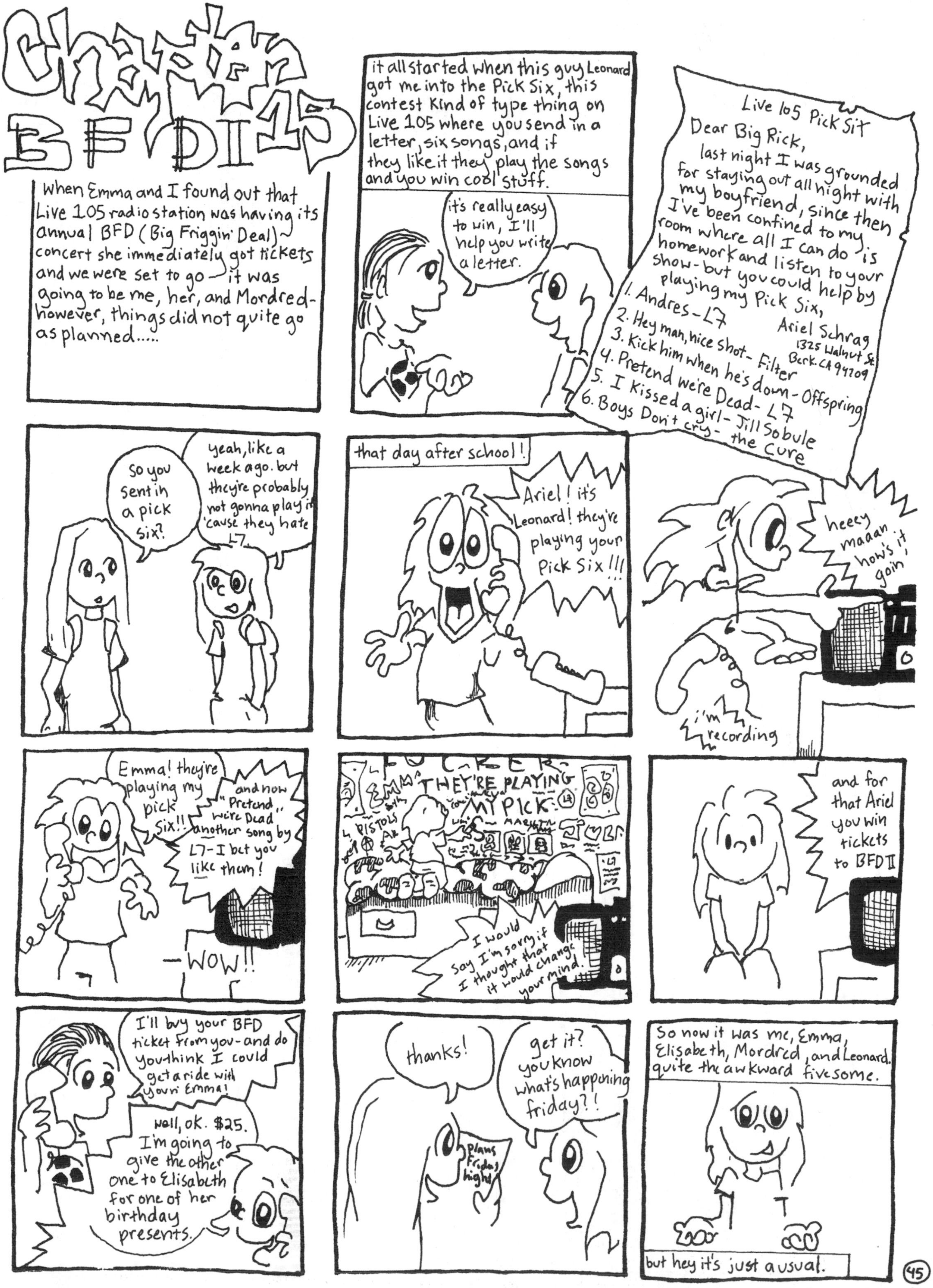

Chapter 15
BFD II
When Emma and I found out that Live 105 radio station was having its annual BFD (Big Friggin' Deal) concert she immediately got tickets and we were set to go— it was going to be me, her, and Mordred— however, things did not quite go as planned.....
it all started when this guy Leonard got me into the Pick Six, this contest kind of type thing on Live 105 where you send in a letter, six songs, and if they like it they play the songs and you win cool stuff.
it's really easy to win, I'll help you write a letter.
Live 105 Pick Sit
Dear Big Rick,
last night I was grounded for staying out all night with my boyfriend, since then I've been confined to my room where all I can do is homework and listen to your show- but you could help by playing my Pick Six,
Ariel Schrag
1325 Walnut St.
Berk. CA 94709
1. Andres - L7
2. Hey man, nice shot - Filter
3. Kick him when he's down - Offspring
4. Pretend we're Dead - L7
5. I Kissed a girl - Jill Sobule
6. Boys Don't cry - the Cure
So you sent in a pick six?
yeah, like a week ago. but they're probably not gonna play it 'cause they hate L7.
that day after school!
Ariel! it's Leonard! they're playing your Pick Six!!!
heeey maaan how's it goin'
i'm recording
Emma! they're playing my pick Six!!
and now "Pretend we're Dead," another song by L7 - I bet you like them!
—WOW!!
THEY'RE PLAYING MY PICK
I would say I'm sorry if I thought that it would change your mind.
and for that Ariel you win tickets to BFD II
I'll buy your BFD ticket from you - and do you think I could get a ride with you 'n' Emma?
well, ok. $25. I'm going to give the other one to Elisabeth for one of her birthday presents.
thanks!
get it? you know what's happening friday?!
Plans Friday night
So now it was me, Emma, Elisabeth, Mordred, and Leonard. quite the awkward fivesome.
but hey it's just a usual.

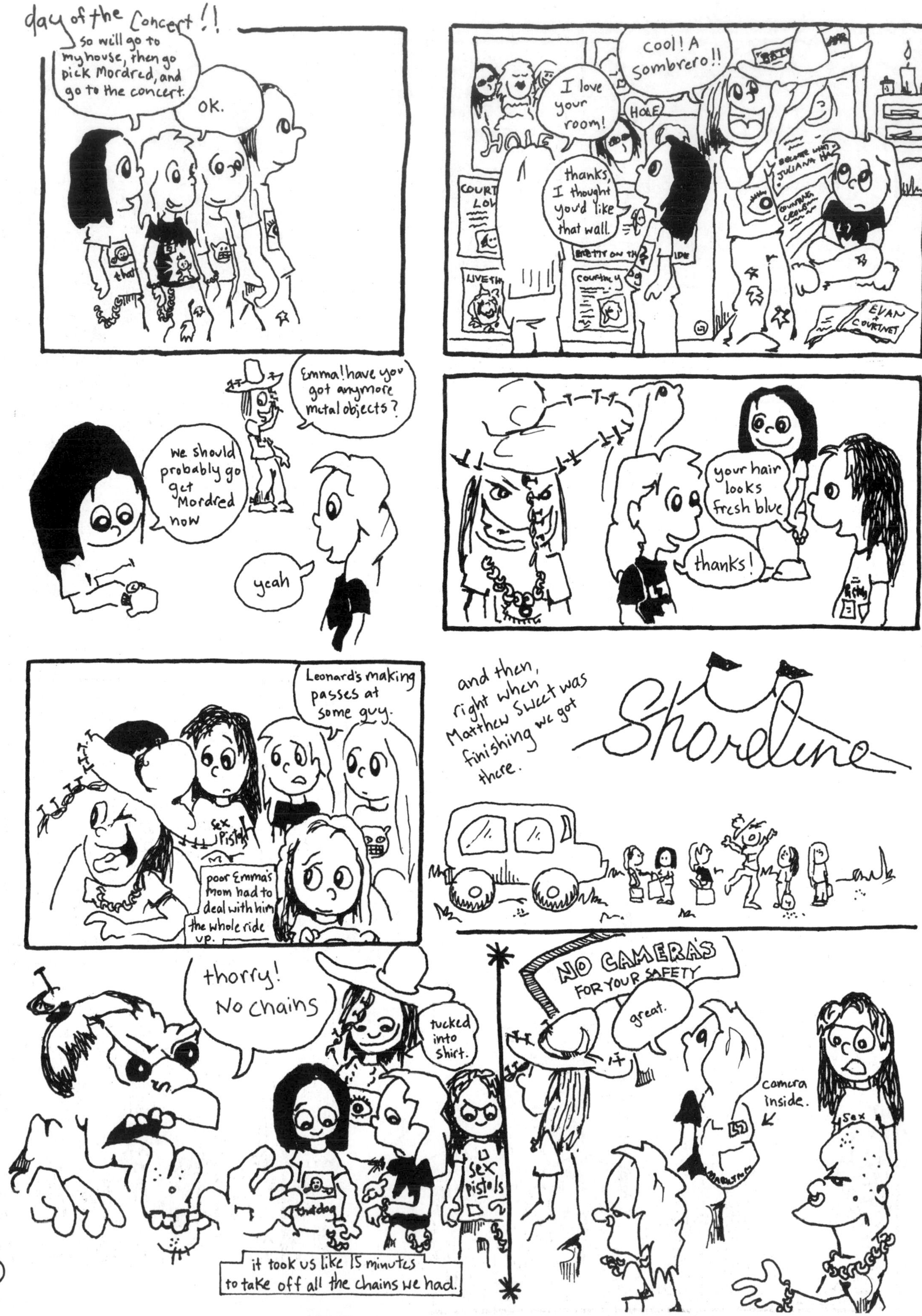

day of the Concert!!
so we'll go to my house, then go pick Mordred, and go to the concert.
OK.
cool! A sombrero!!
I love your room!
thanks, I thought you'd like that wall.
HOLE
Emma! have you got anymore metal objects?
we should probably go get Mordred now
yeah
your hair looks fresh blue
thanks!
Leonard's making passes at some guy.
poor Emma's mom had to deal with him the whole ride up.
and then, right when Matthew Sweet was finishing we got there.
Shoreline
thorry! No chains
tucked into shirt.
it took us like 15 minutes to take off all the chains we had.
NO CAMERAS FOR YOUR SAFETY
great.
camera inside.

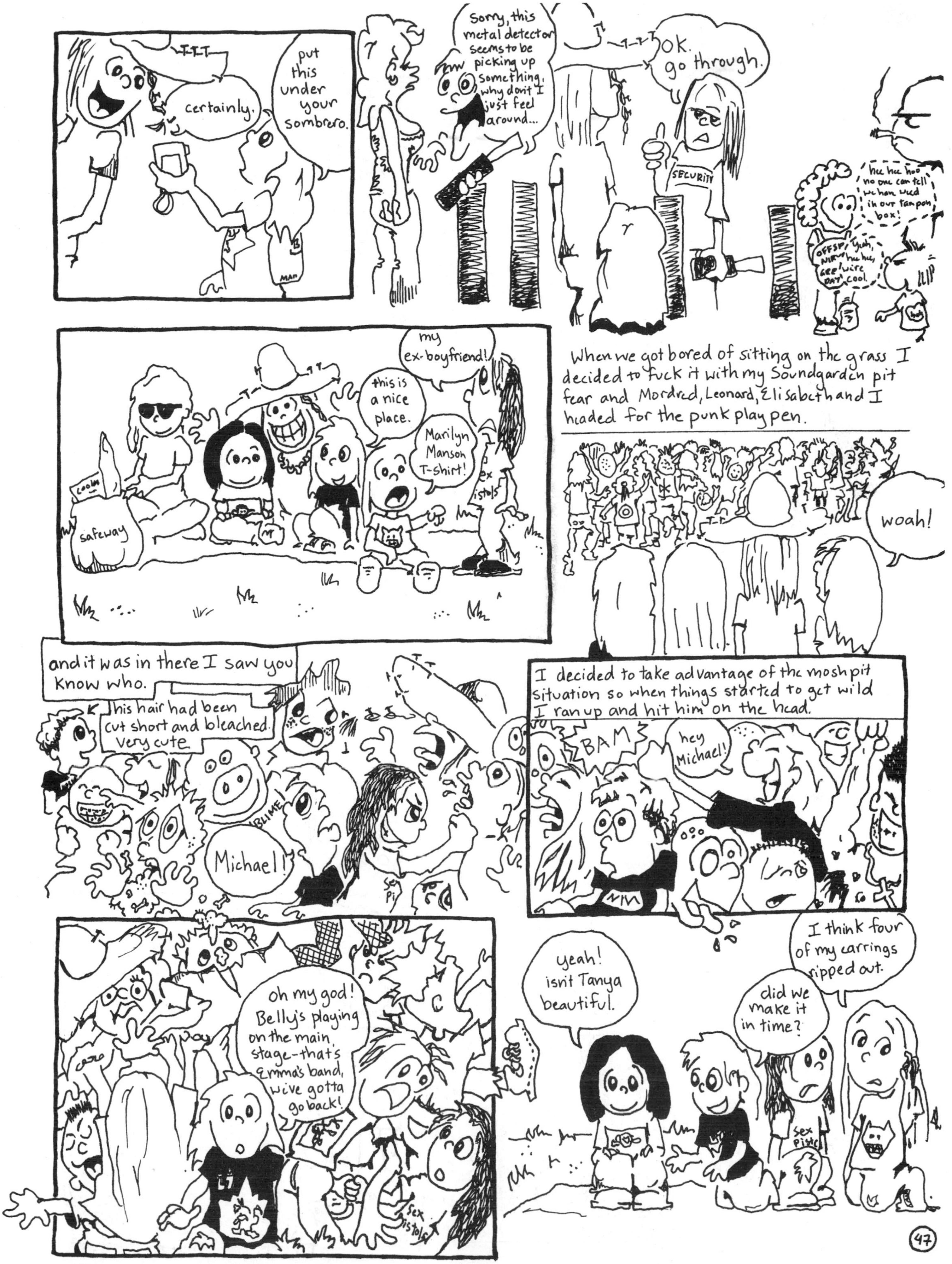
certainly.
put this under your sombrero.
Sorry, this metal detector seems to be picking up something. why don't I just feel around...
ok. go through.
SECURITY
hee hee hoo no one can tell we have weed in our tampon box!
yeah, hee hee, we're cool.
my ex-boyfriend!
this is a nice place.
Marilyn Manson T-shirt!
safeway
When we got bored of sitting on the grass I decided to fuck it with my Soundgarden pit fear and Mordred, Leonard, Elisabeth and I headed for the punk playpen.
woah!
and it was in there I saw you know who.
his hair had been cut short and bleached. very cute.
SUBLIME
Michael!
I decided to take advantage of the mosh pit situation so when things started to get wild I ran up and hit him on the head.
BAM
hey Michael!
NIN
oh my god! Belly's playing on the main stage—that's Emma's band, we've gotta go back!
Sex Pistols
yeah! isn't Tanya beautiful.
I think four of my earrings ripped out.
did we make it in time?
Sex Pistols

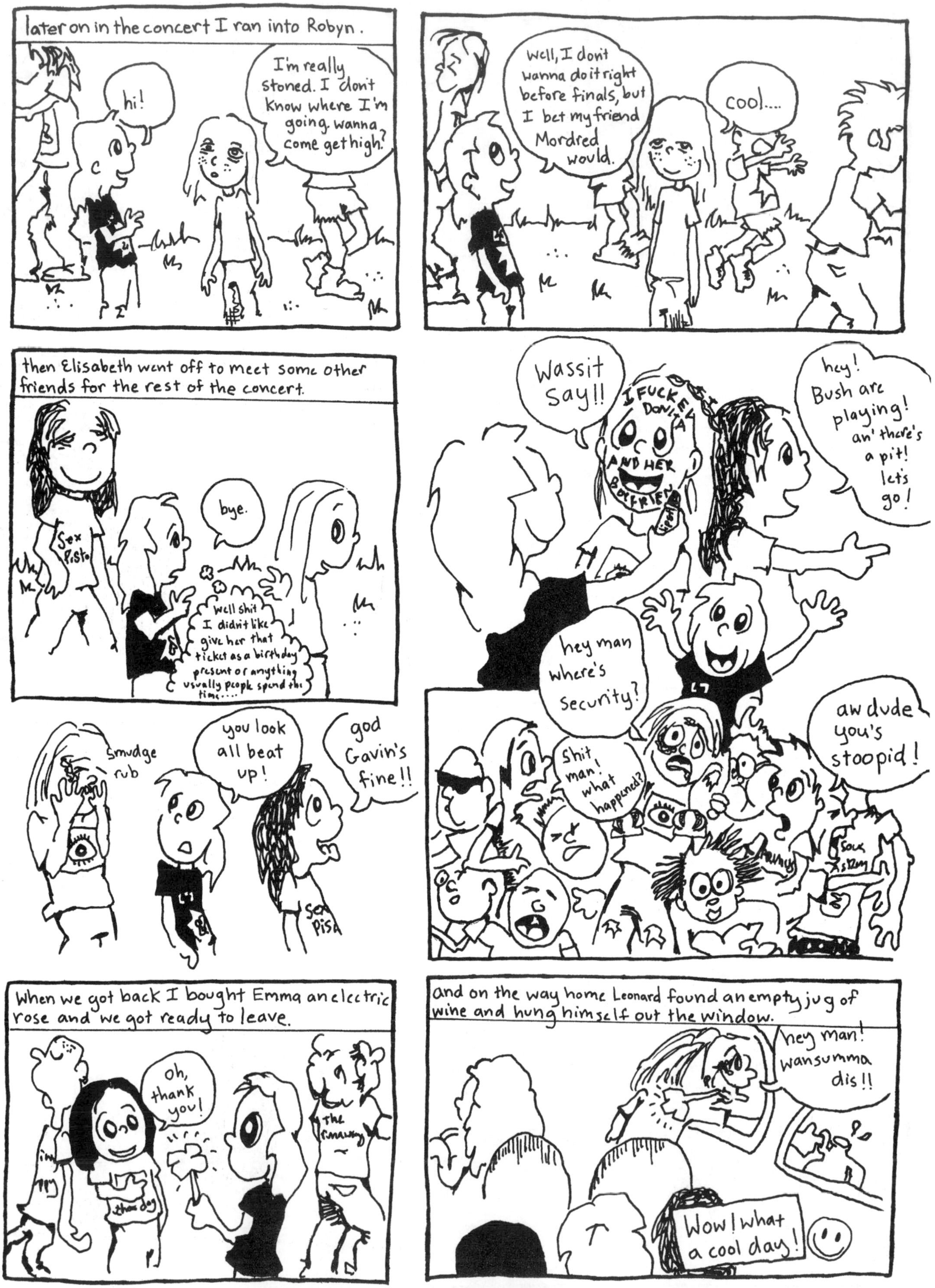

later on in the concert I ran into Robyn.
hi!
I'm really stoned. I don't know where I'm going. wanna come get high?
Well, I don't wanna do it right before finals, but I bet my friend Mordred would.
cool....
then Elisabeth went off to meet some other friends for the rest of the concert.
Sex Pisto
bye.
well shit I didn't like give her that ticket as a birthday present or anything usually people spend the time....
Wassit say!!
I FUCKED DONITA AND HER BOYFRIEND
hey! Bush are playing! an' there's a pit! let's go!
hey man where's security?
Smudge rub
you look all beat up!
god Gavin's fine!!
Shit man! what happened?
aw dude you's stoopid!
Sex Pisa
When we got back I bought Emma an electric rose and we got ready to leave.
oh, thank you!
the runaways
and on the way home Leonard found an empty jug of wine and hung himself out the window.
hey man! wansumma dis!!
Wow! what a cool day!

Chapter 16

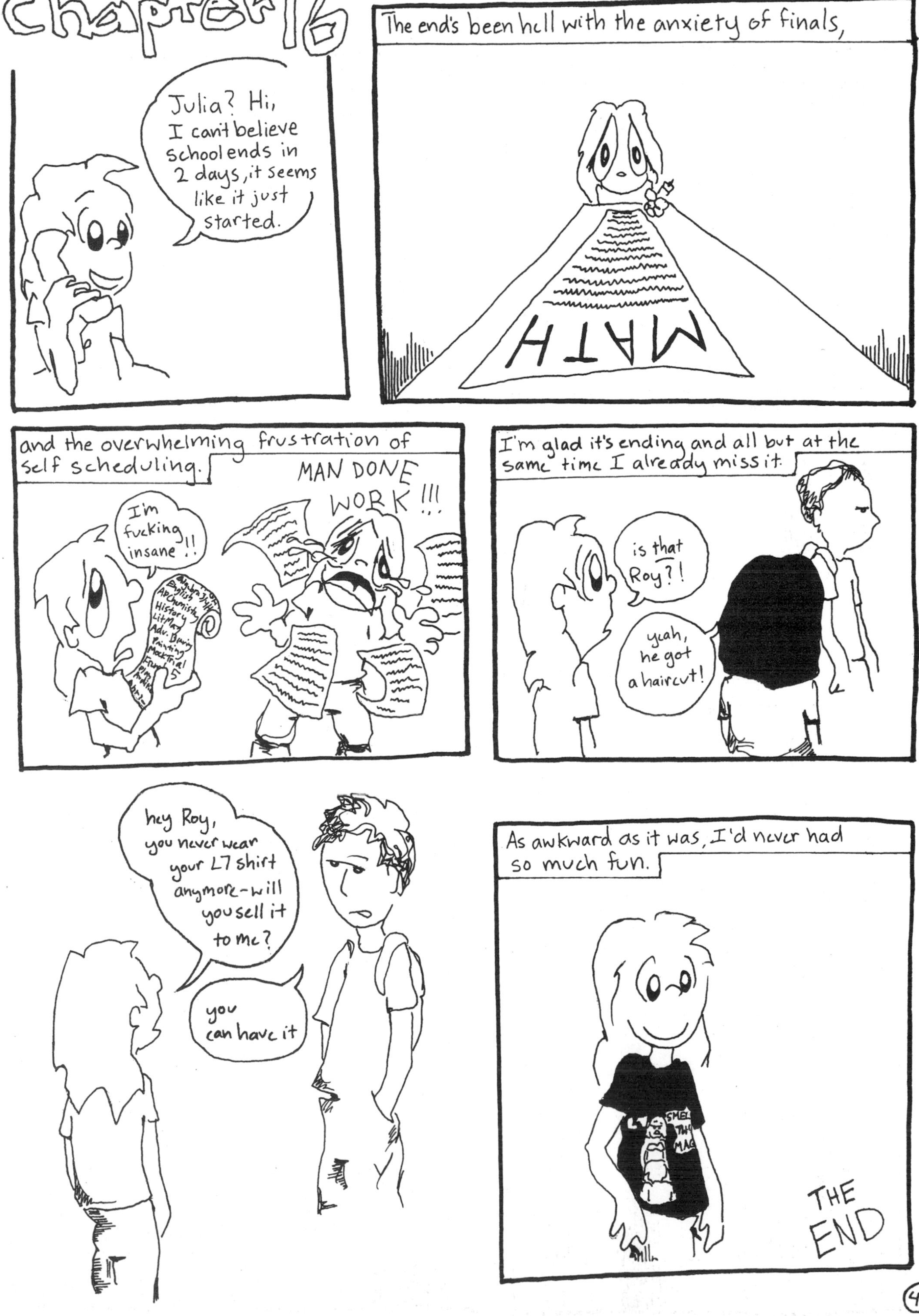

Julia? Hi, I can't believe school ends in 2 days, it seems like it just started.
The end's been hell with the anxiety of finals,
MATH
and the overwhelming frustration of self scheduling.
I'm fucking insane!!
MAN DONE WORK!!!
I'm glad it's ending and all but at the same time I already miss it.
is that Roy?!
yeah, he got a haircut!
hey Roy, you never wear your L7 shirt anymore-will you sell it to me?
you can have it
As awkward as it was, I'd never had so much fun.
THE END

DEFINITION

by Ariel schrag

For
Tania

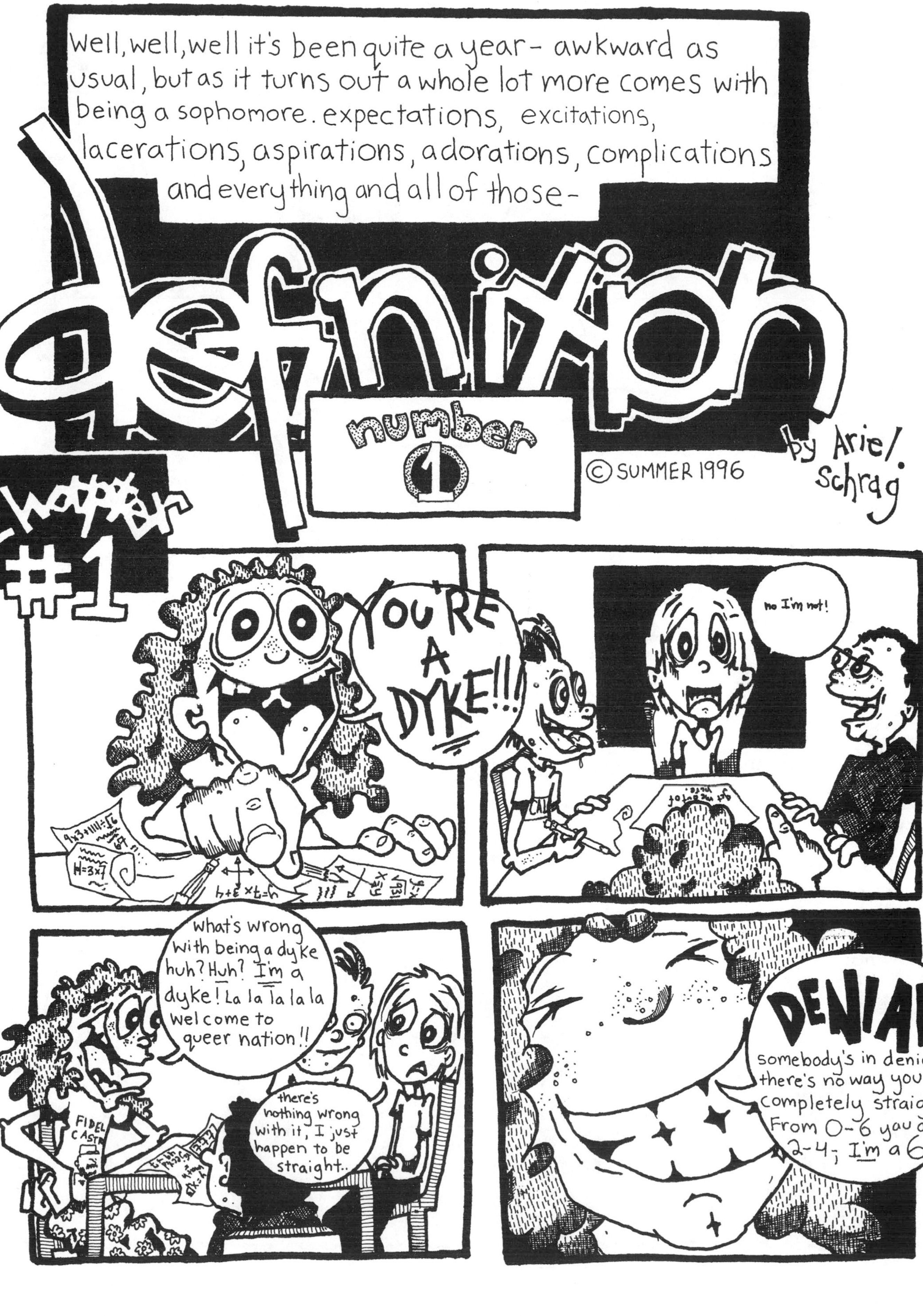

Well, well, well it's been quite a year - awkward as usual, but as it turns out a whole lot more comes with being a sophomore. expectations, excitations, lacerations, aspirations, adorations, complications and everything and all of those -
definition
number 1
© SUMMER 1996
by Ariel Schrag
chapter #1
YOU'RE A DYKE!!!
no I'm not!
what's wrong with being a dyke huh? Huh? I'm a dyke! La la la la la welcome to queer nation!!
there's nothing wrong with it, I just happen to be straight..
DENIAL!
somebody's in denial! there's no way you are completely straight! From 0-6 you are 2-4; I'm a 6!

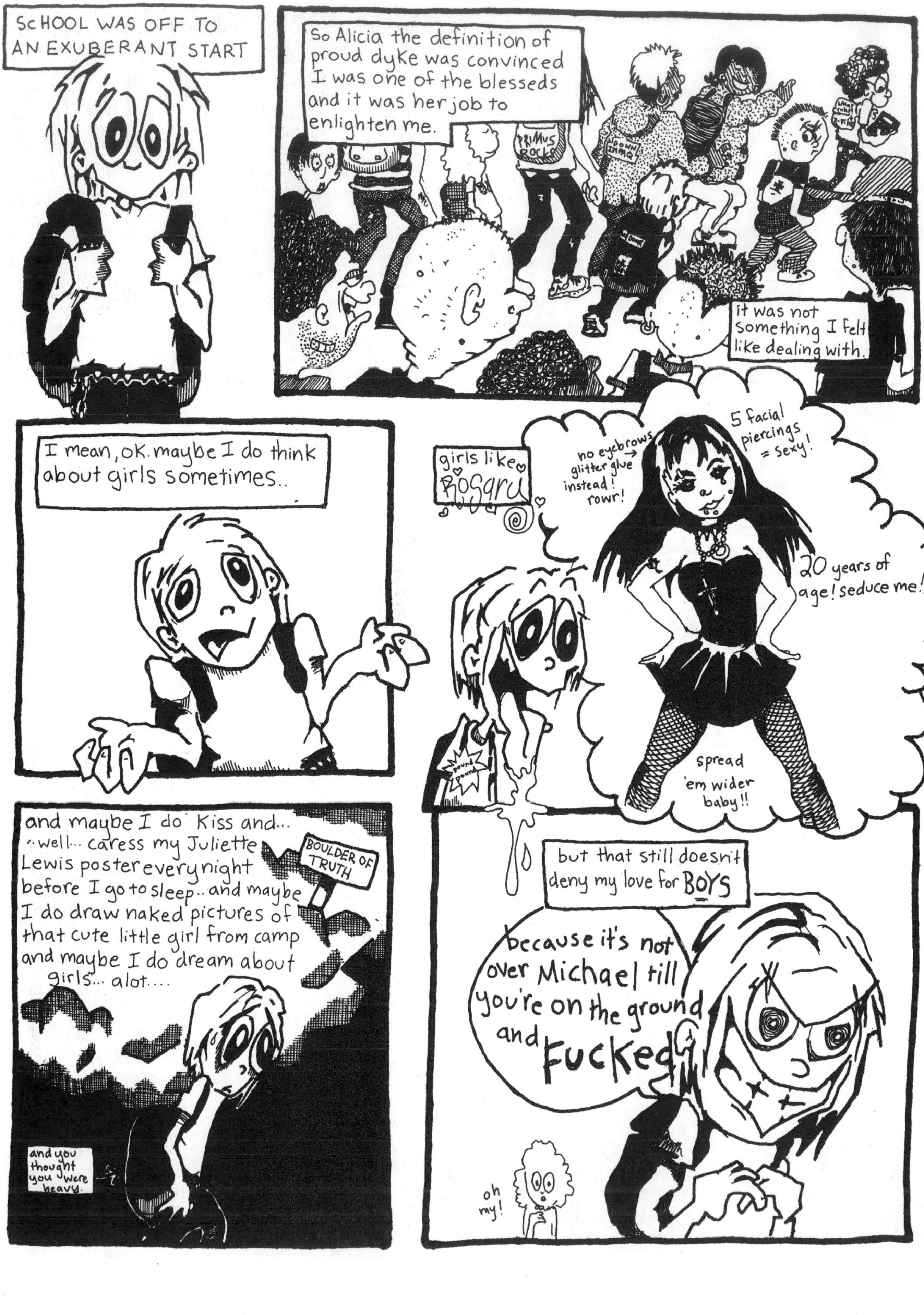

SCHOOL WAS OFF TO AN EXUBERANT START
So Alicia the definition of proud dyke was convinced I was one of the blesseds and it was her job to enlighten me.
PRIMUS ROCKS
it was not something I felt like dealing with.
I mean, OK. maybe I do think about girls sometimes..
girls like Rosaru
no eyebrows → glitter glue instead! rowr!
5 facial piercings = sexy!
20 years of age! seduce me!!
spread 'em wider baby!!
and maybe I do kiss and... ..well... caress my Juliette Lewis poster every night before I go to sleep.. and maybe I do draw naked pictures of that cute little girl from camp and maybe I do dream about girls... alot....
BOULDER OF TRUTH
and you thought you were heavy.
but that still doesn't deny my love for BOYS
because it's not over Michael till you're on the ground and Fucked
oh my!

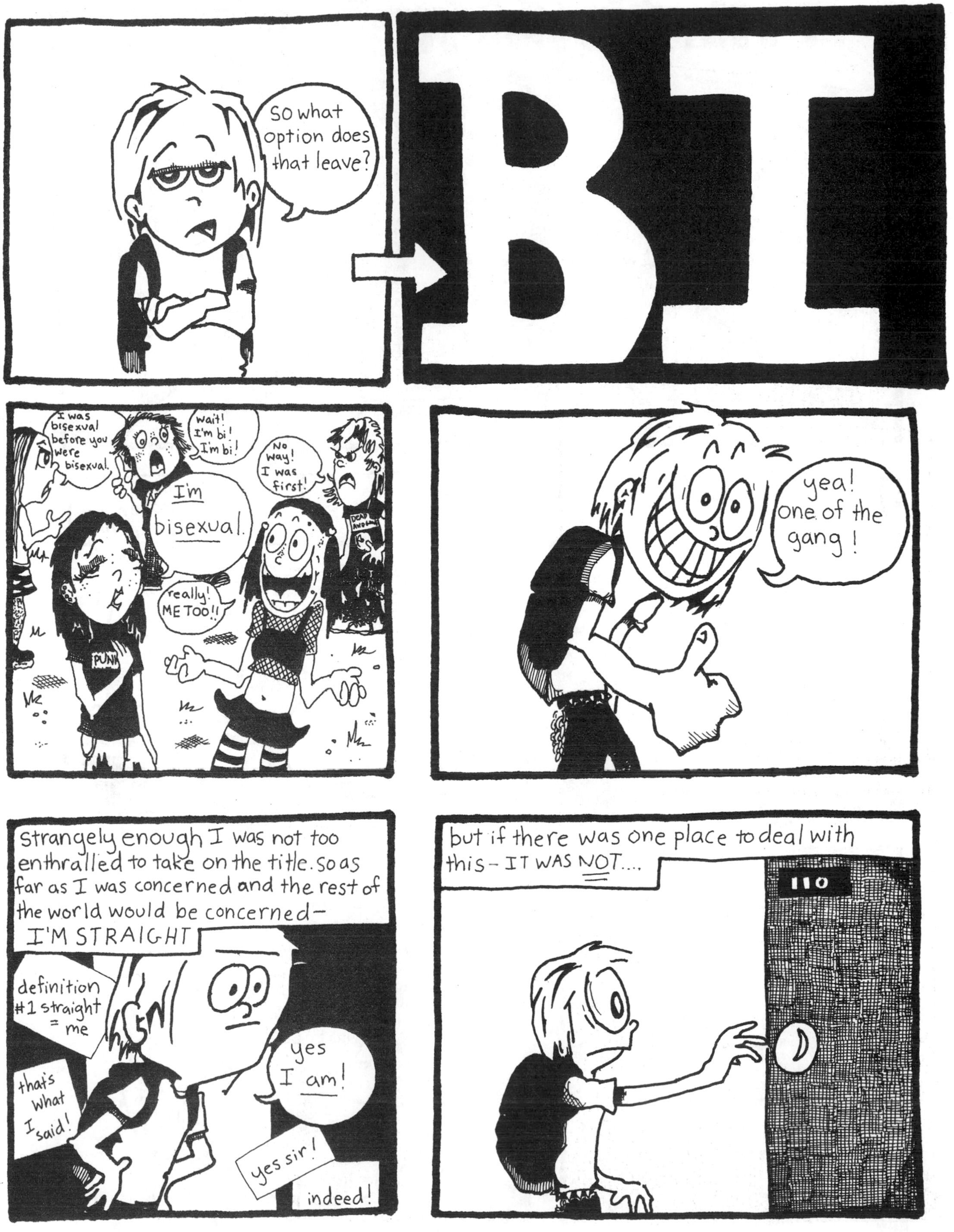
So what option does that leave?
BI
I was bisexual before you were bisexual.
wait! I'm bi! I'm bi!
No way! I was first!
I'm bisexual.
really! ME TOO!!
PUNK
yea! one of the gang!
strangely enough I was not too enthralled to take on the title. so as far as I was concerned and the rest of the world would be concerned—
I'M STRAIGHT
definition #1 straight = me
yes I am!
that's what I said!
yes sir!
indeed!
but if there was one place to deal with this— IT WAS NOT....
110

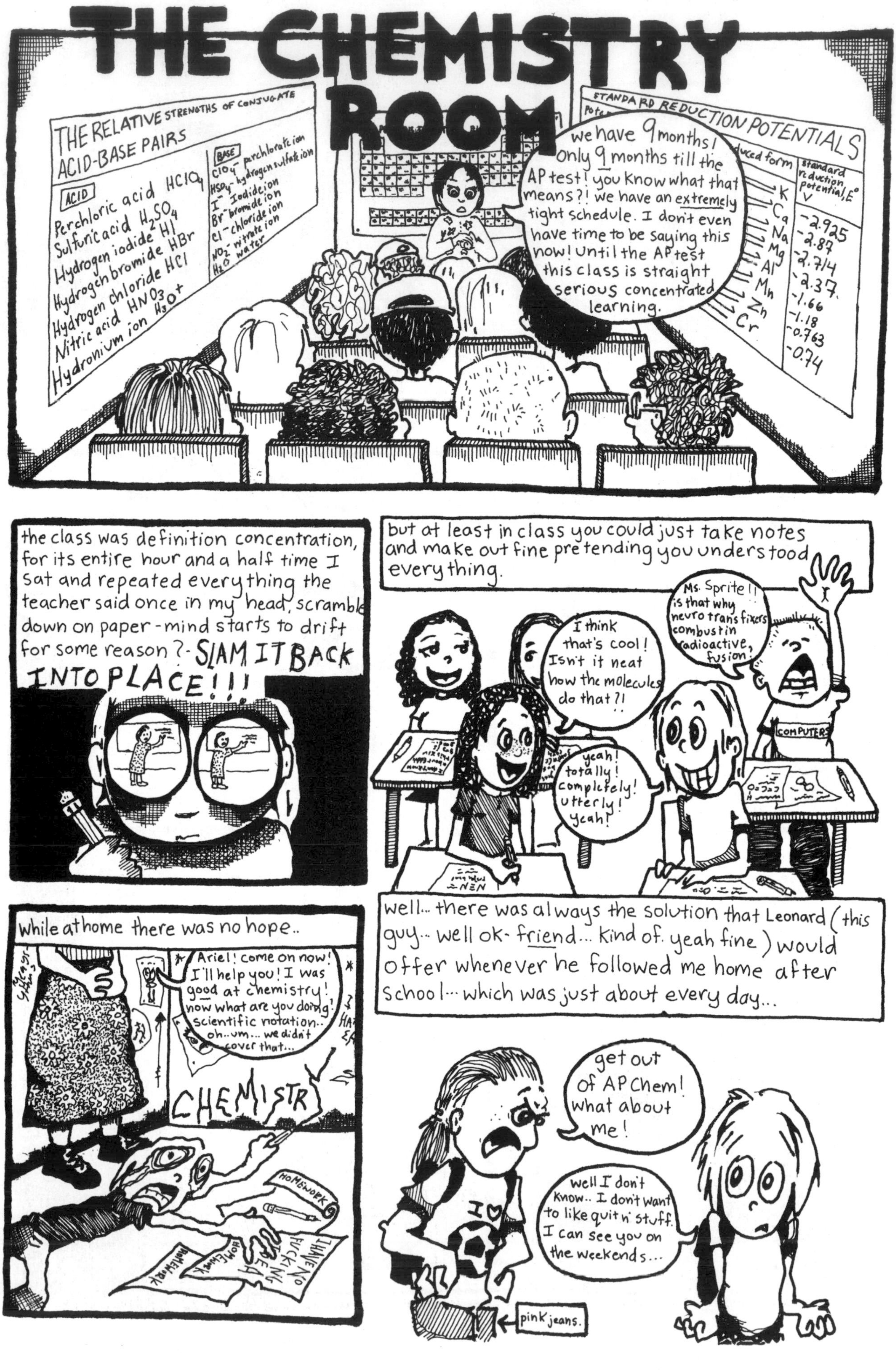
THE CHEMISTRY ROOM
THE RELATIVE STRENGTHS OF CONJUGATE ACID-BASE PAIRS
ACID
Perchloric acid $HClO_4$
Sulfuric acid H_2SO_4
Hydrogen iodide HI
Hydrogen bromide HBr
Hydrogen chloride HCl
Nitric acid HNO_3
Hydronium ion H_3O^+
BASE
ClO_4^- perchlorate ion
HSO_4^- hydrogen sulfate ion
I^- iodide ion
Br^- bromide ion
Cl^- chloride ion
NO_3^- nitrate ion
H_2O water
STANDARD REDUCTION POTENTIALS
standard reduction potential, E° V
K -2.925
Ca -2.87
Na -2.714
Mg -2.37
Al -1.66
Mn -1.18
Zn -0.763
Cr -0.74
we have 9 months! only 9 months till the AP test! you know what that means?! we have an extremely tight schedule. I don't even have time to be saying this now! until the AP test this class is straight serious concentrated learning.
the class was definition concentration, for its entire hour and a half time I sat and repeated everything the teacher said once in my head, scramble down on paper - mind starts to drift for some reason?- SLAM IT BACK INTO PLACE!!!
but at least in class you could just take notes and make out fine pretending you understood everything.
Ms. Sprite!! is that why neuro trans fixers combustin radioactive, fusion?
I think that's cool! Isn't it neat how the molecules do that?!
yeah! totally! completely! utterly! yeah!
COMPUTERS
While at home there was no hope..
Ariel! come on now! I'll help you! I was good at chemistry! now what are you doing? scientific notation.. oh.. um... we didn't cover that...
CHEMISTRY
HOMEWORK
I HAVE NO FUCKING IDEA
well... there was always the solution that Leonard (this guy.. well ok- friend... kind of. yeah fine) would offer whenever he followed me home after school... which was just about every day...
get out of AP Chem! what about me!
well I don't know.. I don't want to like quit n' stuff. I can see you on the weekends...
pink jeans.

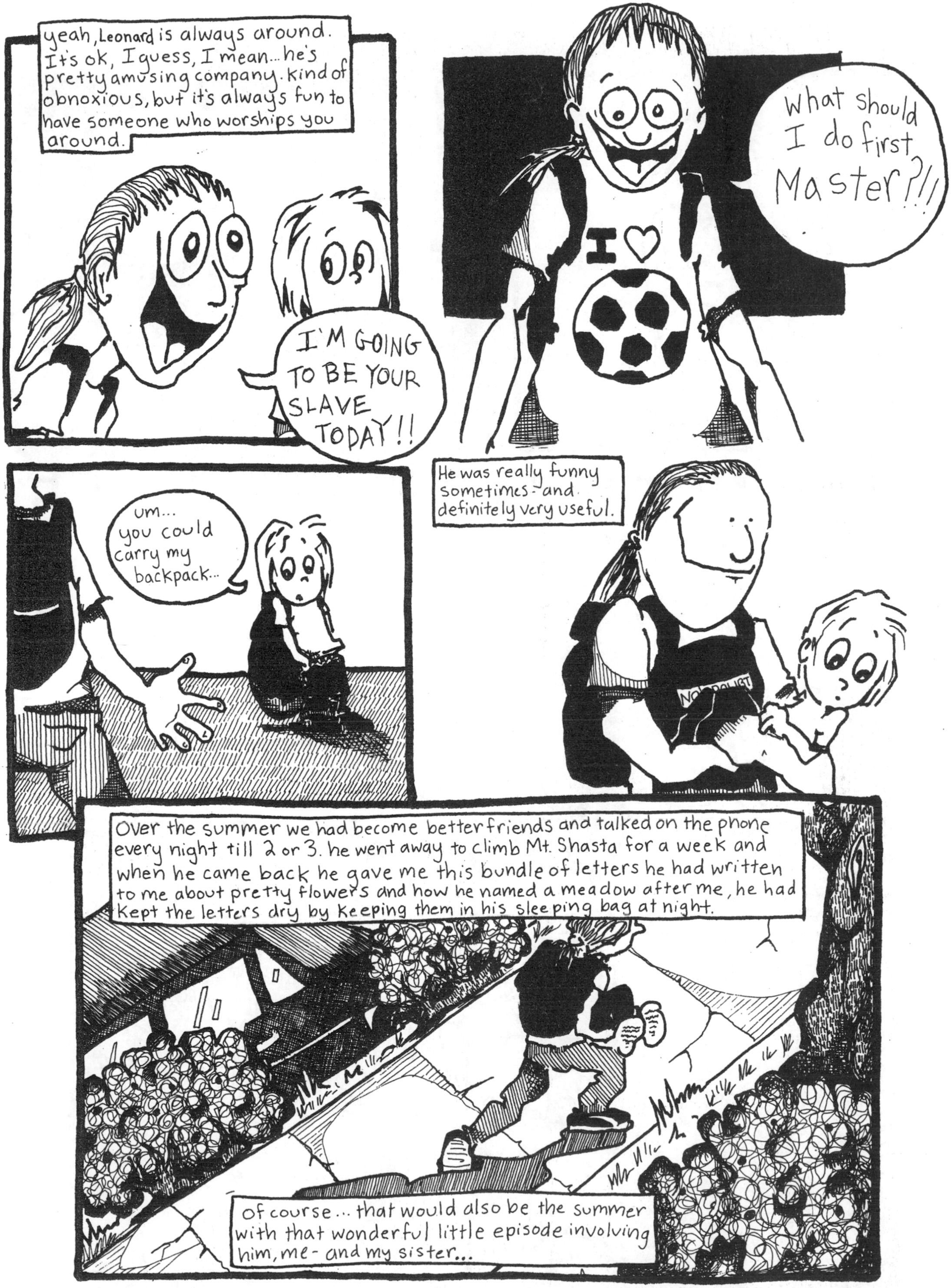

yeah, Leonard is always around. It's ok, I guess, I mean... he's pretty amusing company. kind of obnoxious, but it's always fun to have someone who worships you around.
I'M GOING TO BE YOUR SLAVE TODAY!!
What should I do first Master?!!
um... you could carry my backpack...
He was really funny sometimes - and definitely very useful.
Over the summer we had become better friends and talked on the phone every night till 2 or 3. he went away to climb Mt. Shasta for a week and when he came back he gave me this bundle of letters he had written to me about pretty flowers and how he named a meadow after me, he had kept the letters dry by keeping them in his sleeping bag at night.
Of course... that would also be the summer with that wonderful little episode involving him, me - and my sister...

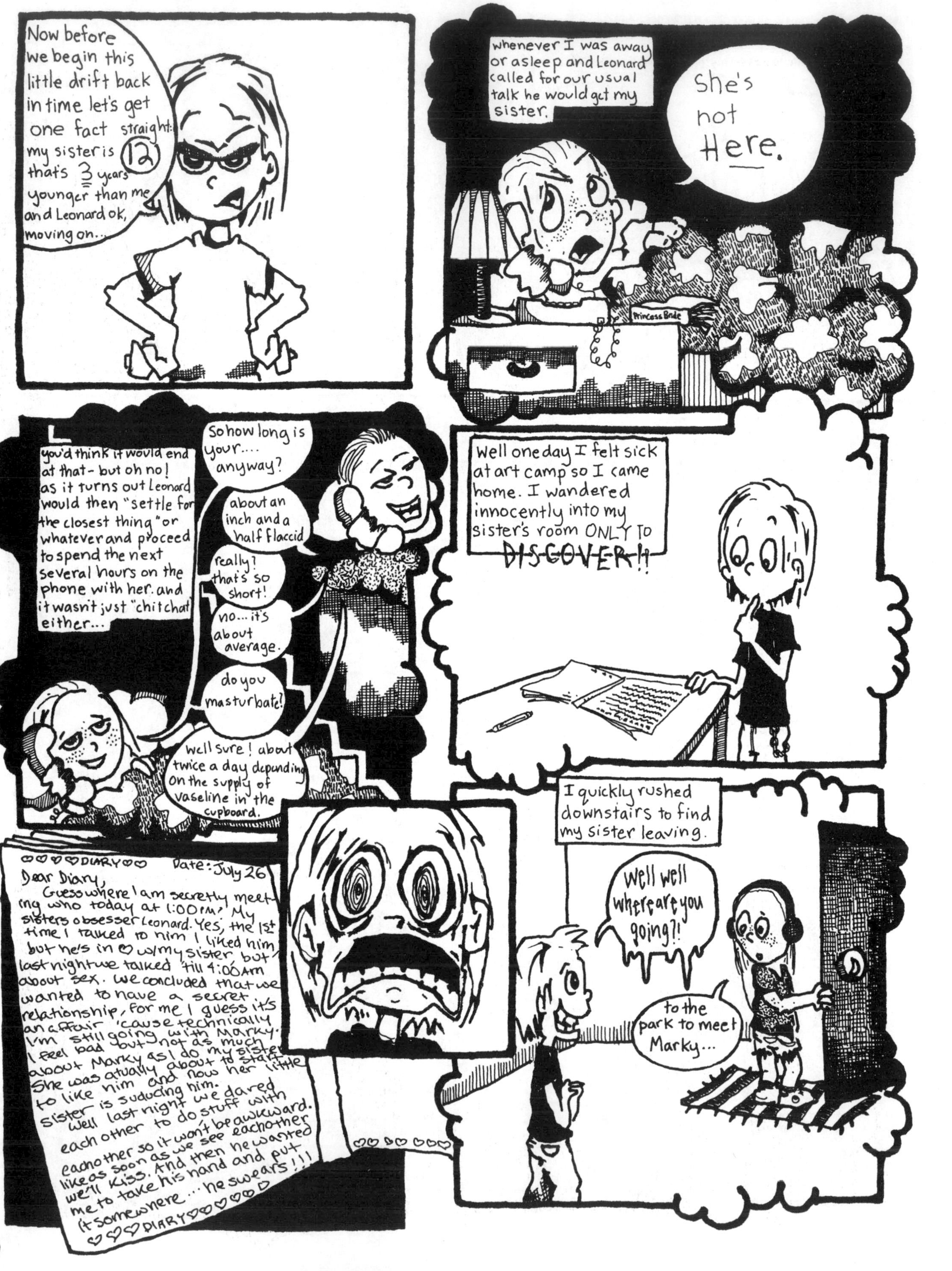
Now before we begin this little drift back in time let's get one fact straight: my sister is 12 that's 3 years younger than me and Leonard ok, moving on...
whenever I was away or asleep and Leonard called for our usual talk he would get my sister.
She's not Here.
Princess Bride
you'd think it would end at that- but oh no! as it turns out Leonard would then "settle for the closest thing" or whatever and proceed to spend the next several hours on the phone with her. and it wasn't just "chit chat" either...
So how long is your.... anyway?
about an inch and a half flaccid
really? that's so short!
no... it's about average.
do you masturbate?
well sure! about twice a day depending on the supply of vaseline in the cupboard.
Well one day I felt sick at art camp so I came home. I wandered innocently into my sister's room ONLY TO DISCOVER!!
DIARY Date: July 26
Dear Diary,
Guess where I am secretly meeting who today at 1:00PM? My sisters obsesser Leonard. Yes, the 1st time I talked to him I liked him but he's in ♡ w/my sister but last night we talked 'till 4:00AM about sex. We concluded that we wanted to have a secret relationship, for me I guess it's an affair 'cause technically I'm still going with Marky. I feel bad but not as much about Marky as I do my sister. She was atually about to start to like him and now her little sister is suducing him.
Well last night we dared each other to do stuff with each other so it won't be awkward. eachother so it won't be awkward. like as soon as we see eachother we'll kiss. And then he wanted me to take his hand and put it somewhere... he swears!!!
DIARY
I quickly rushed downstairs to find my sister leaving.
Well well where are you going?!
to the park to meet Marky...

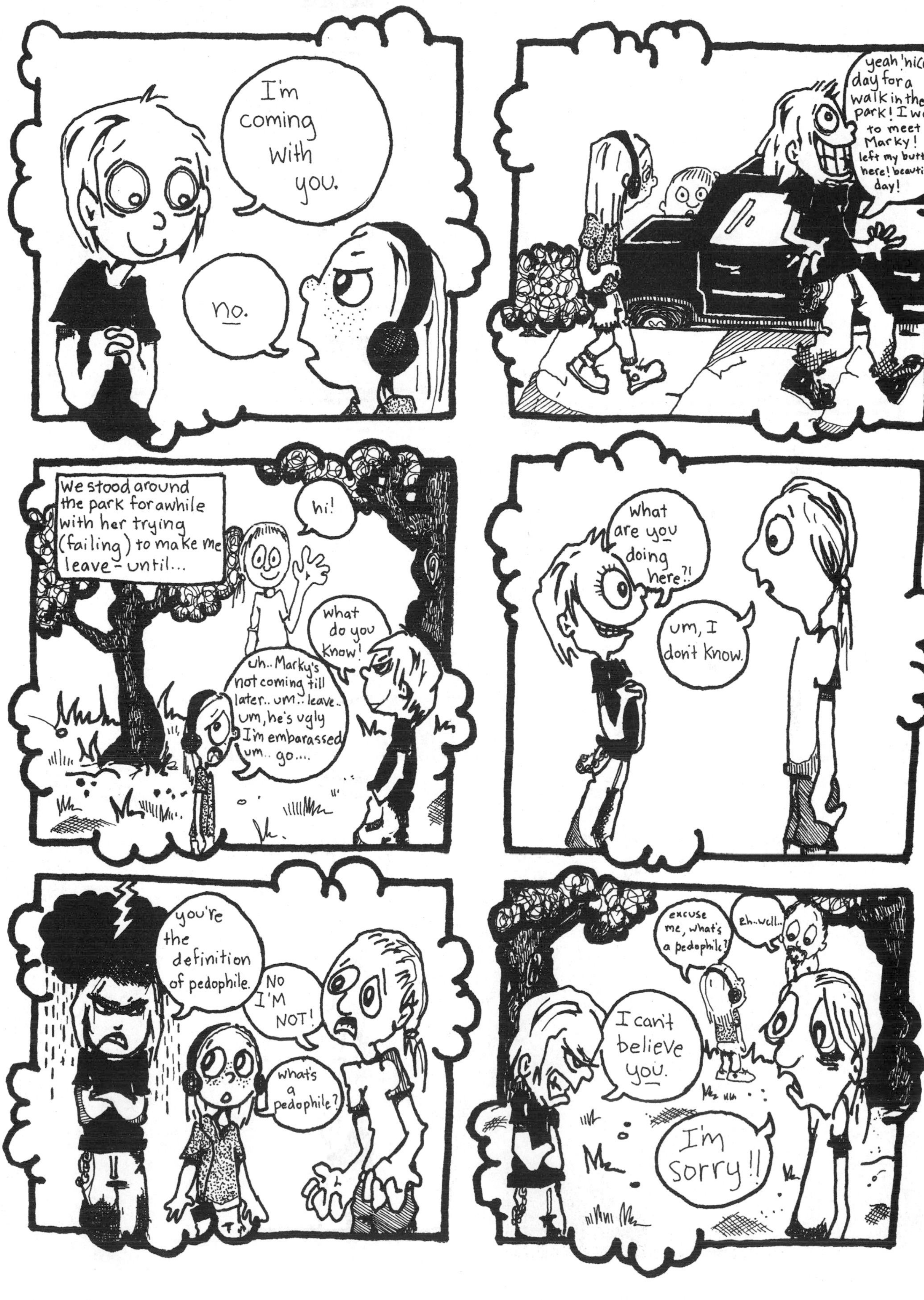
I'm coming with you.
no.
yeah! nice day for a walk in the park! I want to meet Marky! left my button here! beautiful day!
We stood around the park for awhile with her trying (failing) to make me leave - until...
hi!
what do you know!
uh.. Marky's not coming till later.. um.. leave.. um, he's ugly I'm embarassed um.. go....
What are you doing here?!
um, I don't know.
you're the definition of pedophile.
NO I'M NOT!
what's a pedophile?
excuse me, what's a pedophile?
eh..well..
I can't believe you.
I'm sorry!!

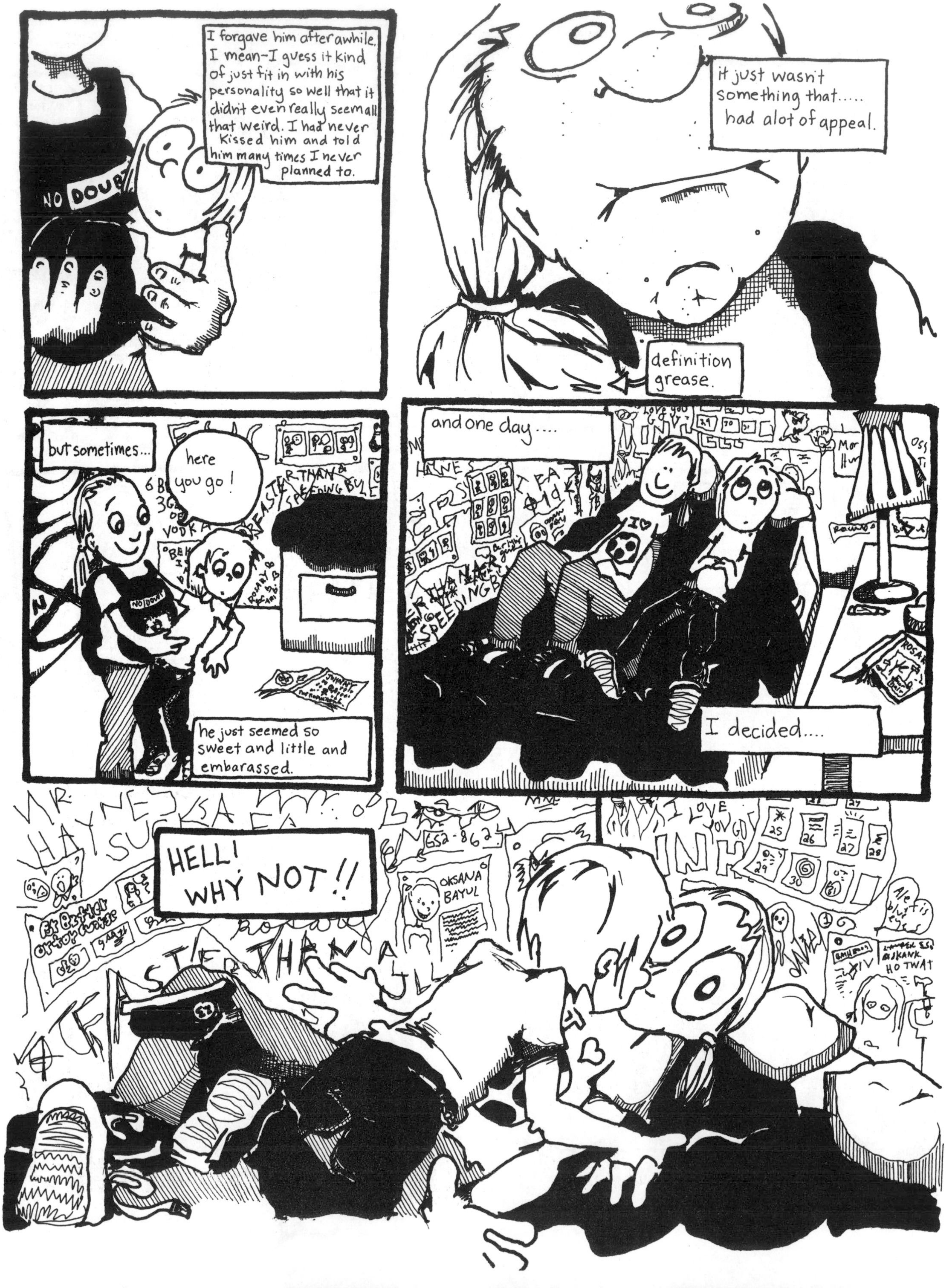
I forgave him after awhile. I mean-I guess it kind of just fit in with his personality so well that it didn't even really seem all that weird. I had never kissed him and told him many times I never planned to.
NO DOUBT
it just wasn't something that..... had alot of appeal.
definition grease.
but sometimes...
here you go!
he just seemed so sweet and little and embarassed.
and one day....
I decided....
HELL! WHY NOT!!
OKSANA BAYUL

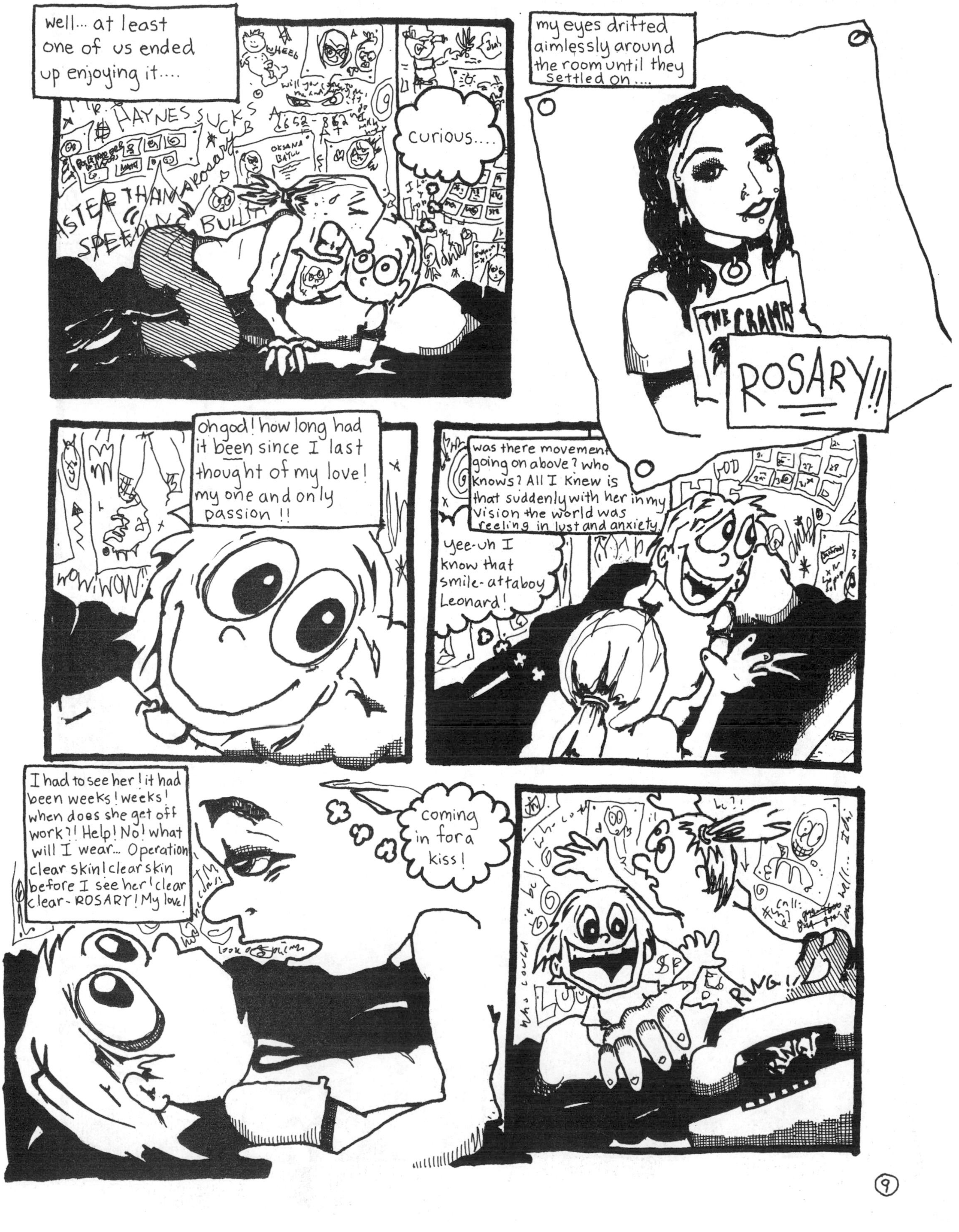
well... at least one of us ended up enjoying it....
curious....
my eyes drifted aimlessly around the room until they settled on....
ROSARY!!
ohgod! how long had it been since I last thought of my love! my one and only passion !!
wow! WOW!!
was there movement going on above? who knows? All I knew is that suddenly with her in my vision the world was reeling in lust and anxiety
yee-uh I know that smile-attaboy Leonard!
I had to see her! it had been weeks! weeks! when does she get off work?! Help! No! what will I wear... Operation clear skin! clear skin before I see her! clear clear- ROSARY! My love!
coming in for a kiss!
RING!!

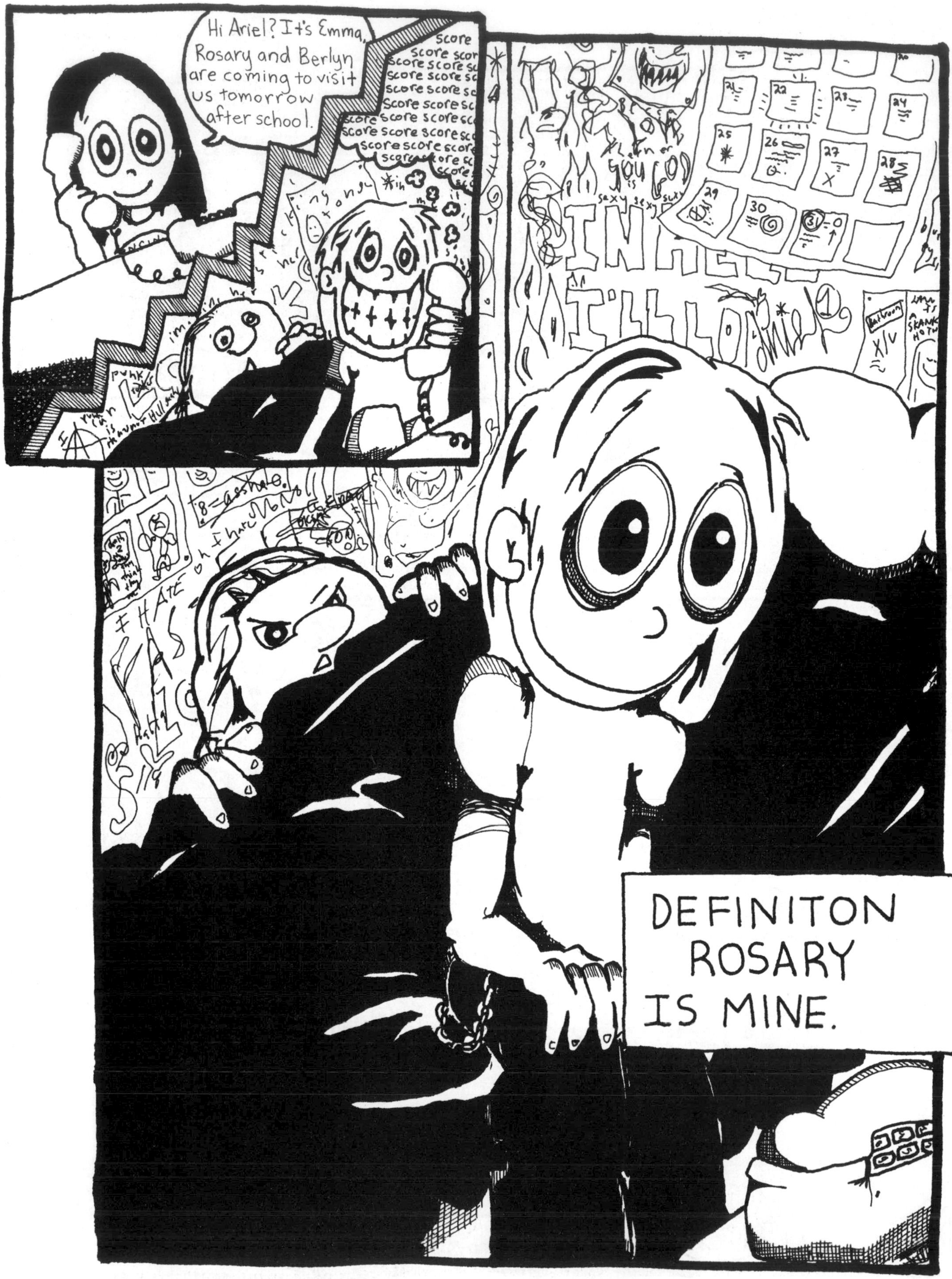
Hi Ariel? It's Emma. Rosary and Berlyn are coming to visit us tomorrow after school.
DEFINITON ROSARY IS MINE.

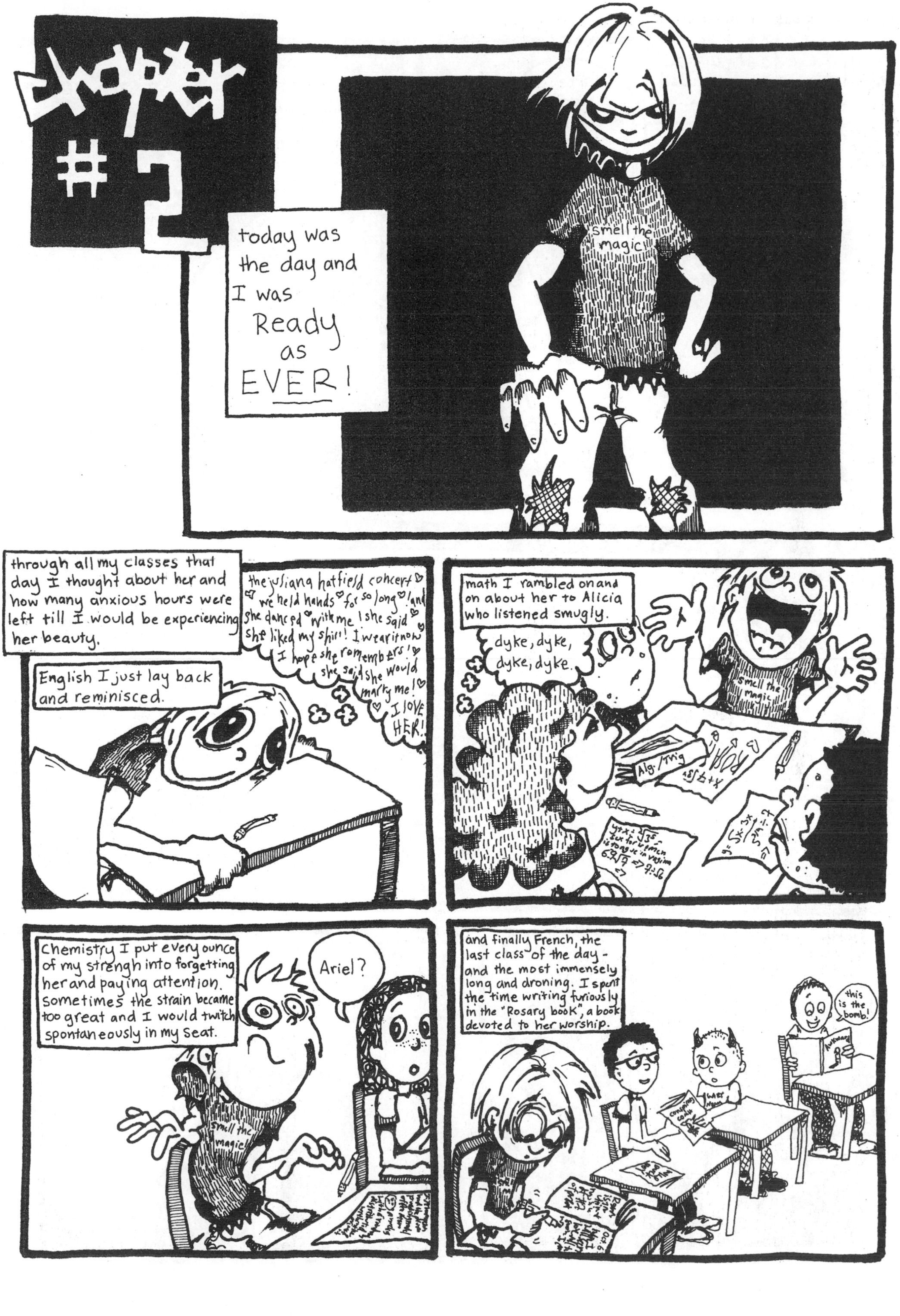
chapter
2
today was the day and I was Ready as EVER!
smell the magic
through all my classes that day I thought about her and how many anxious hours were left till I would be experiencing her beauty.
English I just lay back and reminisced.
the juliana hatfield concert we held hands for so long! and she danced with me! she said she liked my shirt! I wear it now I hope she remembers! she said she would marry me! I LOVE HER!
math I rambled on and on about her to Alicia who listened smugly.
dyke, dyke, dyke, dyke.
smell the magic
Alg./Trig
Chemistry I put every ounce of my strengh into forgetting her and paying attention. Sometimes the strain became too great and I would twitch spontaneously in my seat.
Ariel?
smell the magic
and finally French, the last class of the day - and the most immensely long and droning. I spent the time writing furiously in the "Rosary book", a book devoted to her worship.
this is the bomb!

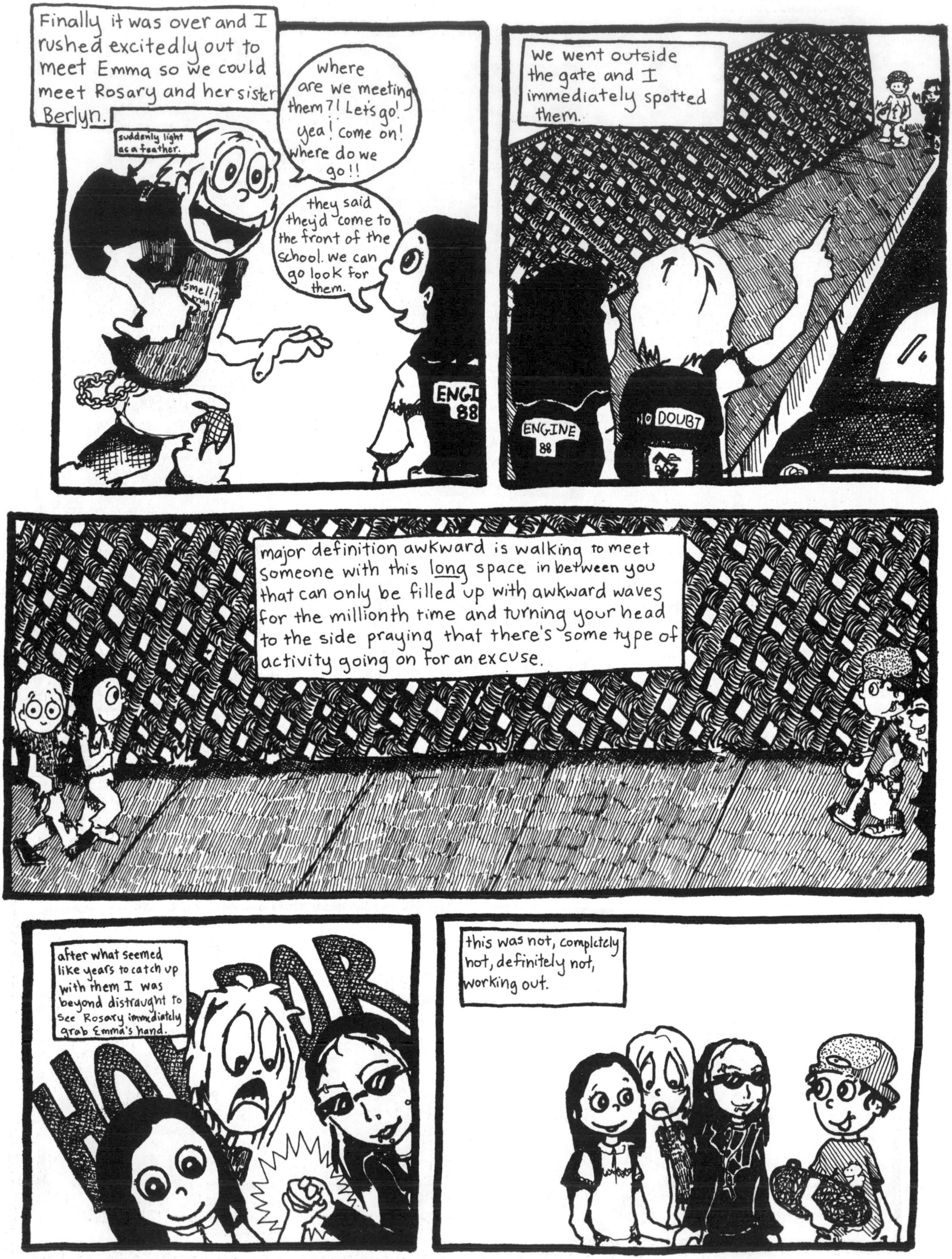
Finally it was over and I rushed excitedly out to meet Emma so we could meet Rosary and her sister Berlyn.
suddenly light as a feather.
where are we meeting them?! Let's go! yea! come on! where do we go!!
they said they'd come to the front of the school. we can go look for them.
ENGI 88
We went outside the gate and I immediately spotted them.
ENGINE 88
NO DOUBT
major definition awkward is walking to meet someone with this long space in between you that can only be filled up with awkward waves for the millionth time and turning your head to the side praying that there's some type of activity going on for an excuse.
after what seemed like years to catch up with them I was beyond distraught to see Rosary immediately grab Emma's hand.
this was not, completely not, definitely not, working out.

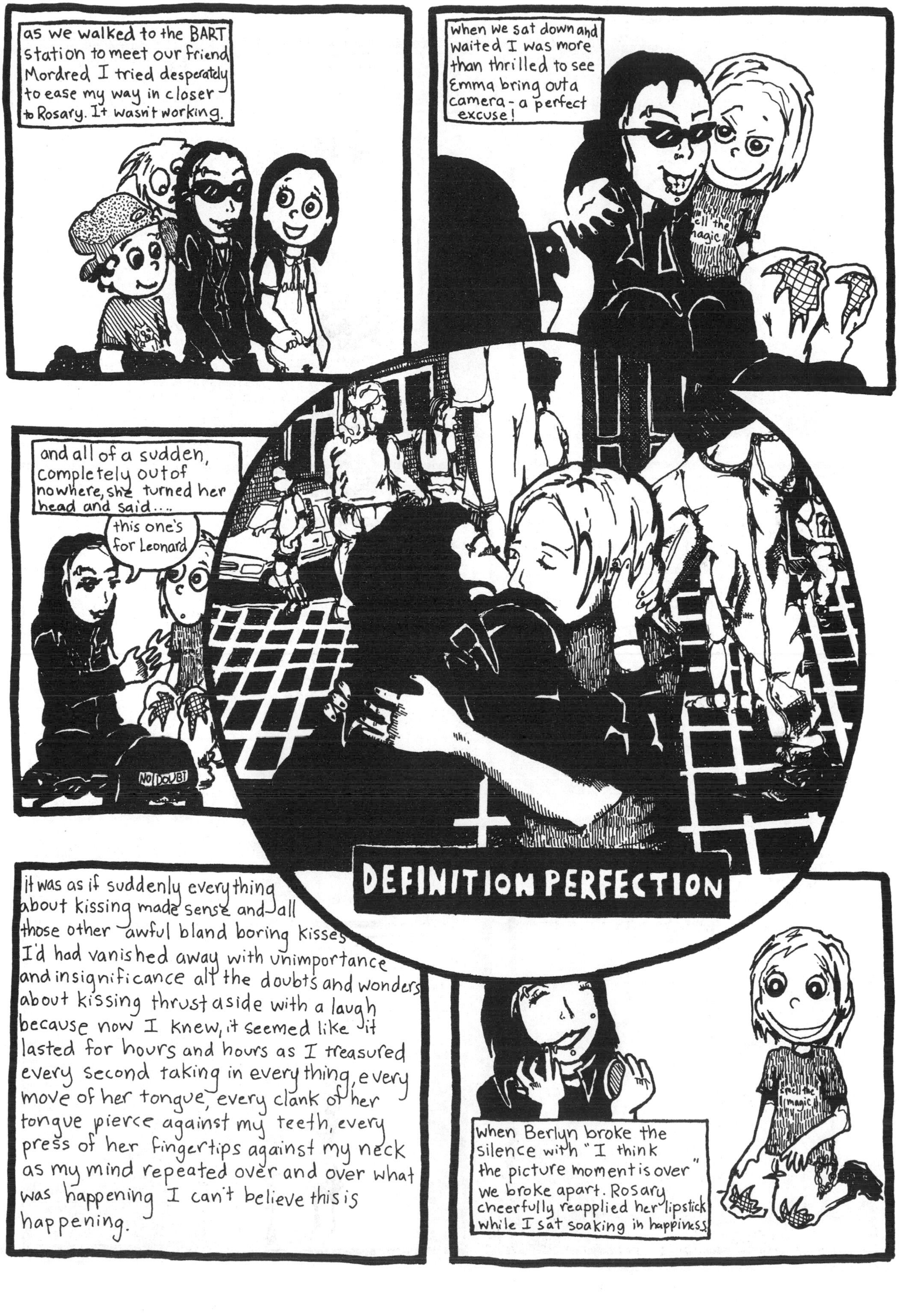
as we walked to the BART station to meet our friend Mordred I tried desperately to ease my way in closer to Rosary. It wasn't working.
when we sat down and waited I was more than thrilled to see Emma bring out a camera - a perfect excuse!
and all of a sudden, completely out of nowhere, she turned her head and said....
this one's for Leonard
NO DOUBT
DEFINITION PERFECTION
it was as if suddenly everything about kissing made sense and all those other awful bland boring kisses I'd had vanished away with unimportance and insignificance all the doubts and wonders about kissing thrust aside with a laugh because now I knew, it seemed like it lasted for hours and hours as I treasured every second taking in everything, every move of her tongue, every clank of her tongue pierce against my teeth, every press of her fingertips against my neck as my mind repeated over and over what was happening I can't believe this is happening.
when Berlyn broke the silence with "I think the picture moment is over" we broke apart. Rosary cheerfully reapplied her lipstick while I sat soaking in happiness.
smell the magic

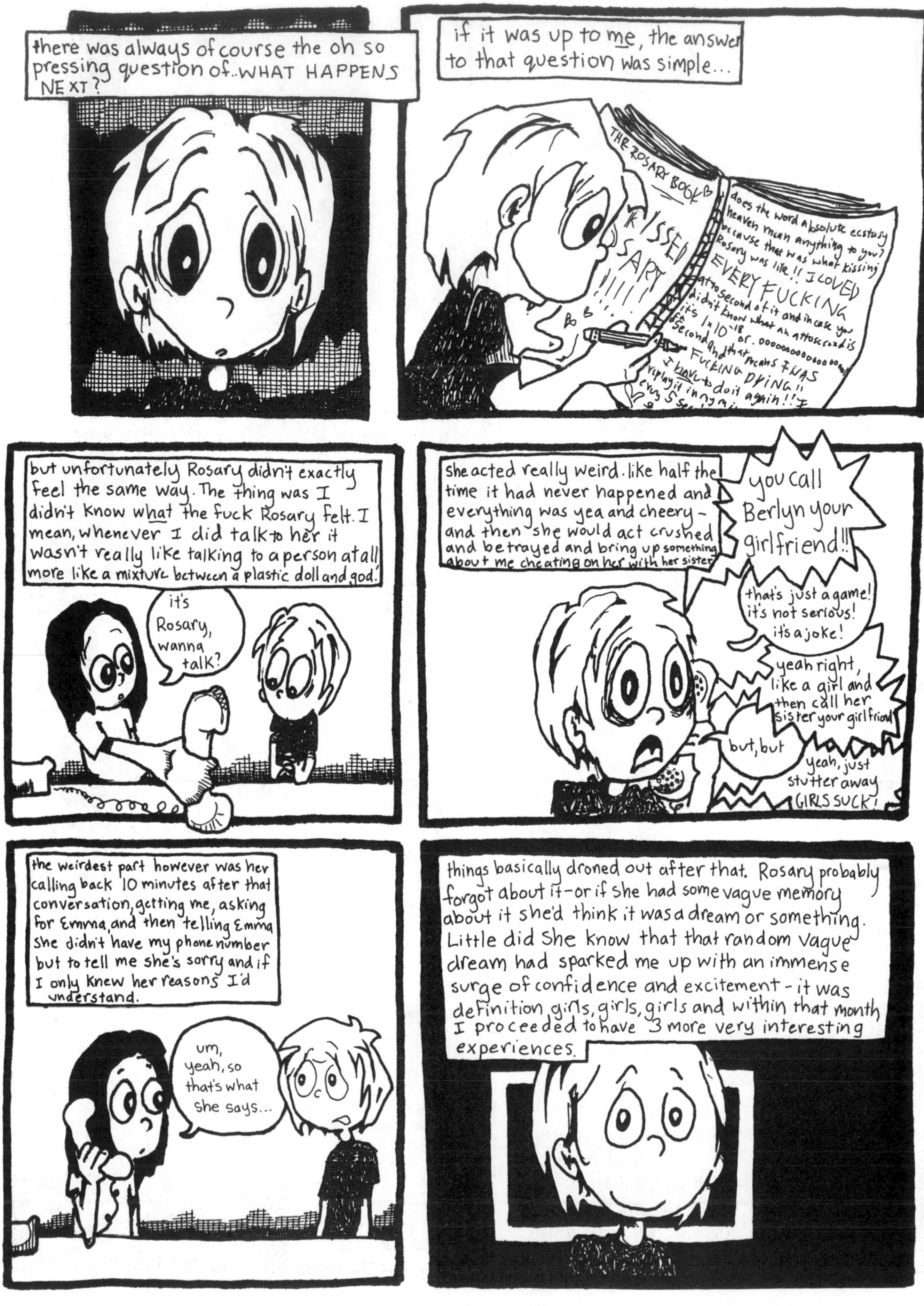

there was always of course the oh so pressing question of..WHAT HAPPENS NEXT?
if it was up to me, the answer to that question was simple...
THE ROSARY BOOK
KISSED SARY!!!!!
does the word absolute ecstasy heaven mean anything to you? because that was what kissing Rosary was like!! I LOVED EVERY FUCKING attosecond of it and in case you didn't know what an attosecond is its 1×10⁻¹⁸ or .000000000000000 of a second and that means I WAS FUCKING DYING!! I have to do it again!!
but unfortunately Rosary didn't exactly feel the same way. The thing was I didn't know what the fuck Rosary felt. I mean, whenever I did talk to her it wasn't really like talking to a person at all more like a mixture between a plastic doll and god.
it's Rosary, wanna talk?
she acted really weird. like half the time it had never happened and everything was yea and cheery - and then she would act crushed and betrayed and bring up something about me cheating on her with her sister
you call Berlyn your girlfriend!!
that's just a game! it's not serious! it's a joke!
yeah right, like a girl and then call her sister your girlfriend
but, but
yeah, just stutter away GIRLS SUCK!
the weirdest part however was her calling back 10 minutes after that conversation, getting me, asking for Emma, and then telling Emma she didn't have my phone number but to tell me she's sorry and if I only knew her reasons I'd understand.
um, yeah, so that's what she says...
things basically droned out after that. Rosary probably forgot about it - or if she had some vague memory about it she'd think it was a dream or something. Little did she know that that random vague dream had sparked me up with an immense surge of confidence and excitement - it was definition girls, girls, girls and within that month I proceeded to have 3 more very interesting experiences.

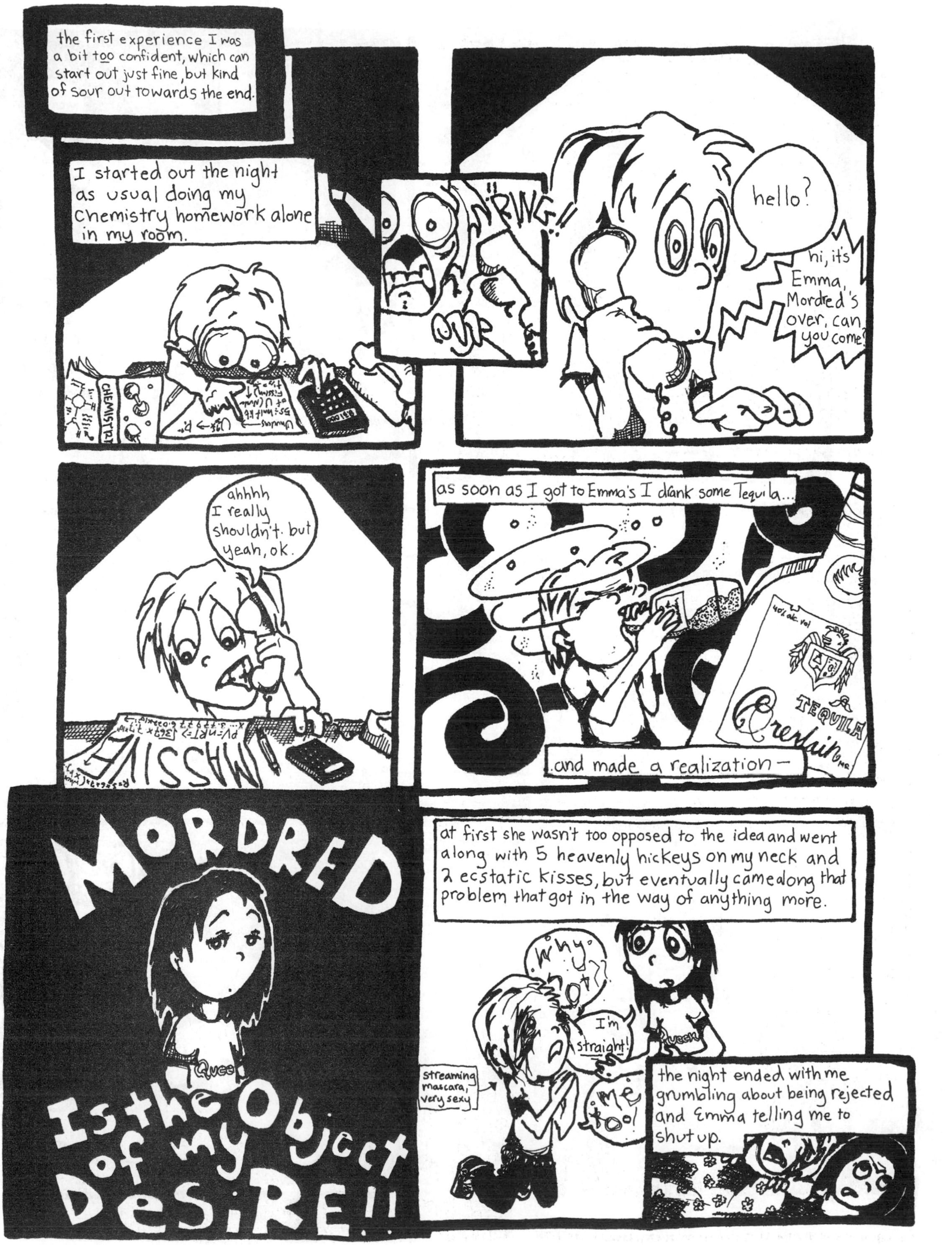

the first experience I was a bit too confident, which can start out just fine, but kind of sour out towards the end.
I started out the night as usual doing my chemistry homework alone in my room.
CHEMISTRY
RING!!
hello?
hi, it's Emma, Mordred's over, can you come?
ahhhh I really shouldn't. but yeah, ok.
MASSIVE
as soon as I got to Emma's I drank some Tequila...
TEQUILA
...and made a realization—
MORDRED Is the Object of my DESiRE!!
at first she wasn't too opposed to the idea and went along with 5 heavenly hickeys on my neck and 2 ecstatic kisses, but eventually came along that problem that got in the way of anything more.
why not?
I'm straight!
me too!
streaming mascara, very sexy
the night ended with me grumbling about being rejected and Emma telling me to shut up.

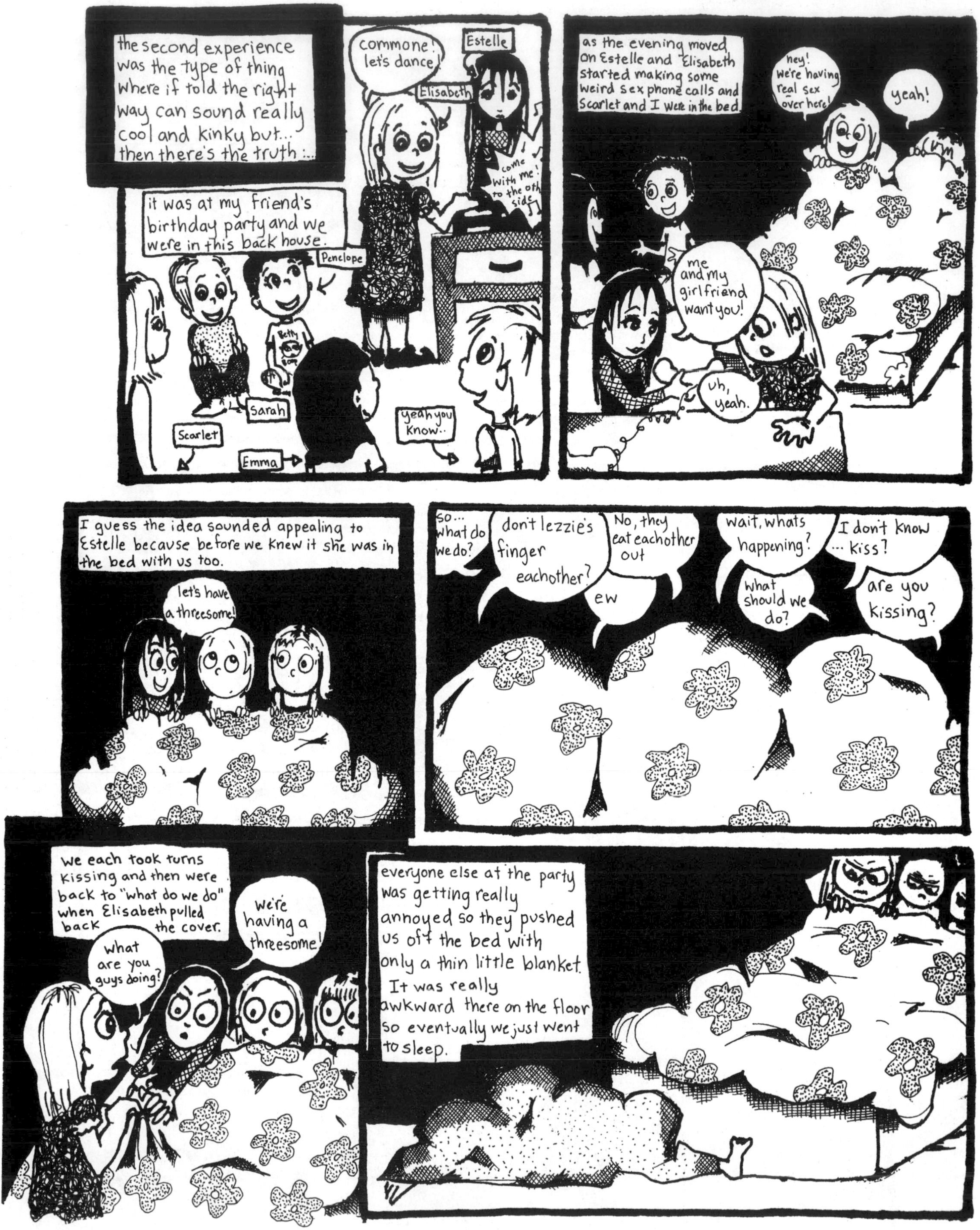
the second experience was the type of thing where if told the right way can sound really cool and kinky but... then there's the truth...
commone! let's dance!
Estelle
Elisabeth
come with me! to the oth side
it was at my friend's birthday party and we were in this back house.
Penelope
Sarah
Scarlet
Emma
yeah you know..
as the evening moved on Estelle and Elisabeth started making some weird sex phone calls and Scarlet and I were in the bed
hey! we're having real sex over here!
yeah!
um
me and my girlfriend want you!
uh, yeah.
I guess the idea sounded appealing to Estelle because before we knew it she was in the bed with us too.
let's have a threesome!
so... what do we do?
don't lezzie's finger eachother?
No, they eat eachother out
ew
wait, whats happening?
what should we do?
I don't know ... kiss?
are you kissing?
We each took turns kissing and then were back to "what do we do" when Elisabeth pulled back the cover.
what are you guys doing?
we're having a threesome!
everyone else at the party was getting really annoyed so they pushed us off the bed with only a thin little blanket. It was really awkward there on the floor so eventually we just went to sleep.

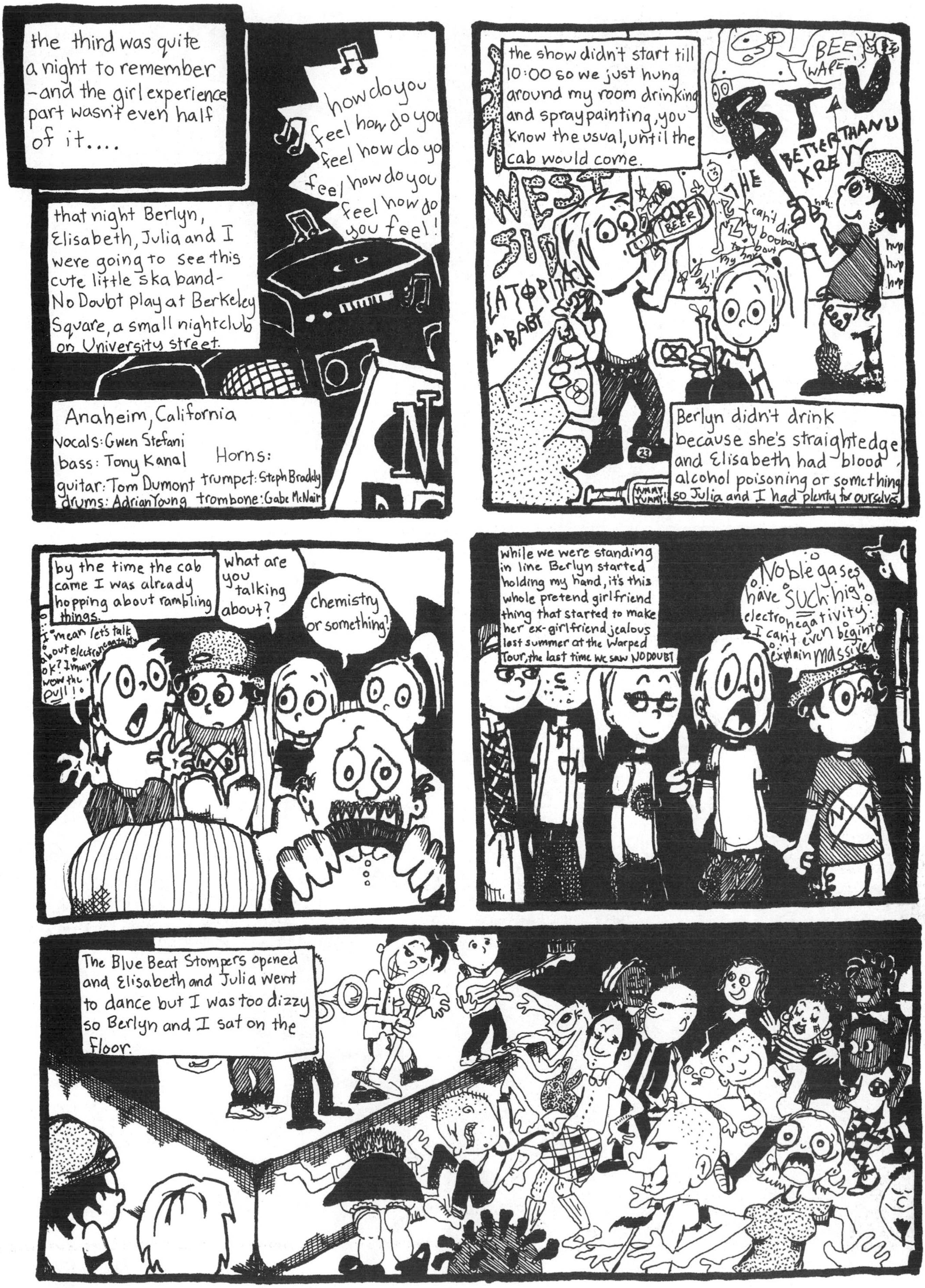

the third was quite a night to remember -and the girl experience part wasn't even half of it....
how do you feel how do you feel how do you feel how do you feel how do you feel!
that night Berlyn, Elisabeth, Julia and I were going to see this cute little ska band- No Doubt play at Berkeley Square, a small nightclub on University street.
Anaheim, California
vocals: Gwen Stefani
bass: Tony Kanal
guitar: Tom Dumont
drums: Adrian Young
Horns:
trumpet: Steph Bradley
trombone: Gabe McNair
the show didn't start till 10:00 so we just hung around my room drinking and spraypainting, you know the usual, until the cab would come.
BEE WARE
BTU
THE BETTER THAN U KREW
WEST SIDE
BEER
hup hup hup
Berlyn didn't drink because she's straightedge and Elisabeth had blood alcohol poisoning or something so Julia and I had plenty for ourselves
by the time the cab came I was already hopping about rambling things.
I mean let's talk about electronegativity ok? I mean wow the pull!
what are you talking about?
chemistry or something?
while we were standing in line Berlyn started holding my hand, it's this whole pretend girlfriend thing that started to make her ex-girlfriend jealous last summer at the Warped Tour, the last time we saw NO DOUBT
Noble gases have SUCH high electronegativity! I can't even begin to explain massive!
The Blue Beat Stompers opened and Elisabeth and Julia went to dance but I was too dizzy so Berlyn and I sat on the floor.

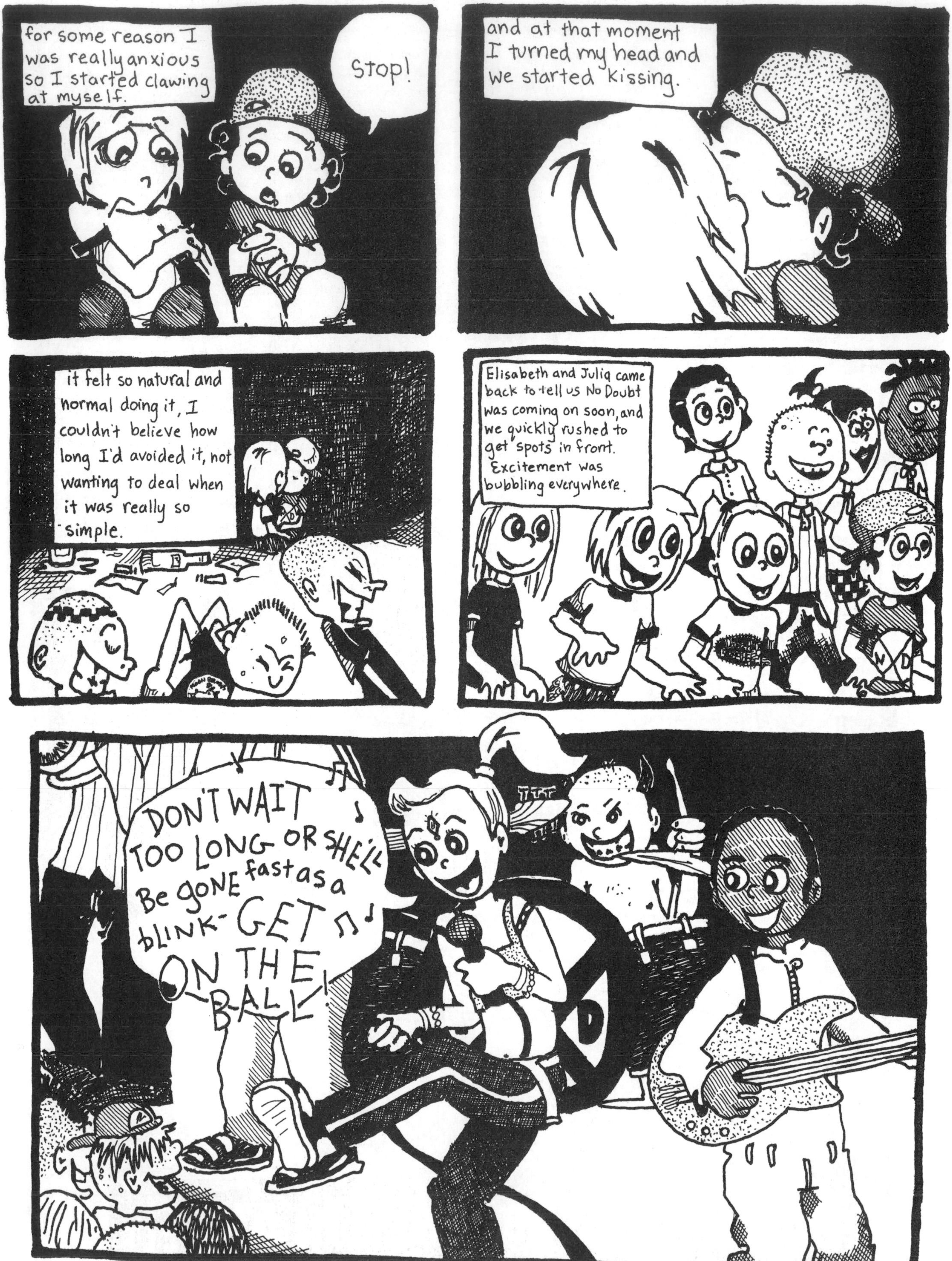
for some reason I was really anxious so I started clawing at myself.
Stop!
and at that moment I turned my head and we started kissing.
it felt so natural and normal doing it, I couldn't believe how long I'd avoided it, not wanting to deal when it was really so simple.
Elisabeth and Julia came back to tell us No Doubt was coming on soon, and we quickly rushed to get spots in front. Excitement was bubbling everywhere.
DON'T WAIT TOO LONG OR SHE'LL Be GONE fast as a bLINK- GET ON THE BALL!

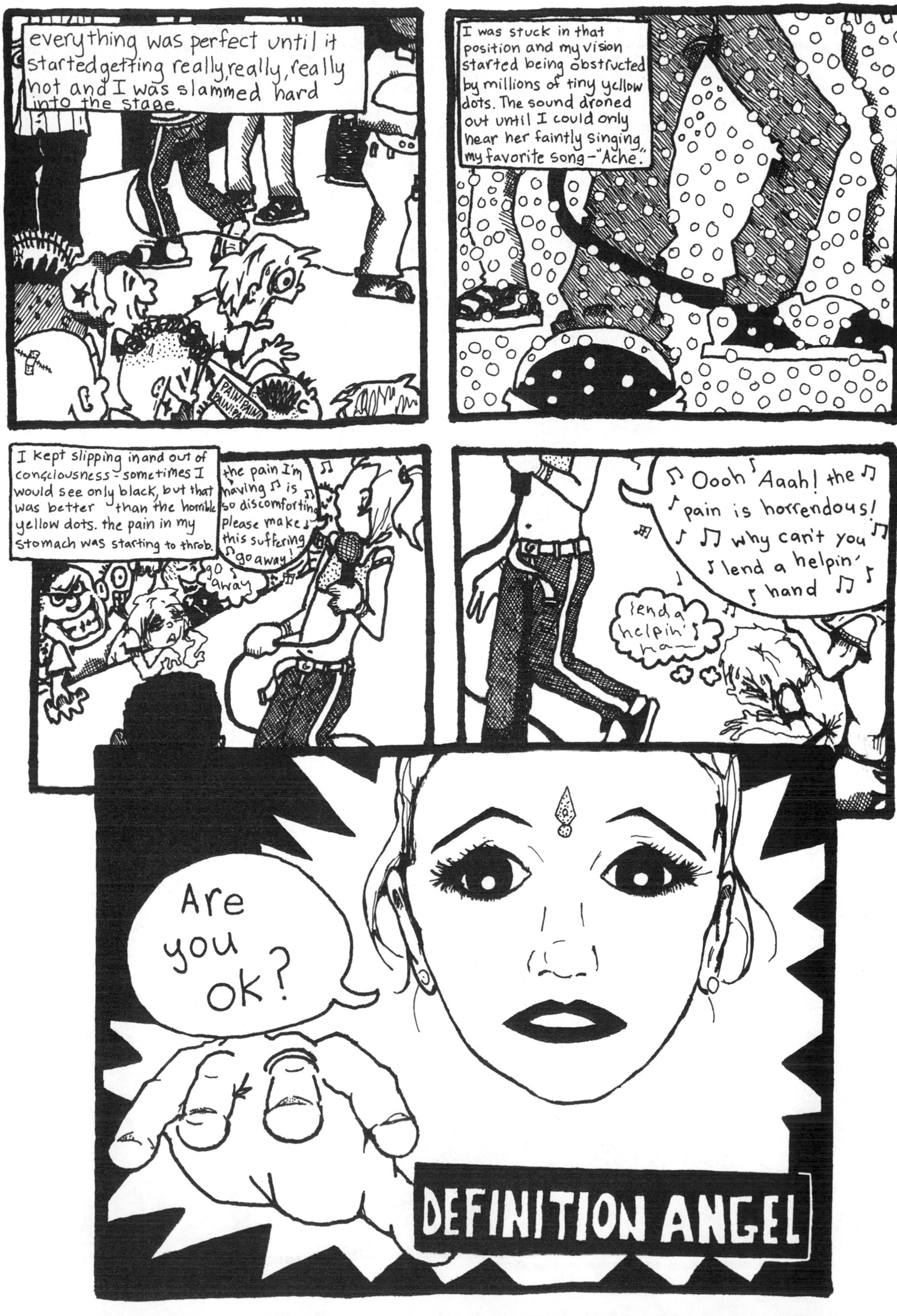
everything was perfect until it started getting really, really, really hot and I was slammed hard into the stage.
PAIN! PAIN! PAIN! PA
I was stuck in that position and my vision started being obstructed by millions of tiny yellow dots. The sound droned out until I could only hear her faintly singing my favorite song—"Ache".
I kept slipping in and out of consciousness—sometimes I would see only black, but that was better than the horrible yellow dots. the pain in my stomach was starting to throb.
the pain I'm having ♫ is so discomforting please make ♪ this suffering ♫ go away!
go away
♪ Oooh ♪ Aaah! the ♫ pain is horrendous! ♪ ♫ why can't you ♪ lend a helpin' ♪ hand ♫
lend a helpin' ♪ ha—
Are you ok?
DEFINITION ANGEL

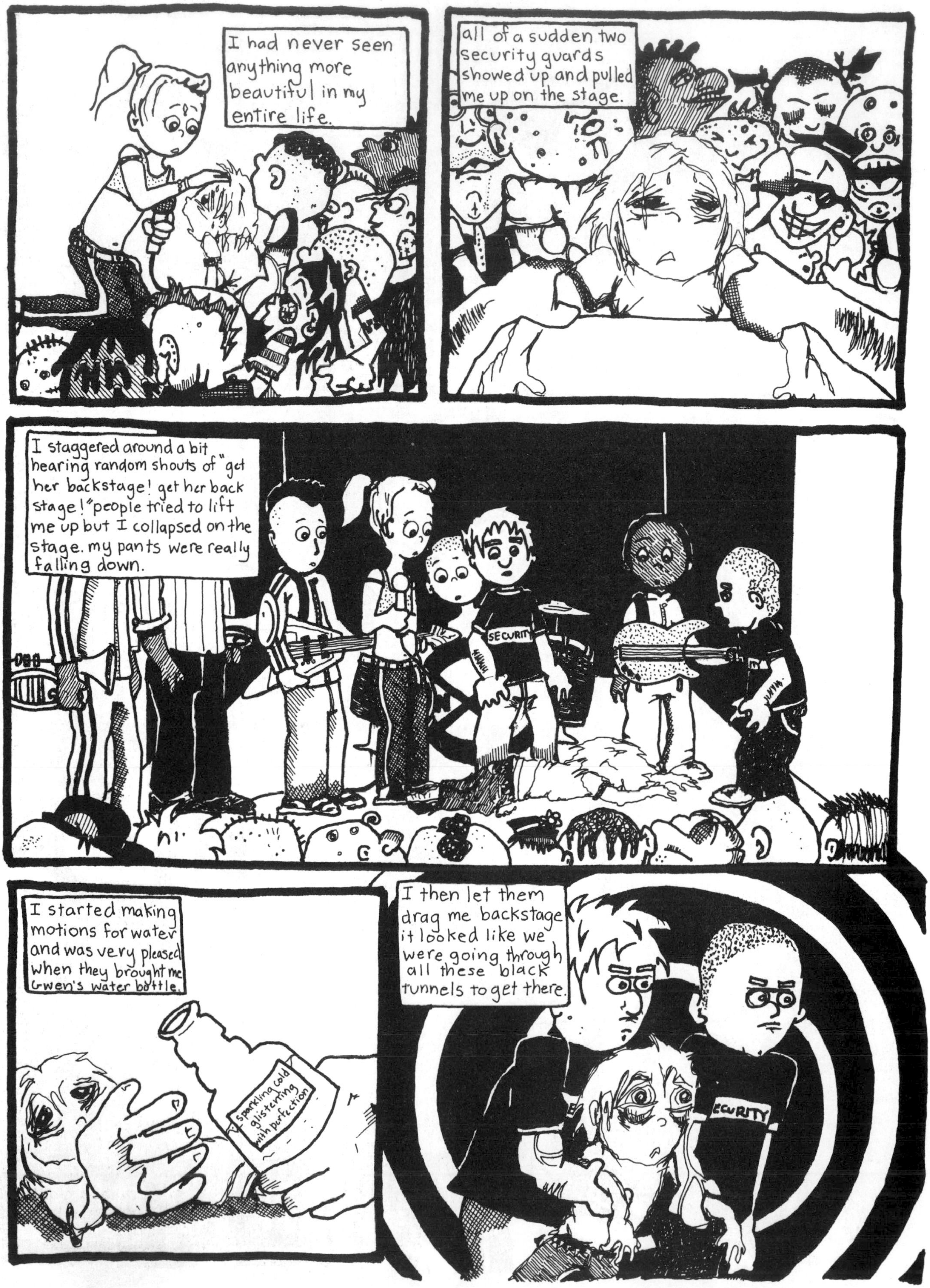
I had never seen anything more beautiful in my entire life.
all of a sudden two security guards showed up and pulled me up on the stage.
I staggered around a bit hearing random shouts of "get her backstage! get her back stage!" people tried to lift me up but I collapsed on the stage. my pants were really falling down.
SECURITY
I started making motions for water and was very pleased when they brought me Gwen's water bottle.
Sparkling cold glistening with perfection
I then let them drag me backstage it looked like we were going through all these black tunnels to get there.
ECURITY

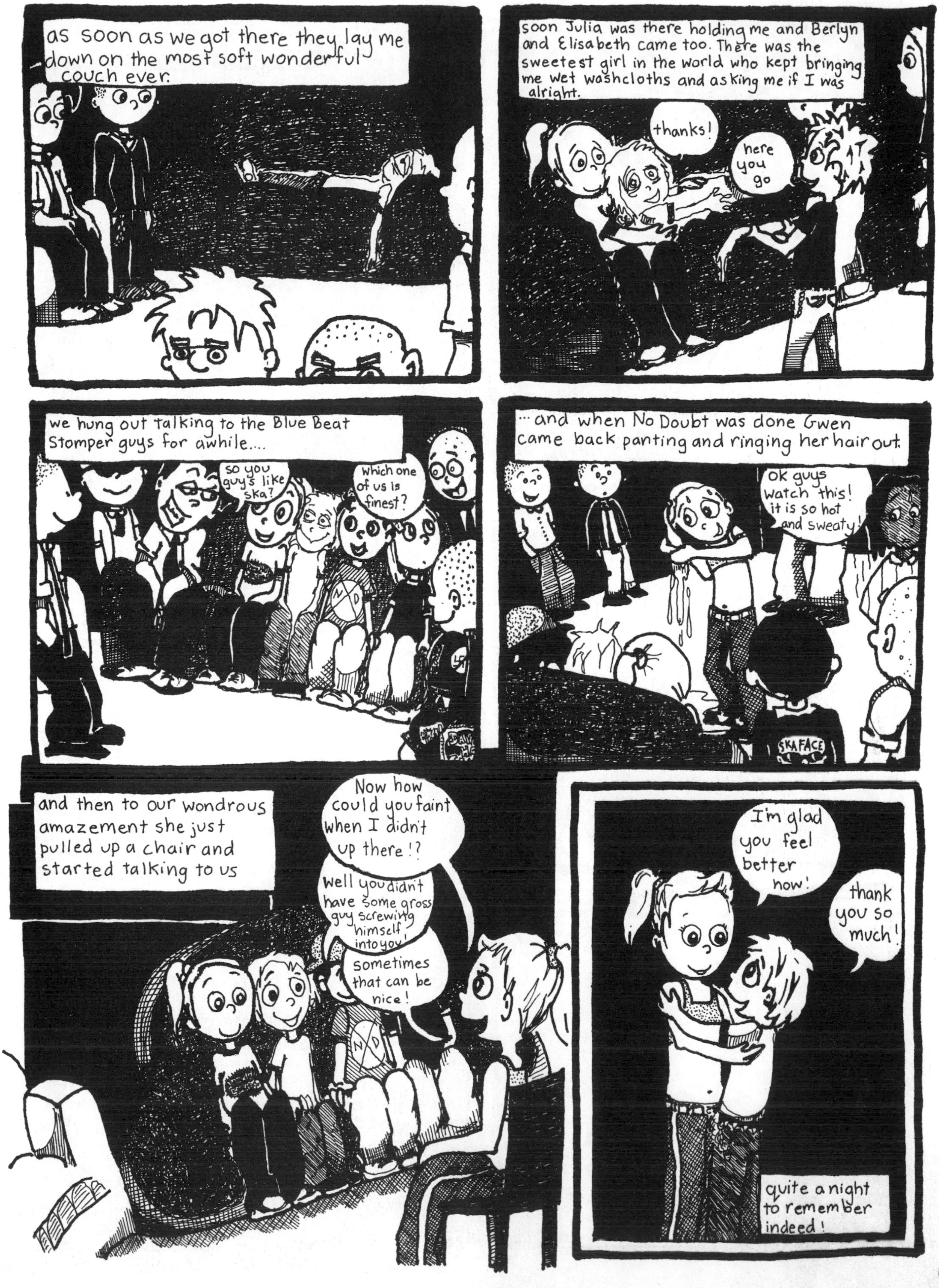
as soon as we got there they lay me down on the most soft wonderful couch ever.
soon Julia was there holding me and Berlyn and Elisabeth came too. There was the sweetest girl in the world who kept bringing me wet washcloths and asking me if I was alright.
thanks!
here you go
we hung out talking to the Blue Beat Stomper guys for awhile....
so you guy's like ska?
which one of us is finest?
...and when No Doubt was done Gwen came back panting and ringing her hair out.
Ok guys watch this! it is so hot and sweaty!
SKAFACE
and then to our wondrous amazement she just pulled up a chair and started talking to us
Now how could you faint when I didn't up there!?
well you didn't have some gross guy screwing himself into you!
sometimes that can be nice!
I'm glad you feel better now!
thank you so much!
quite a night to remember indeed!

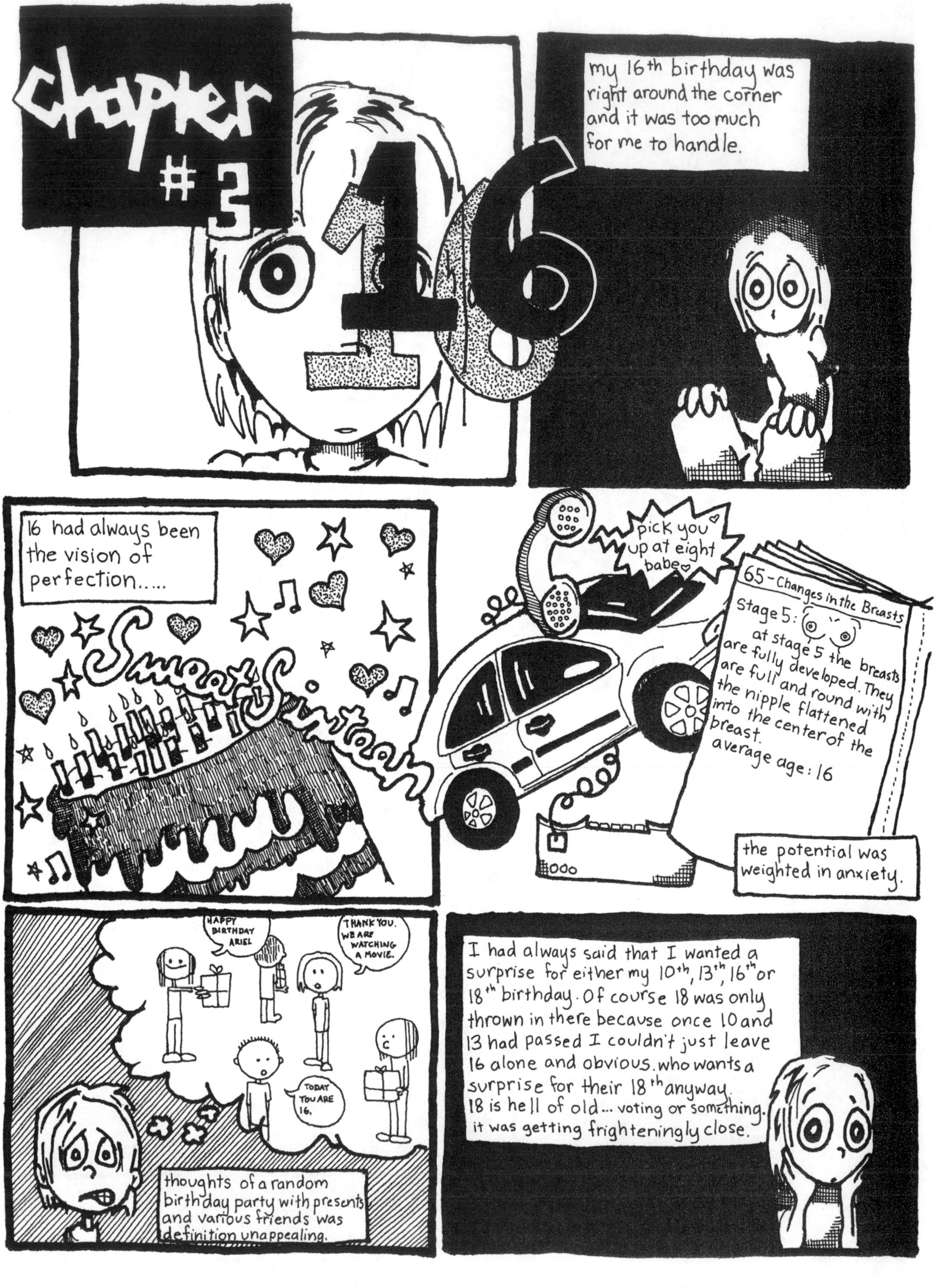
chapter #3
16
my 16th birthday was right around the corner and it was too much for me to handle.
16 had always been the vision of perfection.....
Sweet Sixteen
pick you up at eight babe♡
65 - Changes in the Breasts
Stage 5:
at stage 5 the breasts are fully developed. They are full and round with the nipple flattened into the center of the breast.
average age: 16
the potential was weighted in anxiety.
HAPPY BIRTHDAY ARIEL
THANK YOU. WE ARE WATCHING A MOVIE.
TODAY YOU ARE 16.
thoughts of a random birthday party with presents and various friends was definition unappealing.
I had always said that I wanted a surprise for either my 10th, 13th, 16th or 18th birthday. Of course 18 was only thrown in there because once 10 and 13 had passed I couldn't just leave 16 alone and obvious. who wants a surprise for their 18th anyway. 18 is hell of old... voting or something. it was getting frighteningly close.

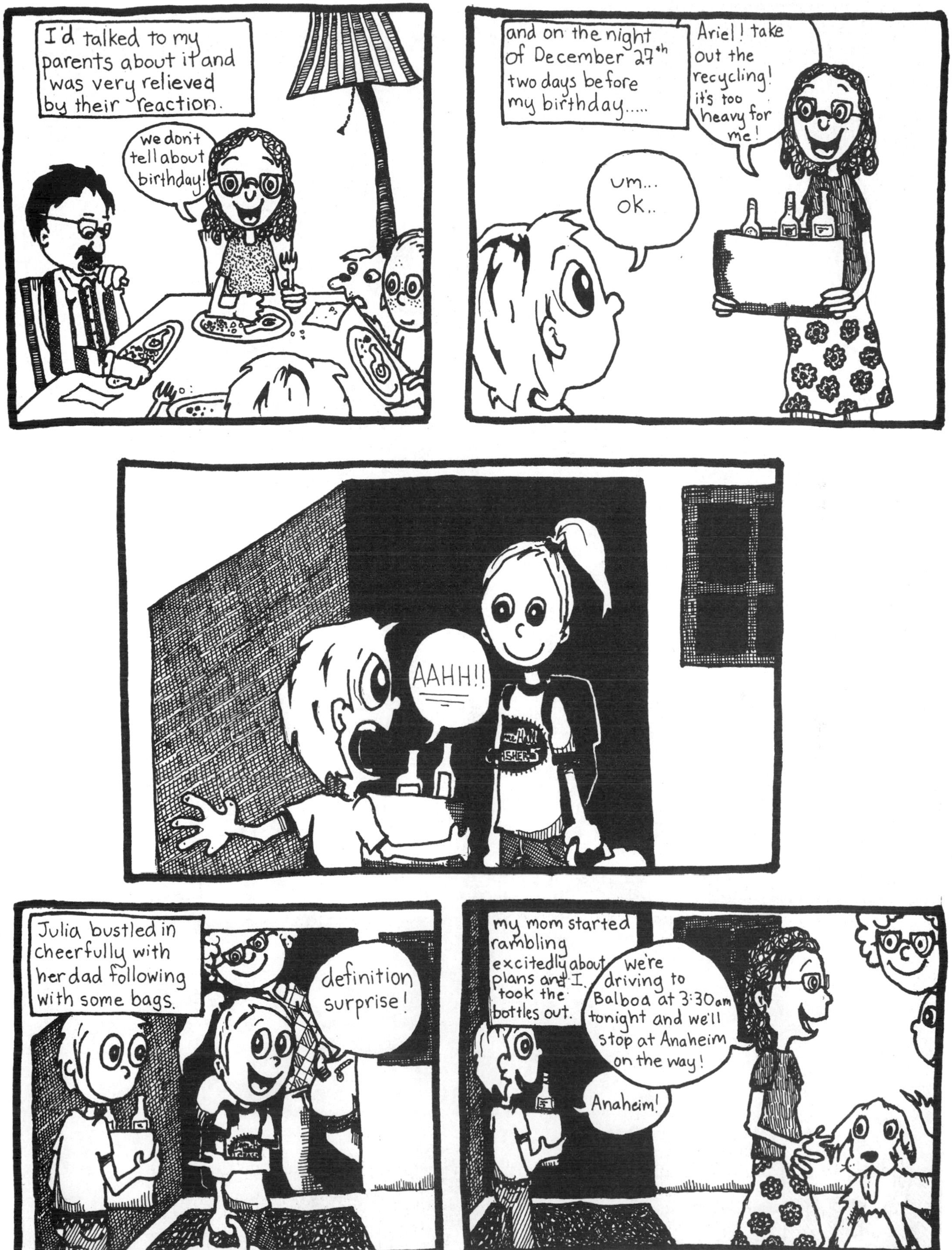
I'd talked to my parents about it and was very relieved by their reaction.
we don't tell about birthday!
and on the night of December 27th two days before my birthday.....
Ariel! take out the recycling! it's too heavy for me!
um... ok..
AAHH!!
Julia bustled in cheerfully with her dad following with some bags.
definition surprise!
my mom started rambling excitedly about plans and I took the bottles out.
we're driving to Balboa at 3:30am tonight and we'll stop at Anaheim on the way!
Anaheim!

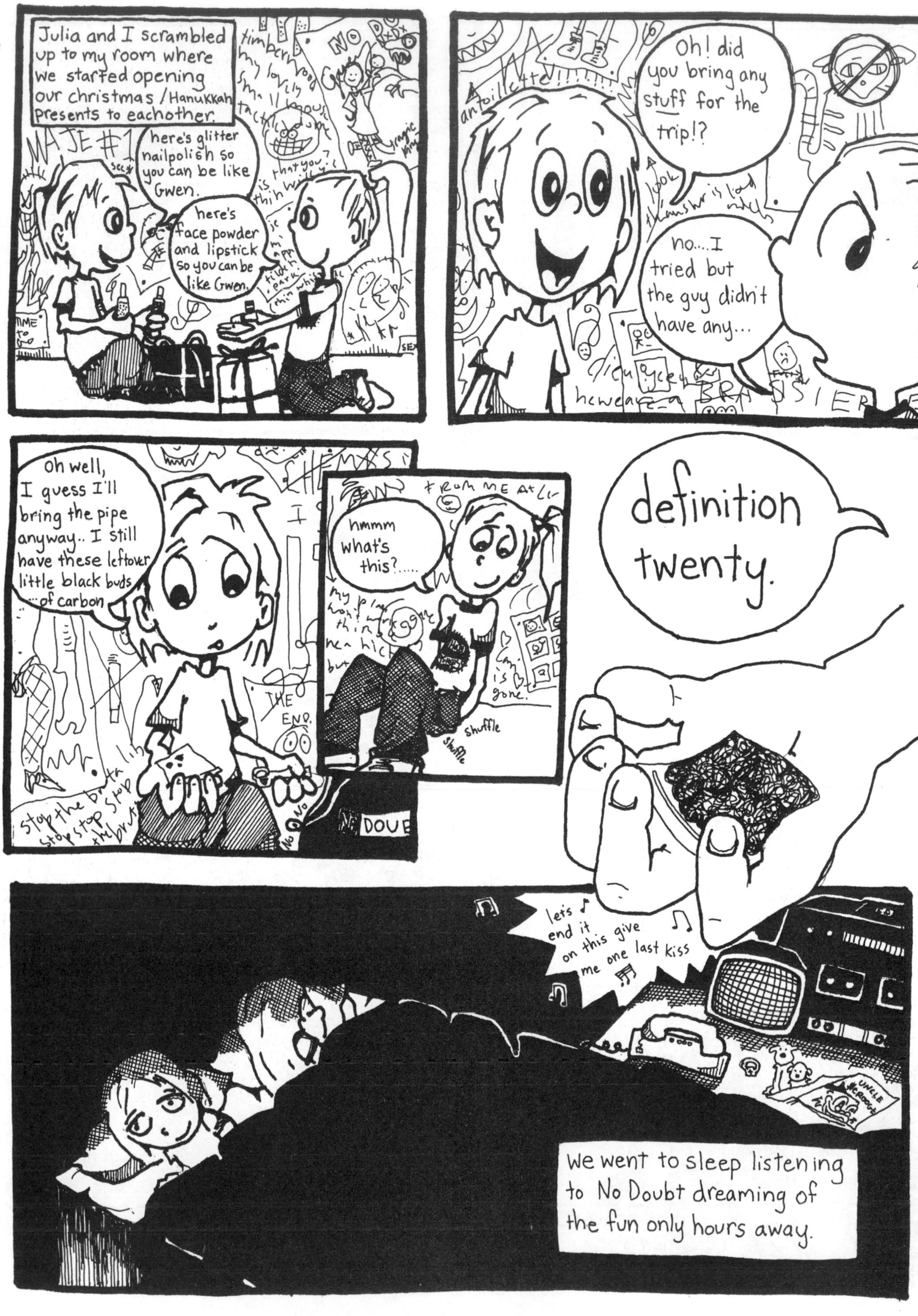
Julia and I scrambled up to my room where we started opening our christmas / Hanukkah presents to eachother.
here's glitter nailpolish so you can be like Gwen.
here's face powder and lipstick so you can be like Gwen.
Oh! did you bring any stuff for the trip!?
no.... I tried but the guy didn't have any...
Oh well, I guess I'll bring the pipe anyway.. I still have these leftover little black buds of carbon
hmmm what's this?.....
shuffle
shuffle
definition twenty.
let's end it on this give me one last kiss
We went to sleep listening to No Doubt dreaming of the fun only hours away.

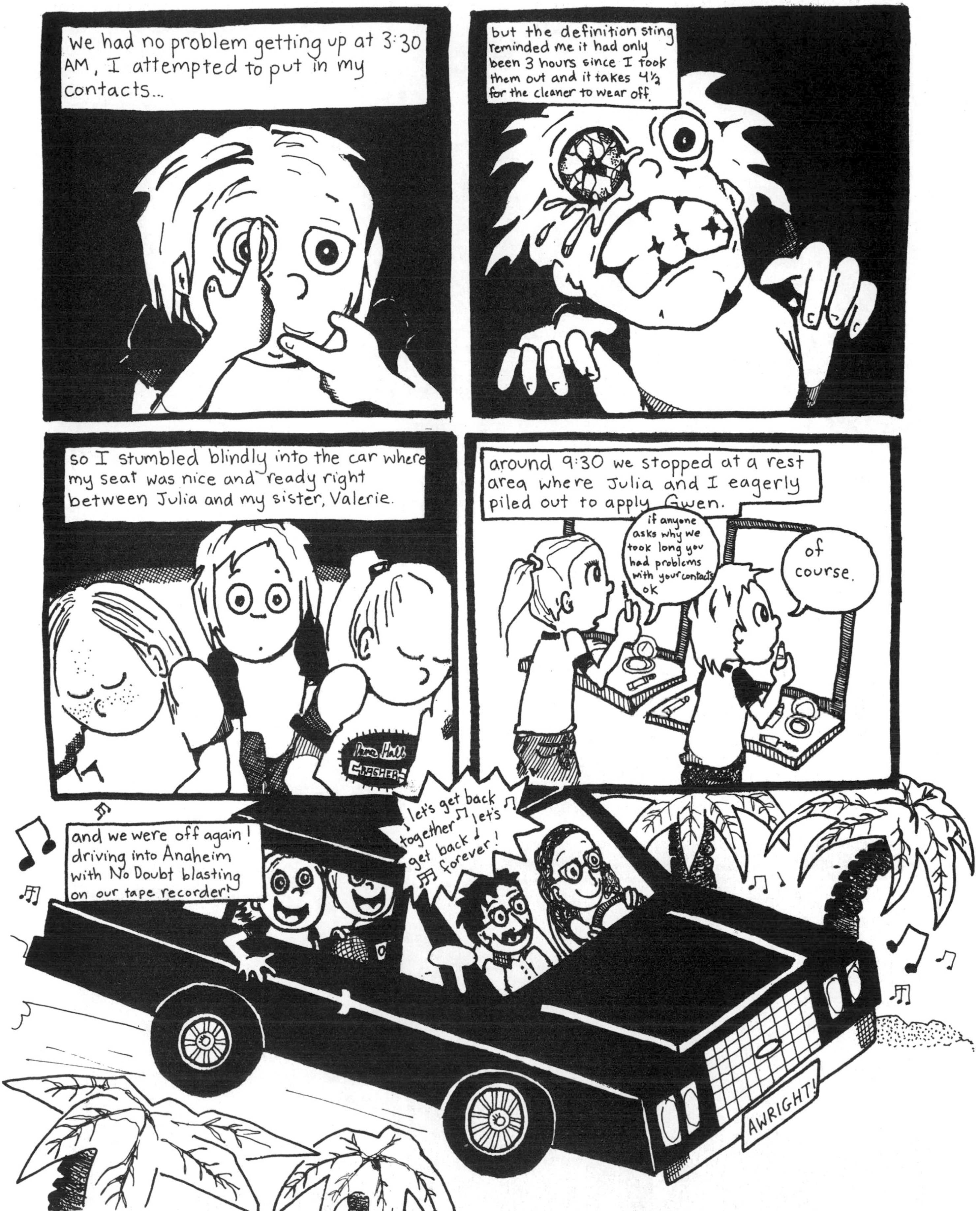

We had no problem getting up at 3:30 AM, I attempted to put in my contacts...
but the definition sting reminded me it had only been 3 hours since I took them out and it takes 4½ for the cleaner to wear off.
so I stumbled blindly into the car where my seat was nice and ready right between Julia and my sister, Valerie.
Dance Hall Crasher
around 9:30 we stopped at a rest area where Julia and I eagerly piled out to apply Gwen.
if anyone asks why we took long you had problems with your contacts ok
of course.
and we were off again! driving into Anaheim with No Doubt blasting on our tape recorder!
let's get back together let's get back forever!
AWRIGHT!

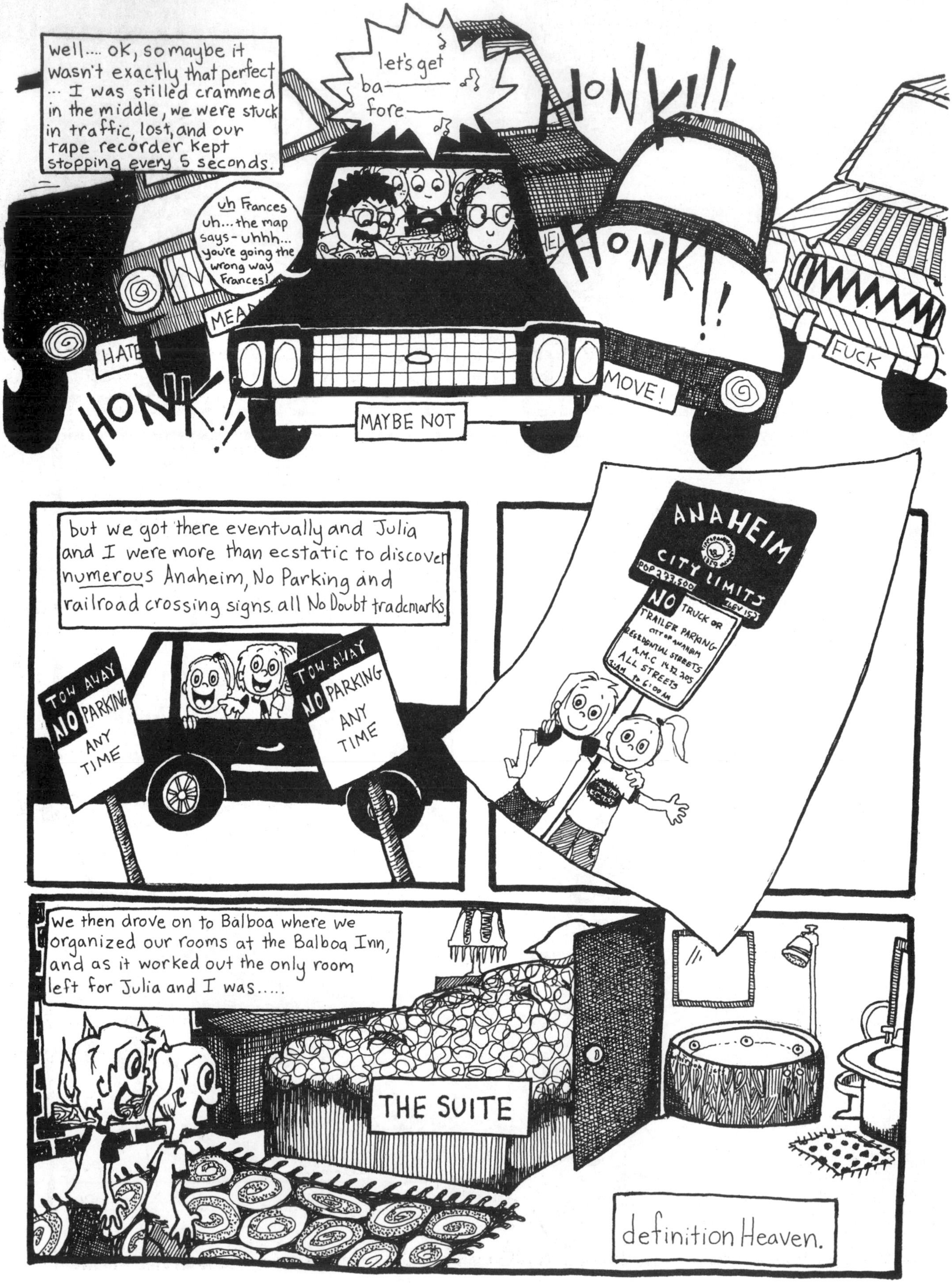
well.... ok, so maybe it wasn't exactly that perfect ... I was stilled crammed in the middle, we were stuck in traffic, lost, and our tape recorder kept stopping every 5 seconds.
let's get ba——— fore———
HONK!!!
uh Frances uh... the map says - uhhh... you're going the wrong way Frances!
HONK!!
HATE
MEAN
HONK!!
MAYBE NOT
MOVE!
FUCK
but we got there eventually and Julia and I were more than ecstatic to discover numerous Anaheim, No Parking and railroad crossing signs. all No Doubt trademarks
TOW AWAY NO PARKING ANY TIME
TOW AWAY NO PARKING ANY TIME
ANAHEIM CITY LIMITS
NO TRUCK OR TRAILER PARKING
We then drove on to Balboa where we organized our rooms at the Balboa Inn, and as it worked out the only room left for Julia and I was.....
THE SUITE
definition Heaven.

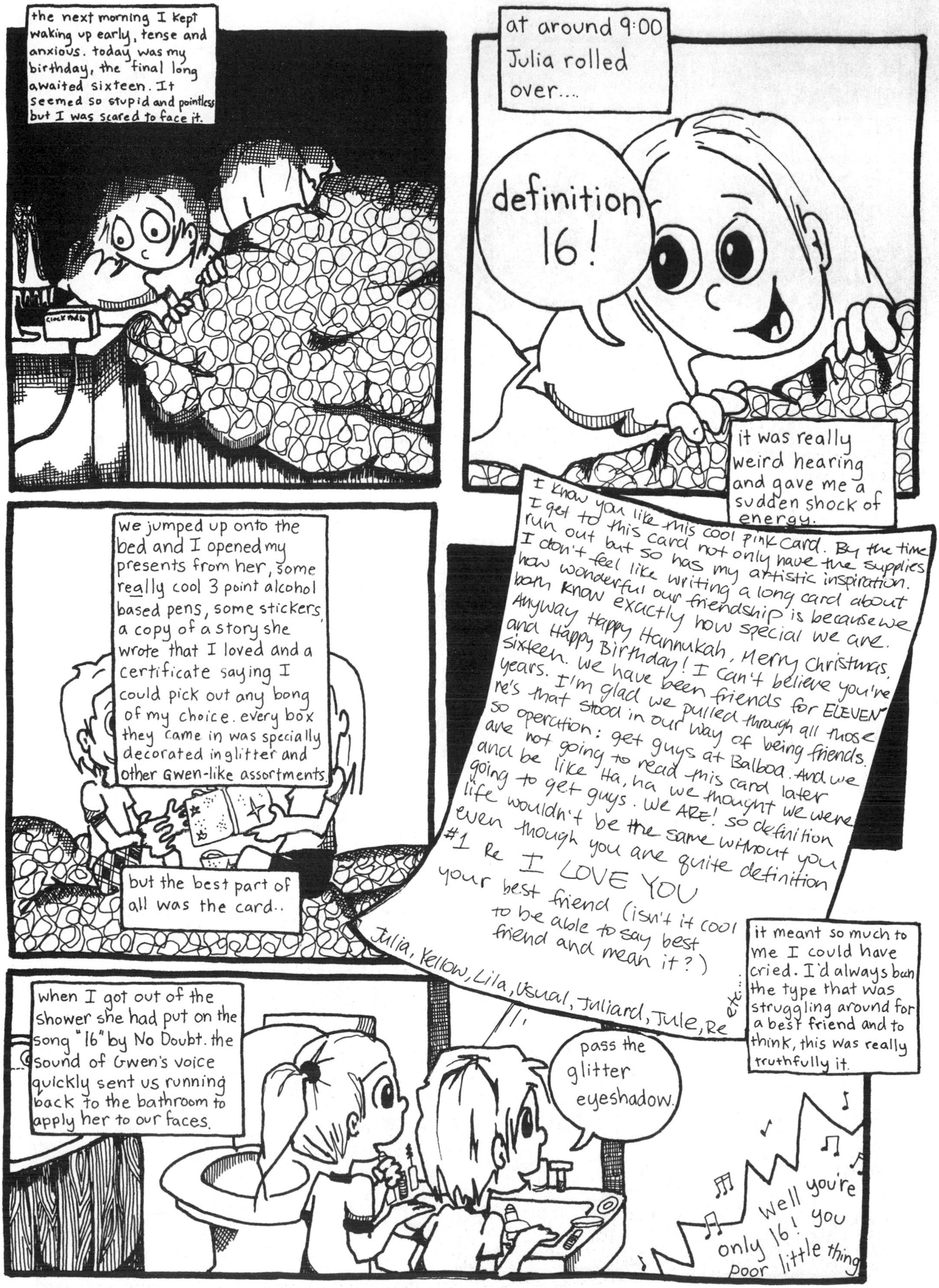

the next morning I kept waking up early, tense and anxious. today was my birthday, the final long awaited sixteen. It seemed so stupid and pointless but I was scared to face it.
at around 9:00 Julia rolled over....
definition 16!
it was really weird hearing and gave me a sudden shock of energy.
we jumped up onto the bed and I opened my presents from her, some really cool 3 point alcohol based pens, some stickers, a copy of a story she wrote that I loved and a certificate saying I could pick out any bong of my choice. every box they came in was specially decorated in glitter and other Gwen-like assortments.
but the best part of all was the card..
I know you like this cool pink card. By the time I get to this card not only have the supplies run out but so has my artistic inspiration. I don't feel like writing a long card about how wonderful our friendship is because we both know exactly how special we are. Anyway Happy Hannukah, Merry Christmas, and Happy Birthday! I can't believe you're sixteen. We have been friends for ELEVEN years. I'm glad we pulled through all those re's that stood in our way of being friends. so operation: get guys at Balboa. And we are not going to read this card later and be like Ha, ha we thought we were going to get guys. WE ARE! so definition life wouldn't be the same without you even though you are quite definition #1 Re I LOVE YOU
your best friend (isn't it cool to be able to say best friend and mean it?)
Julia, Yellow, Lila, Usual, Juliard, Jule, Re etc...
it meant so much to me I could have cried. I'd always been the type that was struggling around for a best friend and to think, this was really truthfully it.
when I got out of the shower she had put on the song "16" by No Doubt. the sound of Gwen's voice quickly sent us running back to the bathroom to apply her to our faces.
pass the glitter eyeshadow.
well you're only 16! you poor little thing

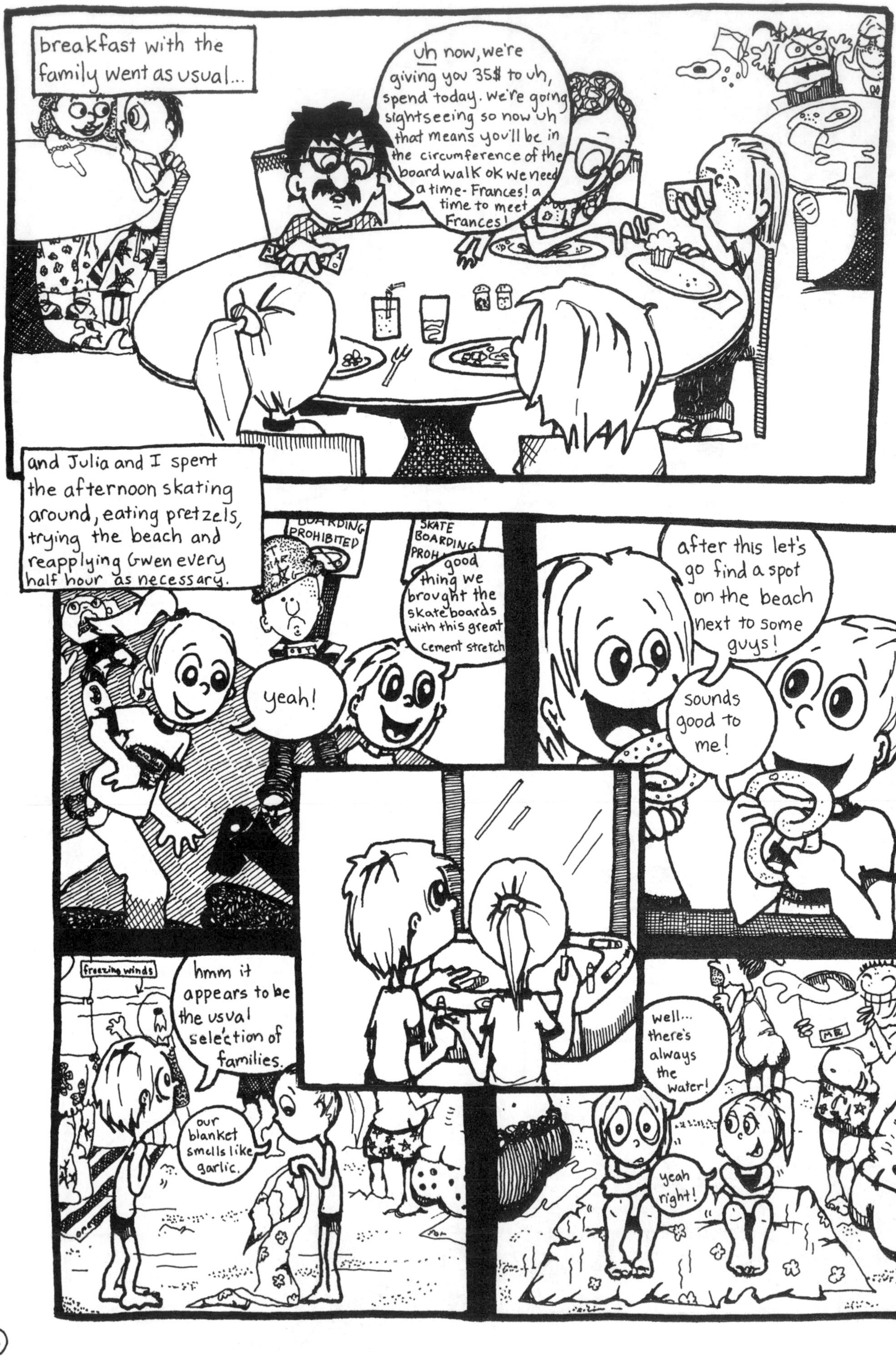

breakfast with the family went as usual...
uh now, we're giving you 35$ to uh, spend today. we're going sightseeing so now uh that means you'll be in the circumference of the board walk ok we need a time- Frances! a time to meet Frances!
and Julia and I spent the afternoon skating around, eating pretzels, trying the beach and reapplying Gwen every half hour as necessary.
BOARDING PROHIBITED
SKATE BOARDING PROH
good thing we brought the skateboards with this great cement stretch
yeah!
after this let's go find a spot on the beach next to some guys!
sounds good to me!
freezing winds
hmm it appears to be the usual selection of families.
our blanket smells like garlic.
well... there's always the water!
yeah right!

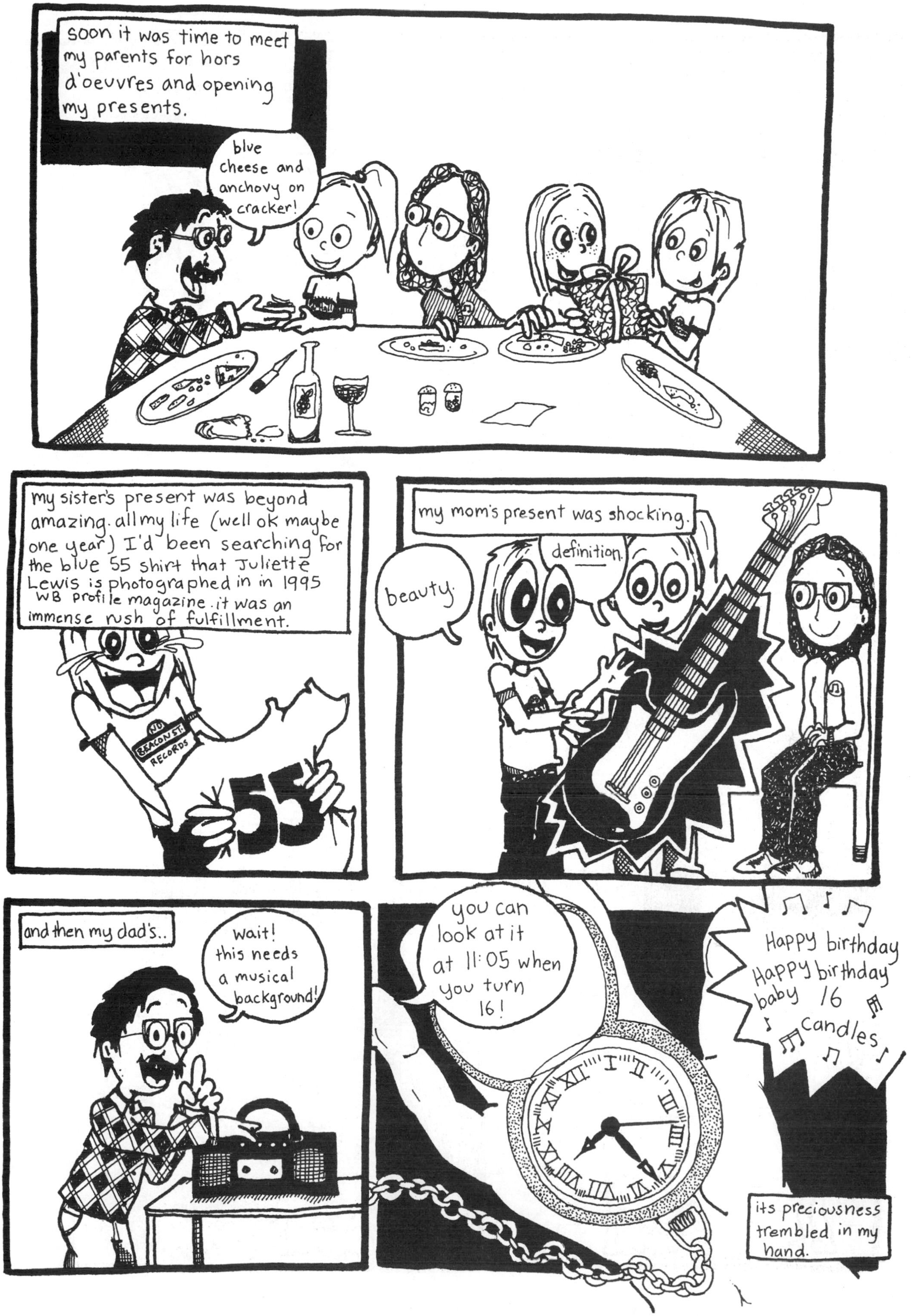
soon it was time to meet my parents for hors d'oeuvres and opening my presents.
blue cheese and anchovy on cracker!
my sister's present was beyond amazing. all my life (well ok maybe one year) I'd been searching for the blue 55 shirt that Juliette Lewis is photographed in in 1995 WB profile magazine. it was an immense rush of fulfillment.
NO BEACON ST. RECORDS
55
my mom's present was shocking.
beauty.
definition.
and then my dad's..
wait! this needs a musical background!
you can look at it at 11:05 when you turn 16!
Happy birthday
Happy birthday
baby 16 candles
its preciousness trembled in my hand.

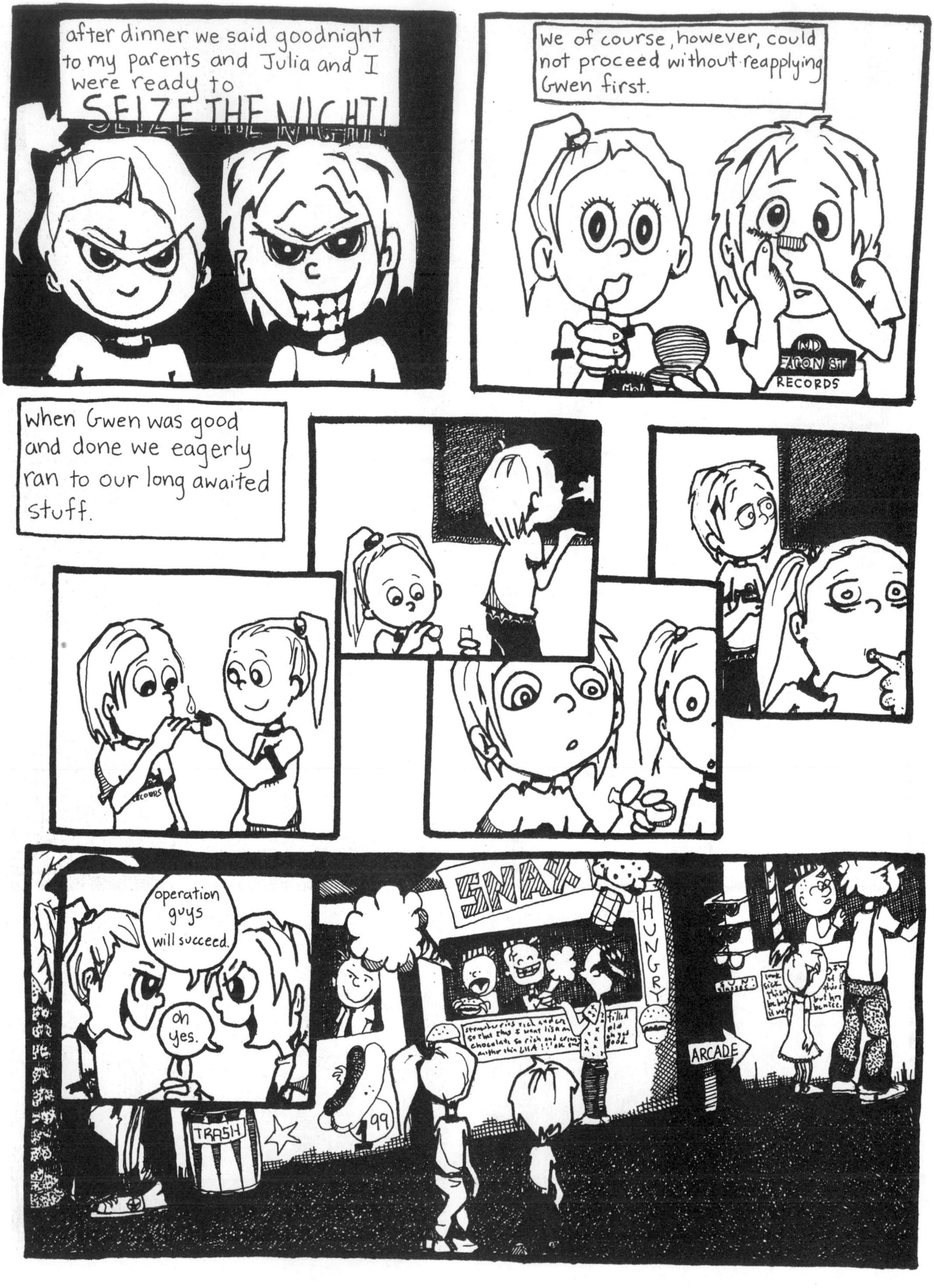
after dinner we said goodnight to my parents and Julia and I were ready to
SEIZE THE NIGHT!
We of course, however, could not proceed without reapplying Gwen first.
RECORDS
when Gwen was good and done we eagerly ran to our long awaited stuff.
RECORDS
operation guys will succeed.
oh yes.
HUNGRY
ARCADE
TRASH
99

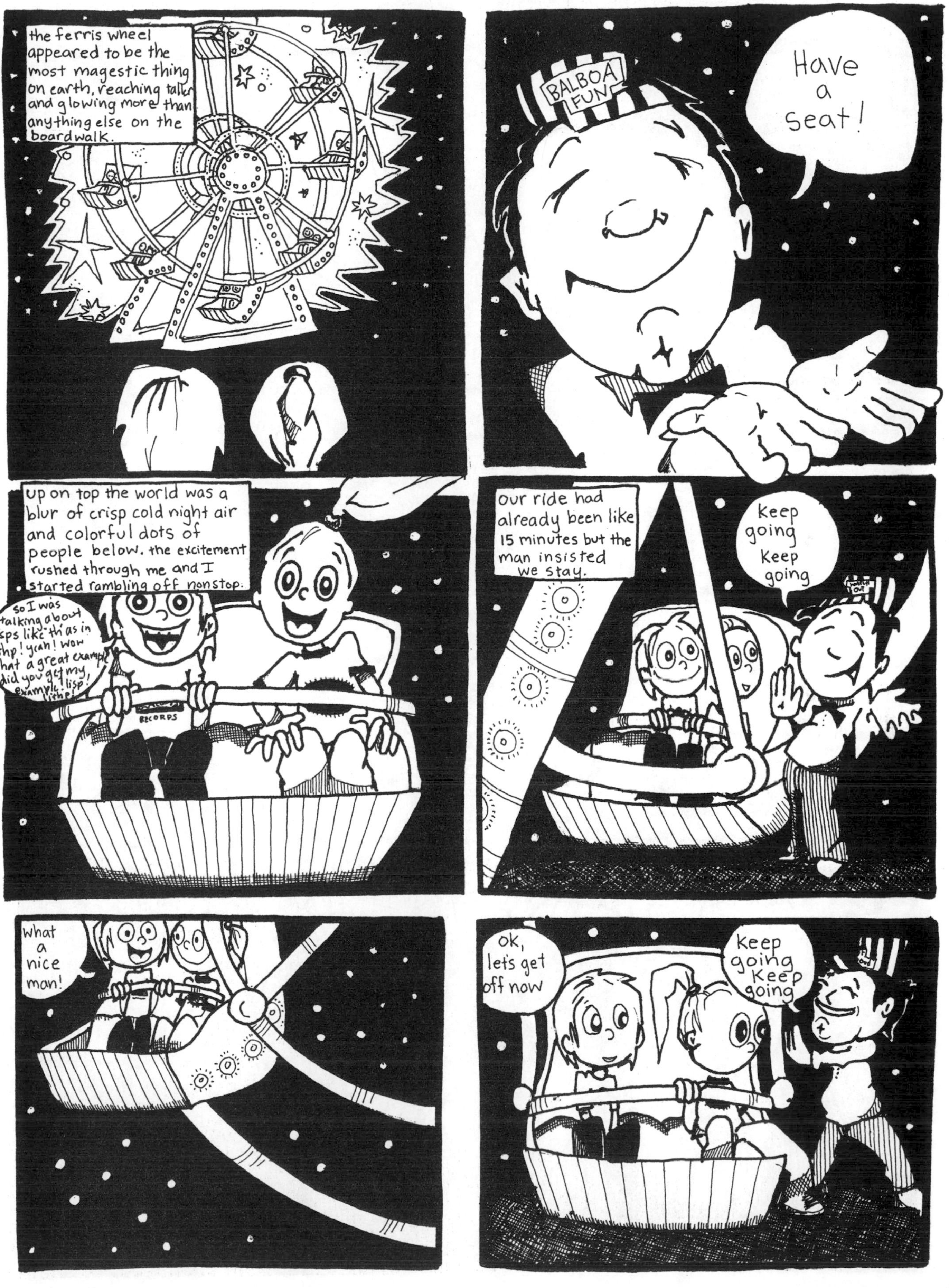

the ferris wheel appeared to be the most magestic thing on earth, reaching taller and glowing more than anything else on the boardwalk.
BALBOA FUN
Have a seat!
up on top the world was a blur of crisp cold night air and colorful dots of people below. the excitement rushed through me and I started rambling off nonstop.
so I was talking about lisps like "th" as in lithp! yeah! wow what a great example did you get my example lisp! lithp!
RECORDS
our ride had already been like 15 minutes but the man insisted we stay.
Keep going Keep going
WATCH OUT
what a nice man!
ok, let's get off now
Keep going Keep going

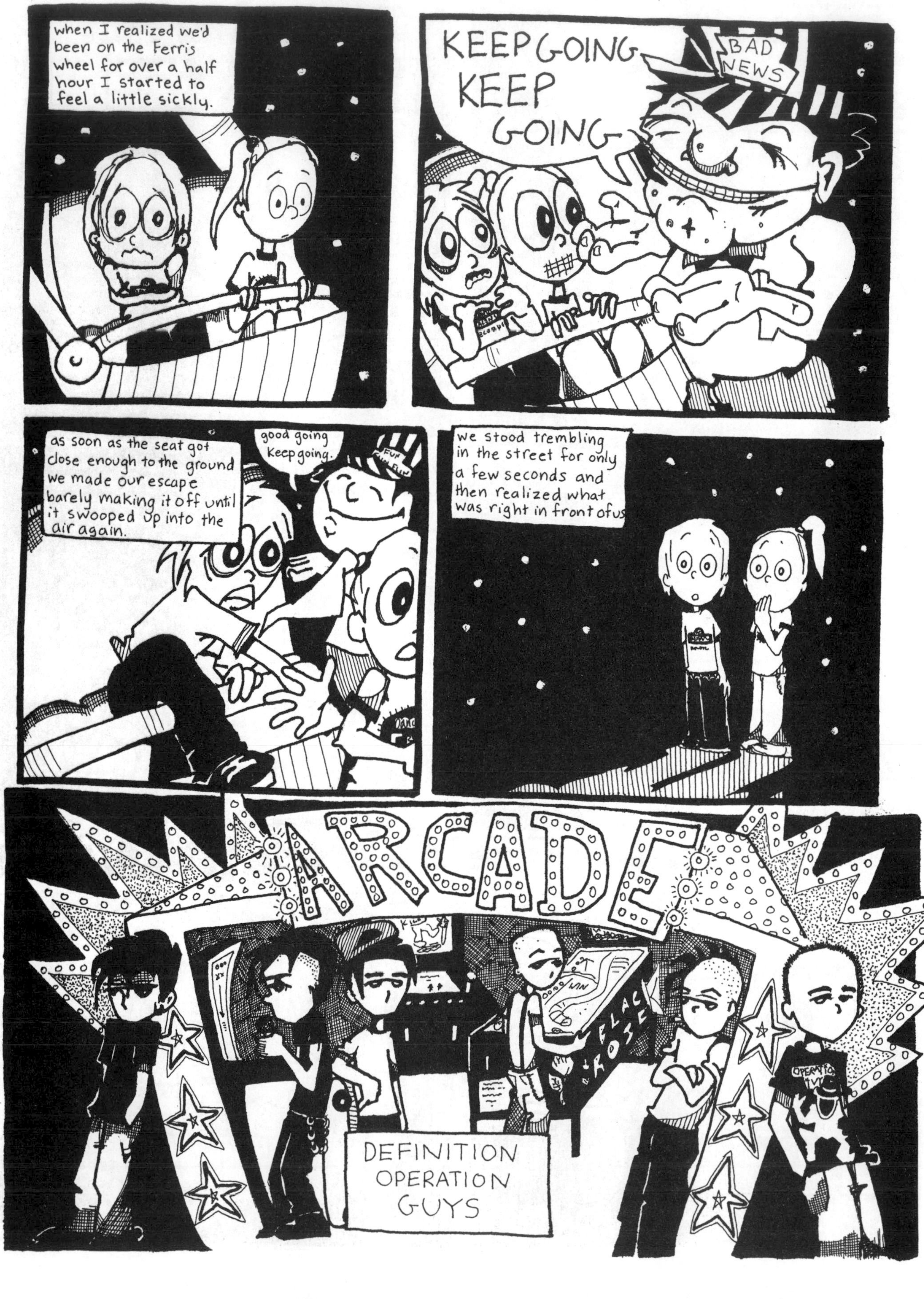
when I realized we'd been on the Ferris wheel for over a half hour I started to feel a little sickly.
KEEP GOING KEEP GOING
BAD NEWS
as soon as the seat got close enough to the ground we made our escape barely making it off until it swooped up into the air again.
good going Keep going.
we stood trembling in the street for only a few seconds and then realized what was right in front of us
ARCADE
DEFINITION OPERATION GUYS

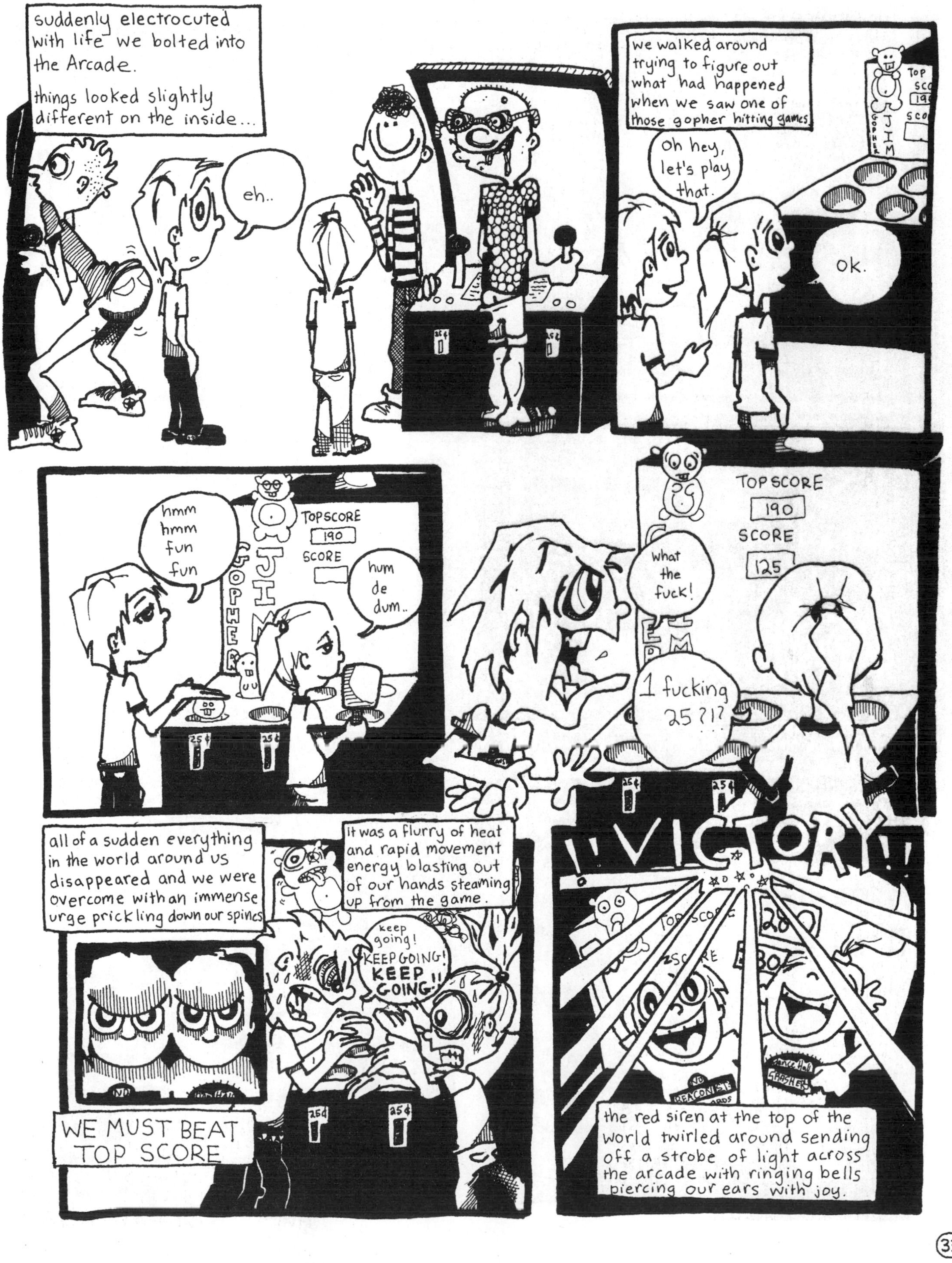

suddenly electrocuted with life we bolted into the Arcade.
things looked slightly different on the inside...
eh..
we walked around trying to figure out what had happened when we saw one of those gopher hitting games
Oh hey, let's play that.
ok.
TOP SCORE
190
SCORE
GOPHER JIM
hmm hmm fun fun
hum de dum..
25¢
TOP SCORE
190
SCORE
125
what the fuck!
1 fucking 25?!?
all of a sudden everything in the world around us disappeared and we were overcome with an immense urge prickling down our spines
it was a flurry of heat and rapid movement energy blasting out of our hands steaming up from the game.
keep going! KEEP GOING! KEEP GOING!!
WE MUST BEAT TOP SCORE
!'VICTORY'!
TOP SCORE
280
SCORE
the red siren at the top of the world twirled around sending off a strobe of light across the arcade with ringing bells piercing our ears with joy.

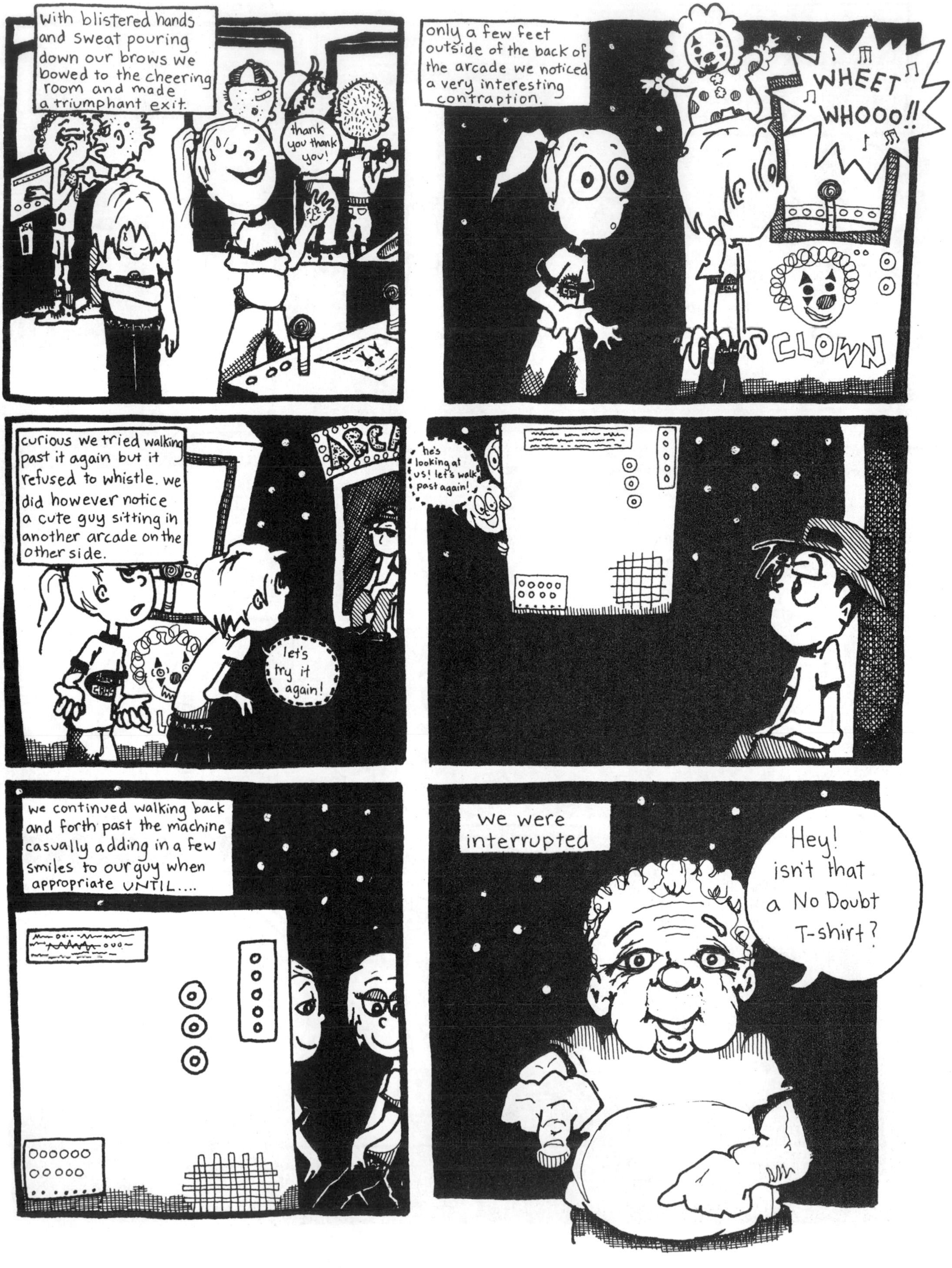
with blistered hands and sweat pouring down our brows we bowed to the cheering room and made a triumphant exit.
thank you thank you!
only a few feet outside of the back of the arcade we noticed a very interesting contraption.
WHEET WHOOO!!
CLOWN
curious we tried walking past it again but it refused to whistle. we did however notice a cute guy sitting in another arcade on the other side.
let's try it again!
he's looking at us! let's walk past again!
we continued walking back and forth past the machine casually adding in a few smiles to our guy when appropriate UNTIL....
we were interrupted
Hey! isn't that a No Doubt T-shirt?

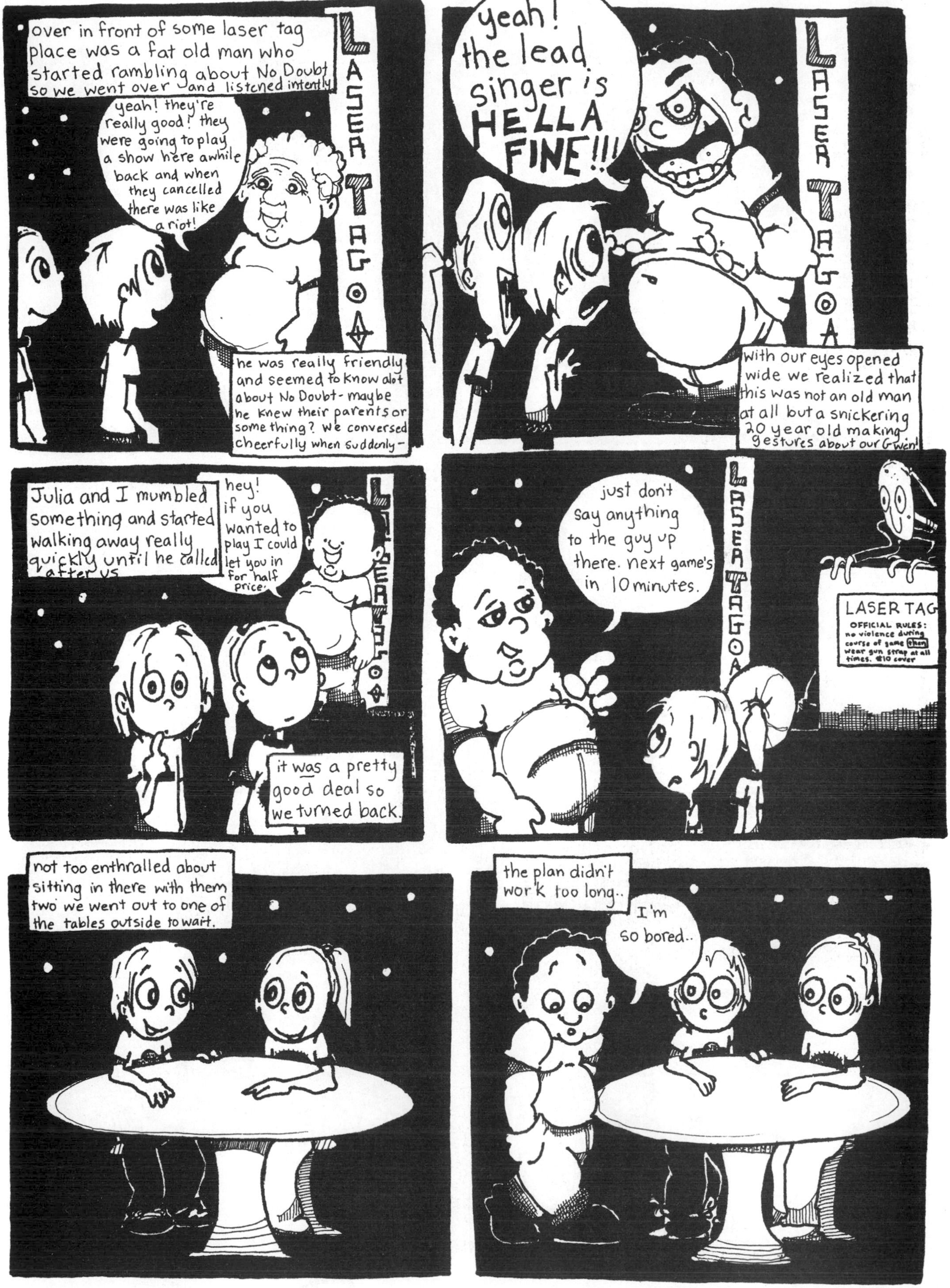
over in front of some laser tag place was a fat old man who started rambling about No Doubt so we went over and listened intently
LASER TAG
yeah! they're really good! they were going to play a show here awhile back and when they cancelled there was like a riot!
he was really friendly and seemed to know alot about No Doubt - maybe he knew their parents or something? we conversed cheerfully when suddenly -
yeah! the lead singer is HELLA FINE!!!
LASER TAG
with our eyes opened wide we realized that this was not an old man at all but a snickering 20 year old making gestures about our Gwen!
Julia and I mumbled something and started walking away really quickly until he called after us
hey! if you wanted to play I could let you in for half price.
it was a pretty good deal so we turned back.
just don't say anything to the guy up there. next game's in 10 minutes.
LASER TAG
LASER TAG
OFFICIAL RULES: no violence during course of game then wear gun strap at all times. $10 cover
not too enthralled about sitting in there with them two we went out to one of the tables outside to wait.
the plan didn't work too long..
I'm so bored..

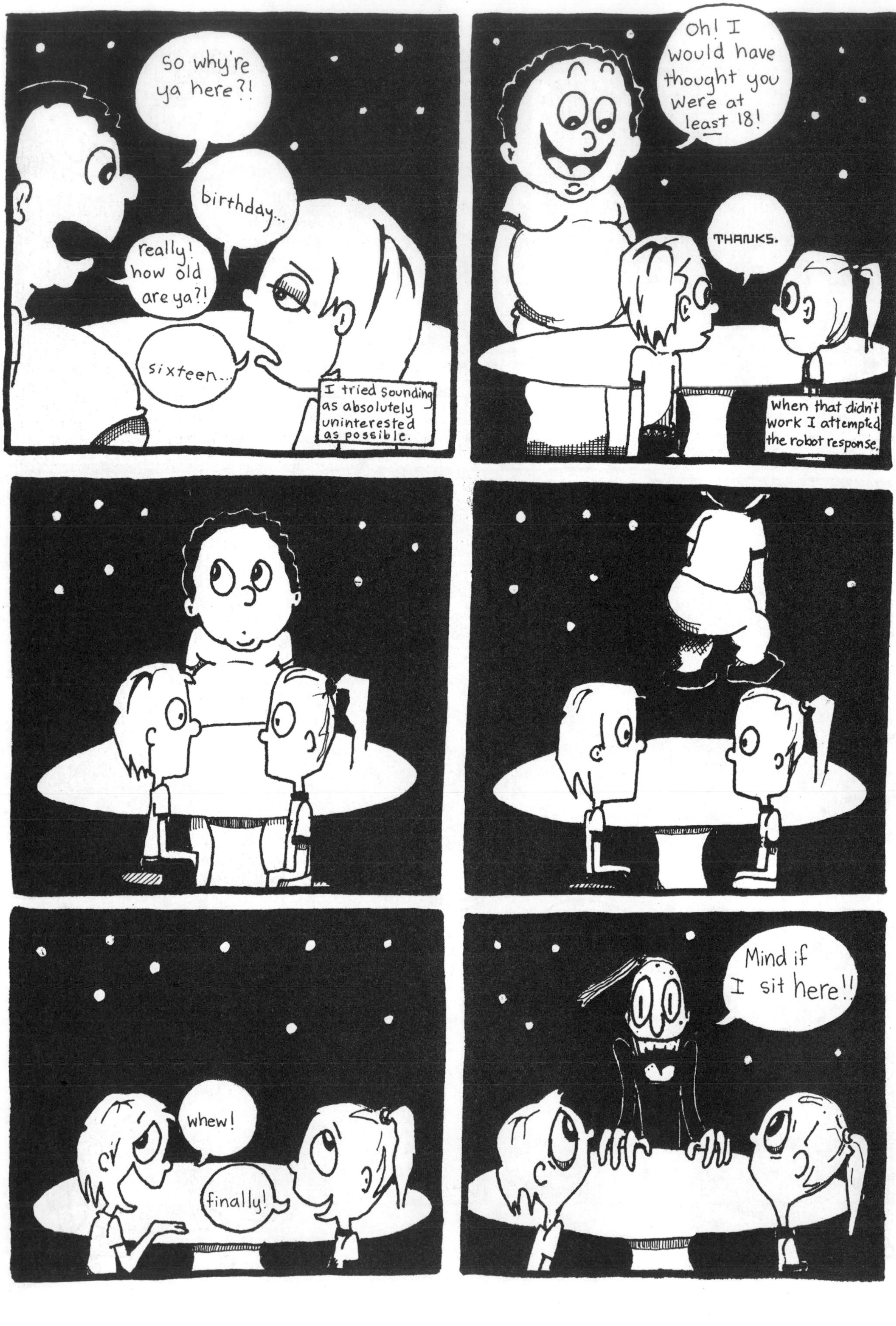
So why're ya here?!
birthday...
really! how old are ya?!
sixteen...
I tried sounding as absolutely uninterested as possible.
Oh! I would have thought you were at least 18!
THANKS.
when that didn't work I attempted the robot response.
whew!
finally!
Mind if I sit here!!

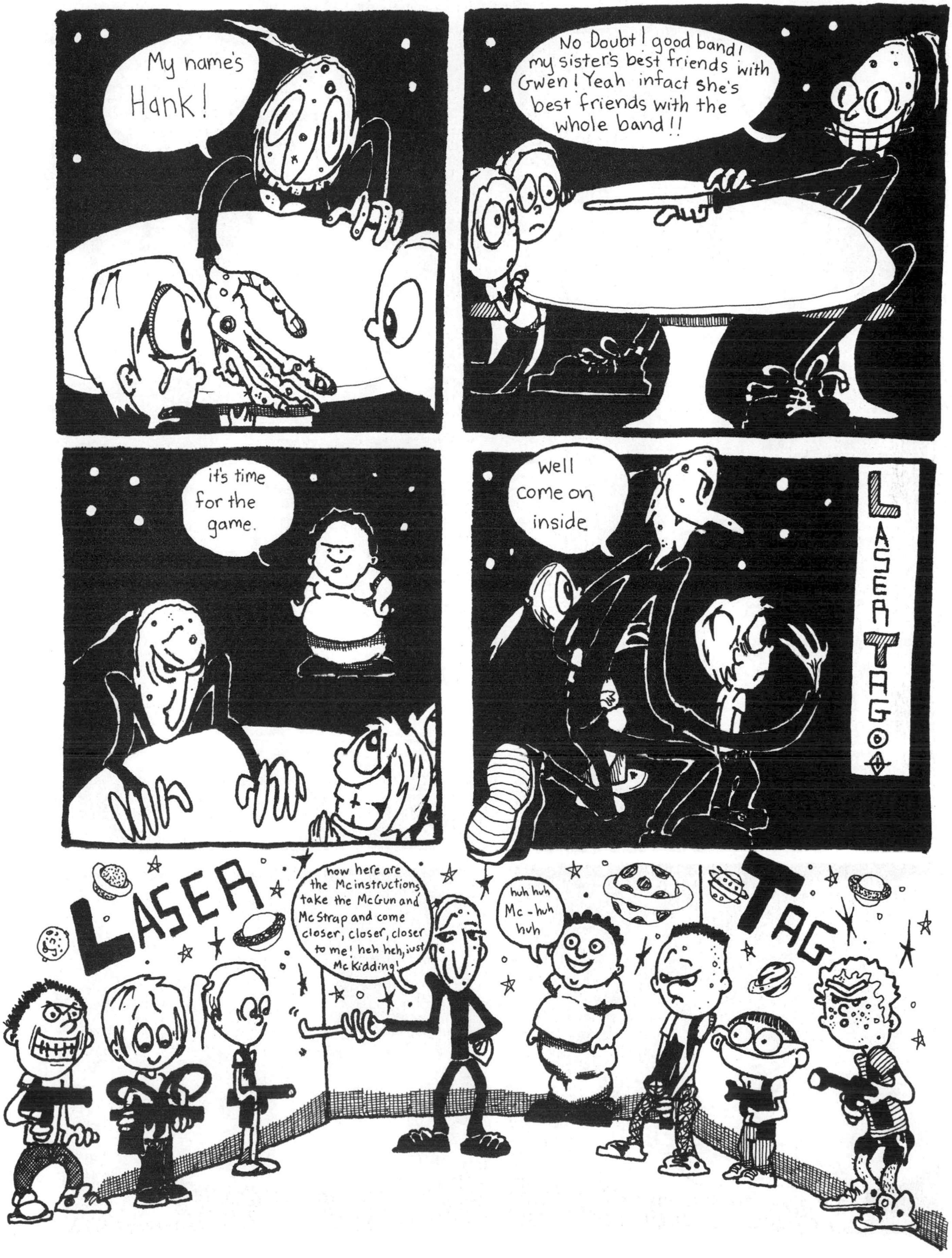

My name's Hank!
No Doubt! good band! my sister's best friends with Gwen! Yeah infact she's best friends with the whole band!!
it's time for the game.
Well come on inside
LASER TAG
LASER
TAG
how here are the Mc instructions take the McGun and McStrap and come closer, closer, closer to me! heh heh, just McKidding!
huh huh Mc-huh huh

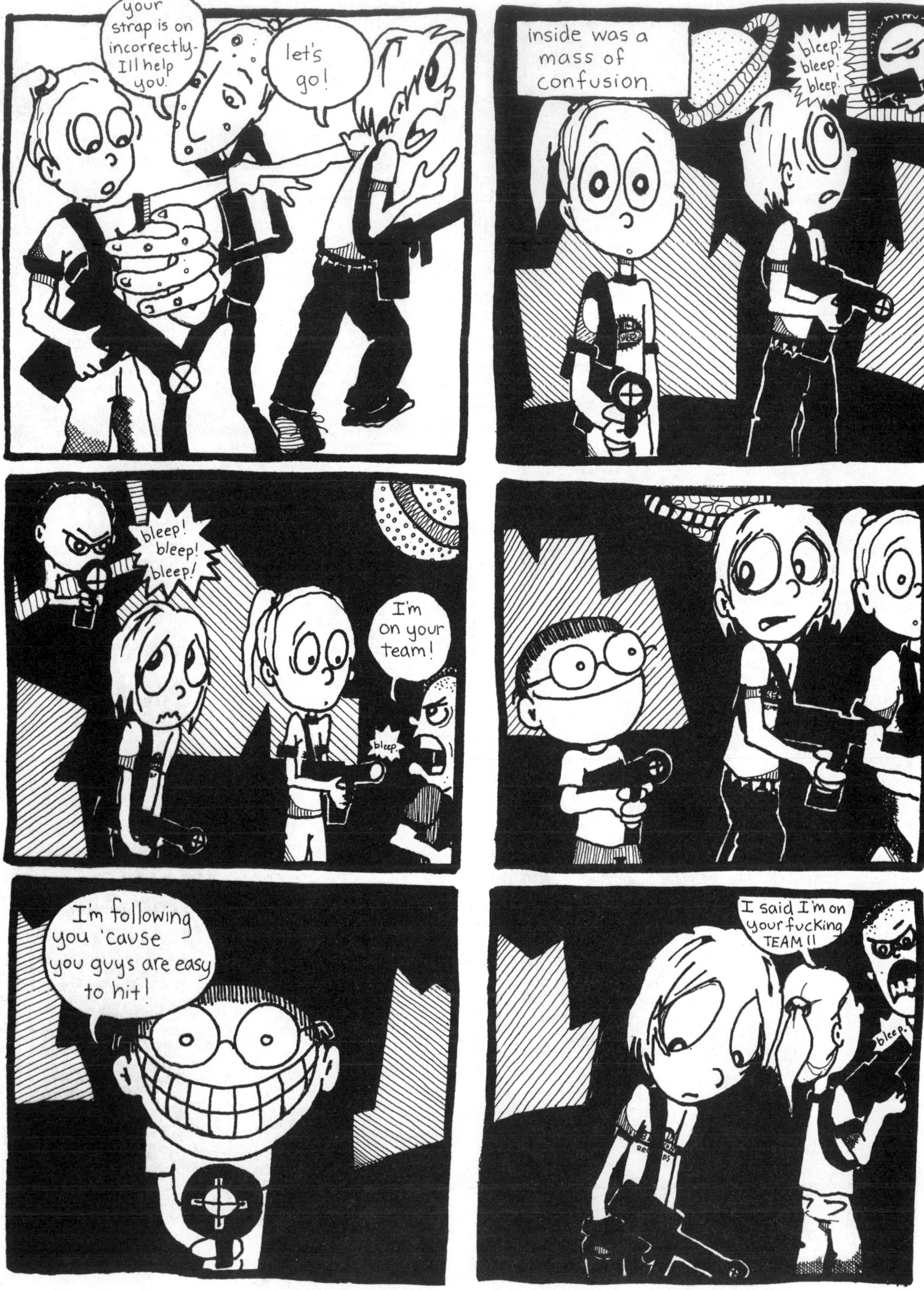
your strap is on incorrectly- Ill help you.
let's go!
inside was a mass of confusion.
bleep! bleep! bleep!
bleep! bleep! bleep!
I'm on your team!
bleep.
I'm following you 'cause you guys are easy to hit!
I said I'm on your fucking TEAM!!
bleep.

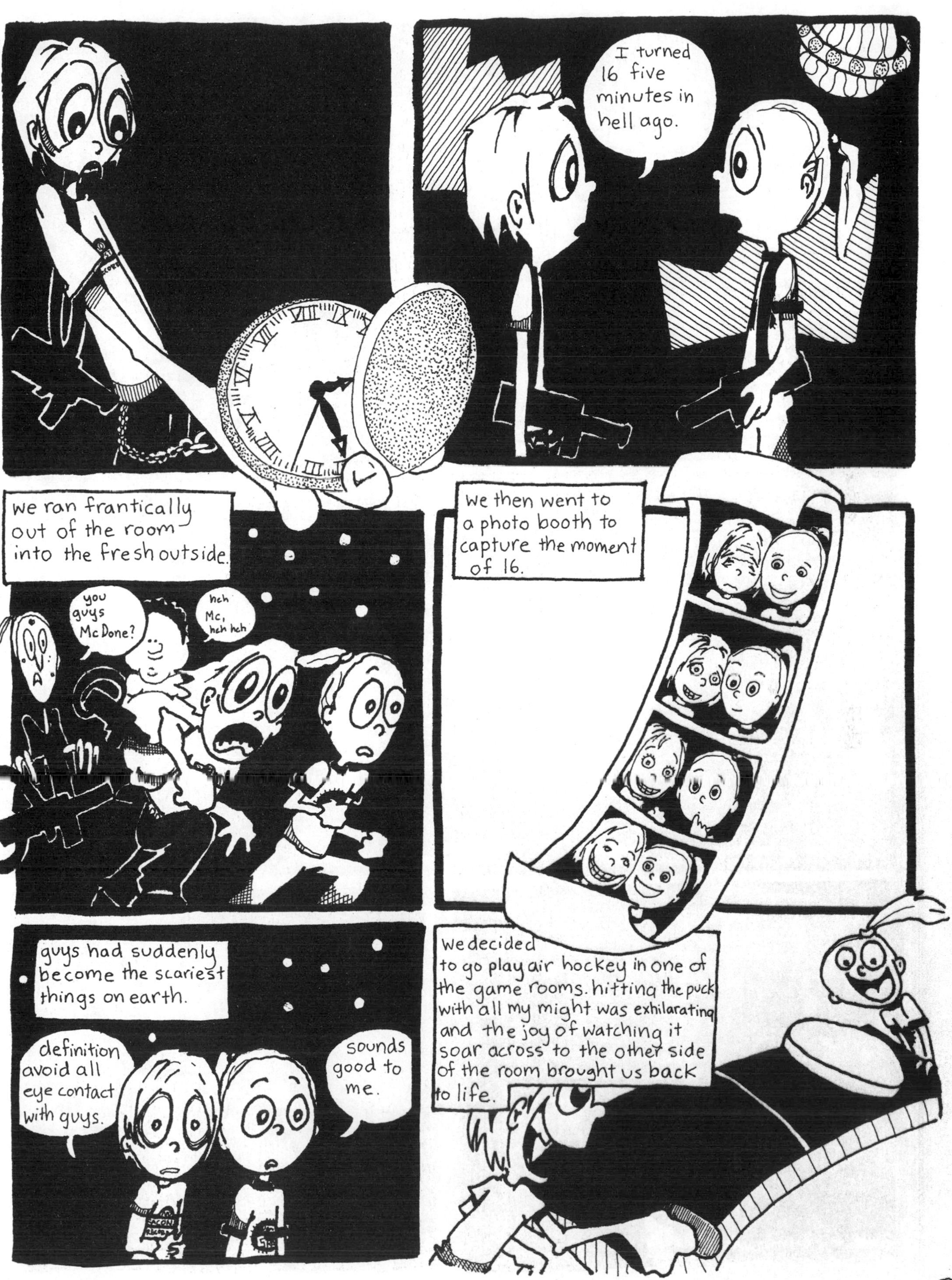
I turned 16 five minutes in hell ago.
we ran frantically out of the room into the fresh outside.
you guys Mc Done?
hch Mc, hch hch
we then went to a photo booth to capture the moment of 16.
guys had suddenly become the scariest things on earth.
definition avoid all eye contact with guys.
sounds good to me.
we decided to go play air hockey in one of the game rooms. hitting the puck with all my might was exhilarating and the joy of watching it soar across to the other side of the room brought us back to life.

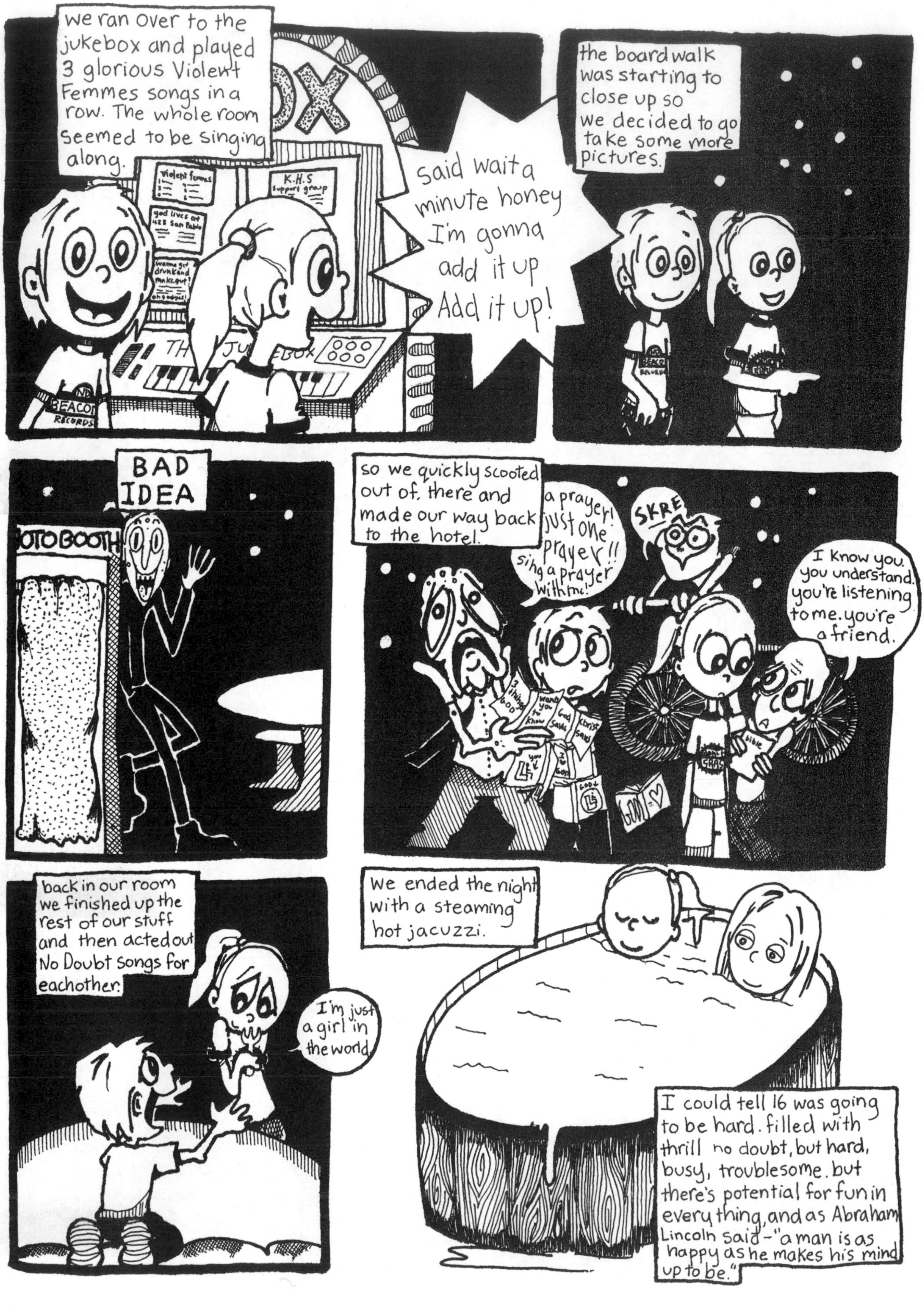
we ran over to the jukebox and played 3 glorious Violent Femmes songs in a row. The whole room seemed to be singing along.
THE JUKEBOX
said wait a minute honey I'm gonna add it up Add it up!
the boardwalk was starting to close up so we decided to go take some more pictures.
BAD IDEA
OTO BOOTH
so we quickly scooted out of there and made our way back to the hotel.
a prayer! just one prayer!! sing a prayer with me!
SKRE
I know you. you understand. you're listening to me. you're a friend.
back in our room we finished up the rest of our stuff and then acted out No Doubt songs for eachother.
I'm just a girl in the world.
We ended the night with a steaming hot jacuzzi.
I could tell 16 was going to be hard. filled with thrill no doubt, but hard, busy, troublesome. but there's potential for fun in every thing, and as Abraham Lincoln said - "a man is as happy as he makes his mind up to be."

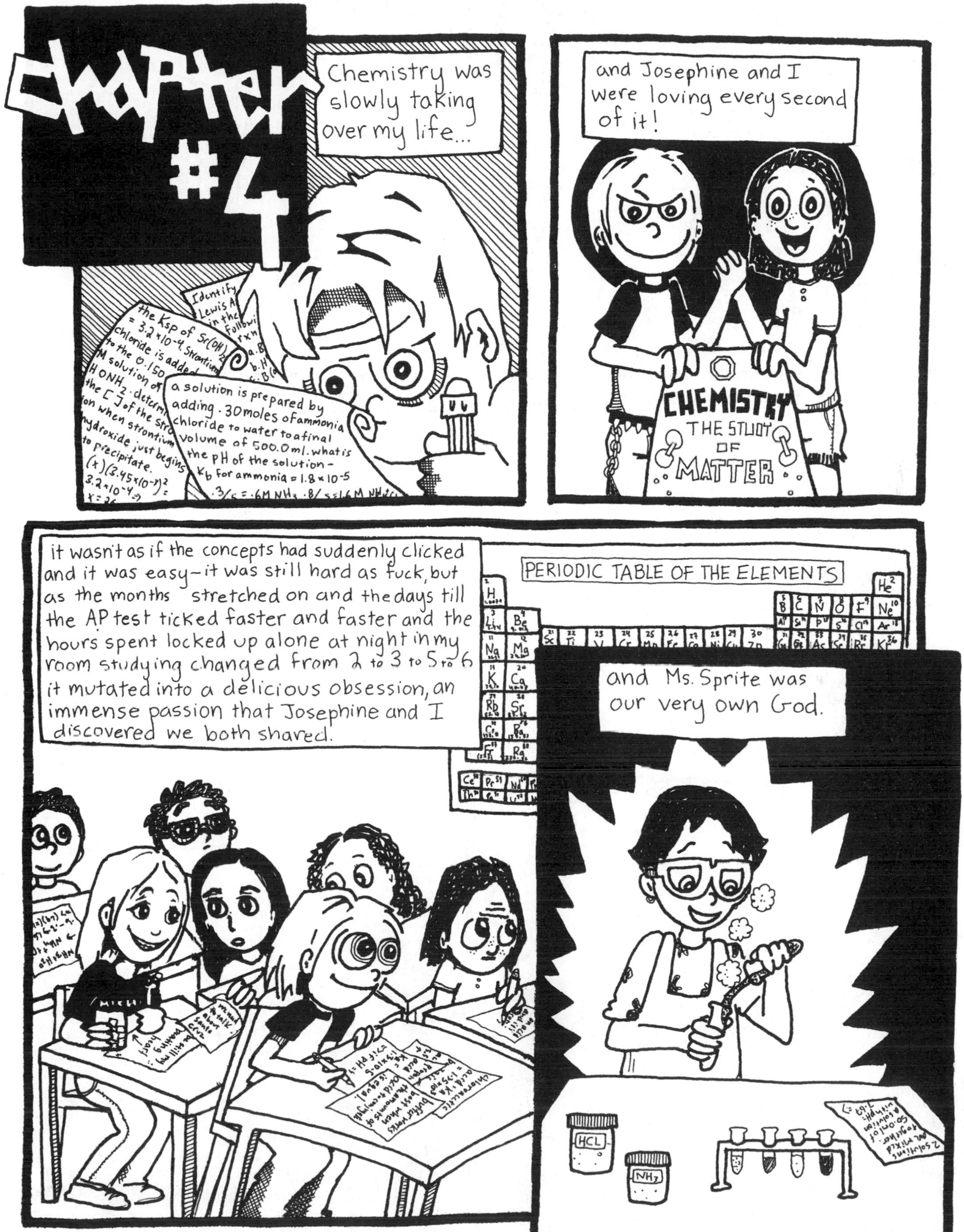
Chapter #4
Chemistry was slowly taking over my life...
and Josephine and I were loving every second of it!
CHEMISTRY THE STUDY OF MATTER
it wasn't as if the concepts had suddenly clicked and it was easy—it was still hard as fuck, but as the months stretched on and the days till the AP test ticked faster and faster and the hours spent locked up alone at night in my room studying changed from 2 to 3 to 5 to 6 it mutated into a delicious obsession, an immense passion that Josephine and I discovered we both shared.
PERIODIC TABLE OF THE ELEMENTS
and Ms. Sprite was our very own God.
HCL

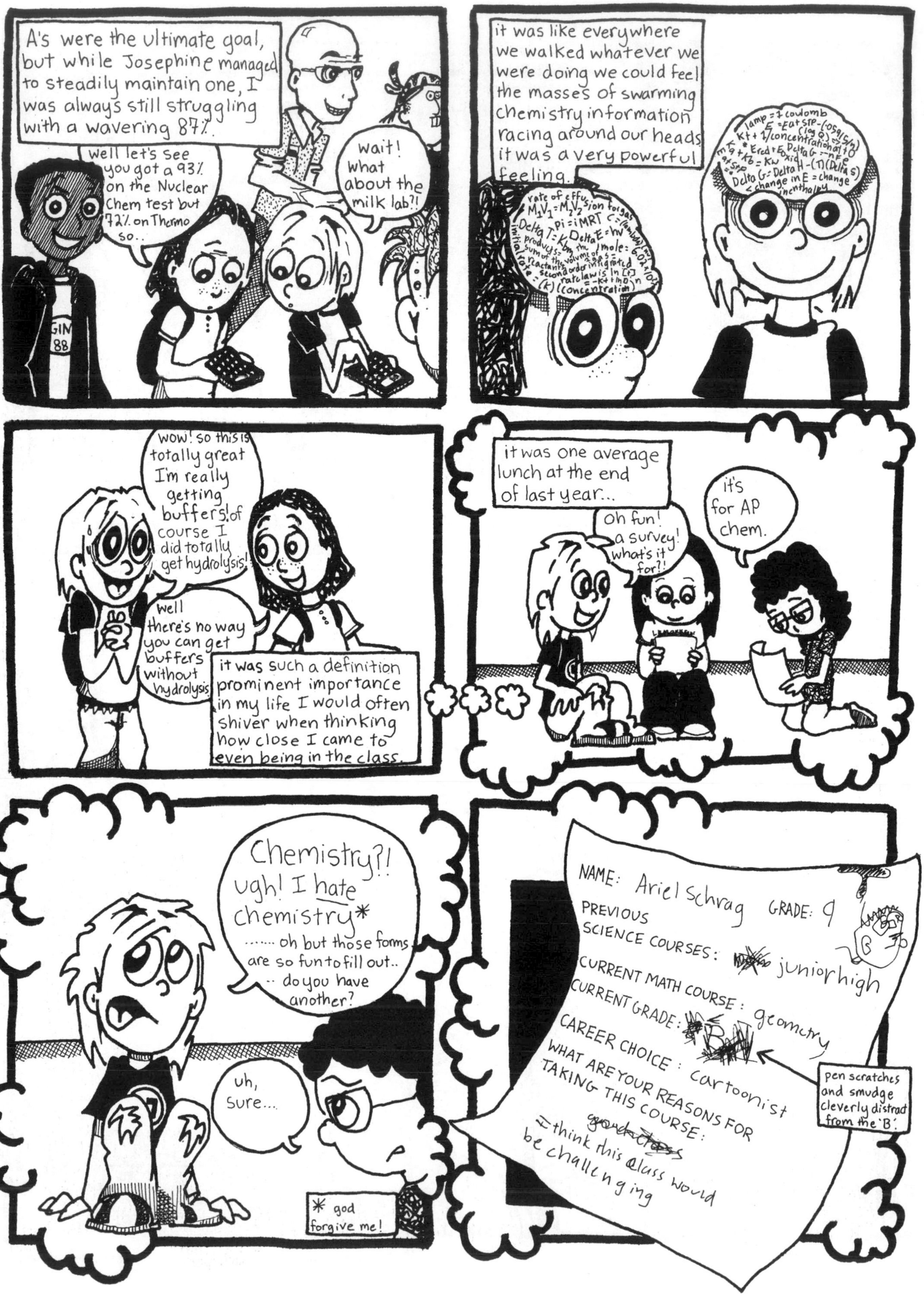
A's were the ultimate goal, but while Josephine managed to steadily maintain one, I was always still struggling with a wavering 87%.
well let's see you got a 93% on the Nuclear Chem test but 72% on Thermo so..
wait! what about the milk lab?!
it was like everywhere we walked whatever we were doing we could feel the masses of swarming chemistry information racing around our heads it was a very powerful feeling.
wow! so this is totally great I'm really getting buffers! of course I did totally get hydrolysis!
well there's no way you can get buffers without hydrolysis
it was such a definition prominent importance in my life I would often shiver when thinking how close I came to even being in the class.
it was one average lunch at the end of last year...
Oh fun! a survey! what's it for?!
it's for AP chem.
Chemistry?! ugh! I hate chemistry* .... oh but those forms are so fun to fill out.. .. do you have another?
uh, sure...
* god forgive me!
NAME: Ariel Schrag GRADE: 9
PREVIOUS SCIENCE COURSES: junior high
CURRENT MATH COURSE: geometry
CURRENT GRADE: B
CAREER CHOICE: cartoonist
WHAT ARE YOUR REASONS FOR TAKING THIS COURSE:
I think this class would be challenging
pen scratches and smudge cleverly distract from the 'B'.

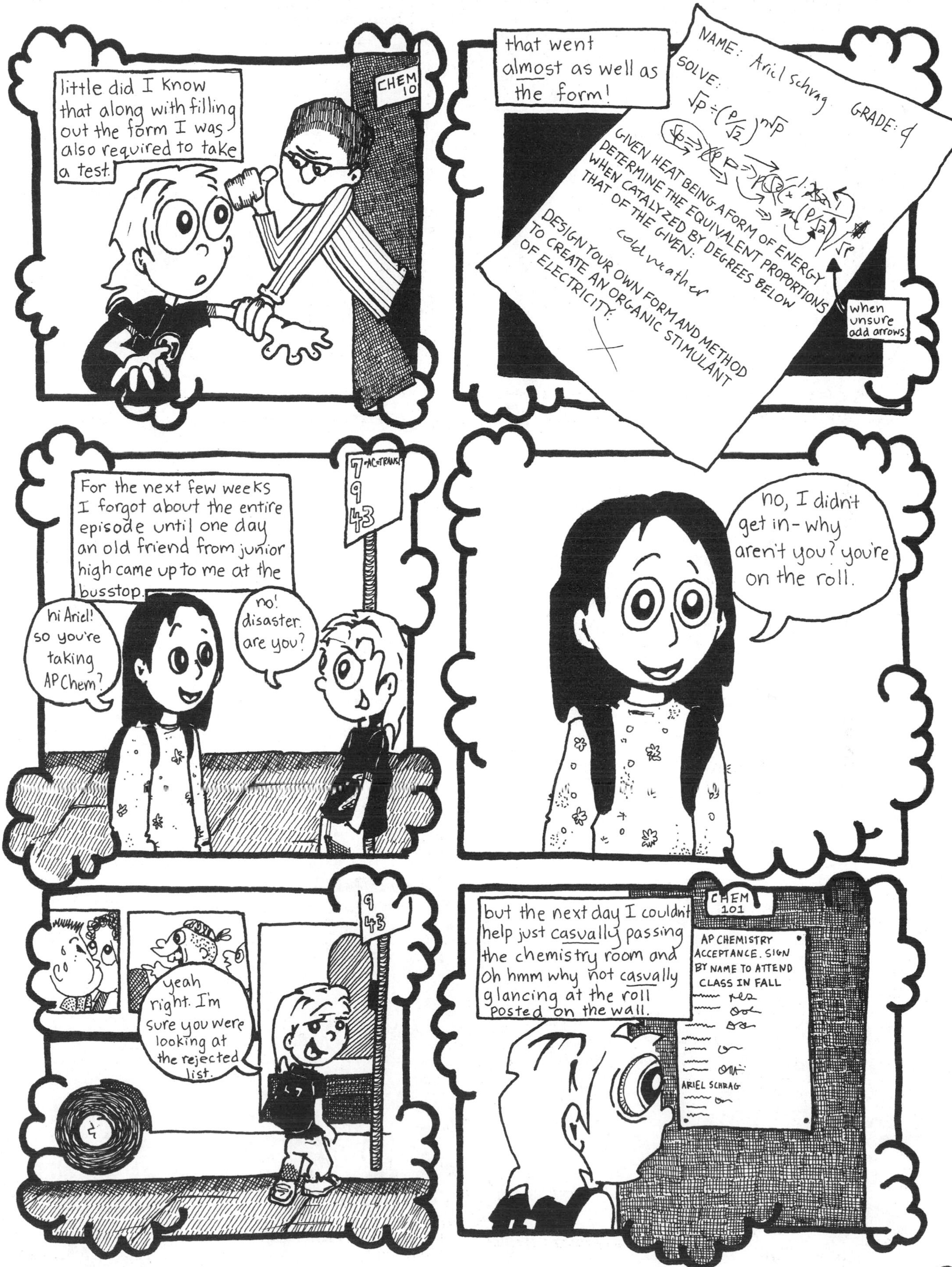

CHEM 10
little did I know that along with filling out the form I was also required to take a test.
that went almost as well as the form!
NAME: Ariel Schrag
GRADE: d
SOLVE:
$\sqrt{p} \div (\frac{p}{\sqrt{2}})^{n\sqrt{p}}$
GIVEN HEAT BEING A FORM OF ENERGY DETERMINE THE EQUIVALENT PROPORTIONS WHEN CATALYZED BY DEGREES BELOW THAT OF THE GIVEN:
cold weather
DESIGN YOUR OWN FORM AND METHOD TO CREATE AN ORGANIC STIMULANT OF ELECTRICITY:
when unsure add arrows.
For the next few weeks I forgot about the entire episode until one day an old friend from junior high came up to me at the busstop.
7 9 43
hi Ariel! so you're taking AP Chem?
no! disaster. are you?
no, I didnt get in- why aren't you? you're on the roll.
9 43
yeah right. I'm sure you were looking at the rejected list.
but the next day I couldn't help just casually passing the chemistry room and oh hmm why not casually glancing at the roll posted on the wall.
CHEM 101
AP CHEMISTRY ACCEPTANCE. SIGN BY NAME TO ATTEND CLASS IN FALL
ARIEL SCHRAG

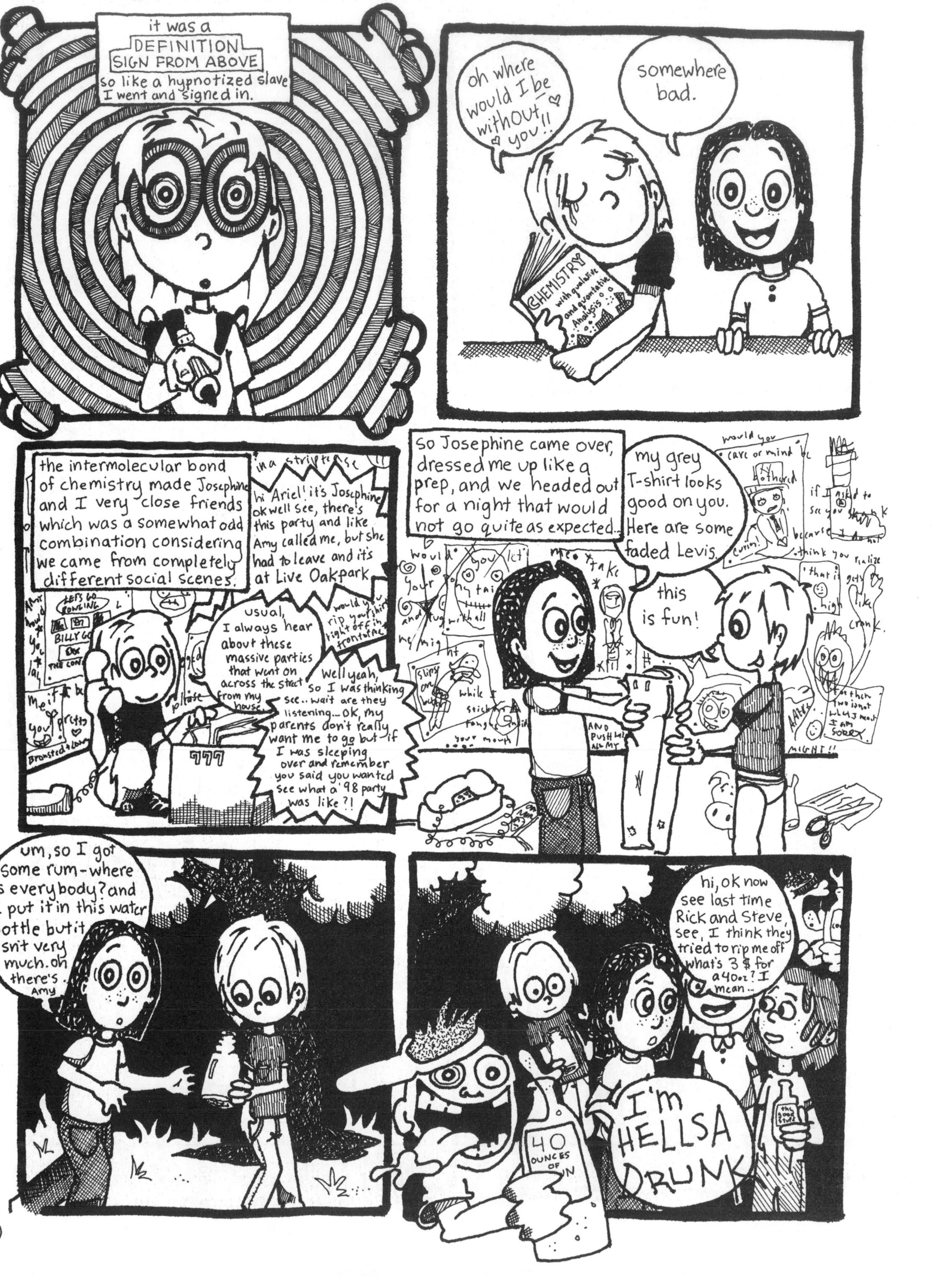

it was a DEFINITION SIGN FROM ABOVE so like a hypnotized slave I went and signed in.
oh where would I be without you!!
somewhere bad.
CHEMISTRY with qualitative and quantitative Analysis
the intermolecular bond of chemistry made Josephine and I very close friends which was a somewhat odd combination considering we came from completely different social scenes.
hi Ariel! it's Josephine ok well see, there's this party and like Amy called me, but she had to leave and it's at Live Oakpark
usual, I always hear about these massive parties that went on across the street from my house
Well yeah, so I was thinking see.. wait are they listening... ok, my parents don't really want me to go but if I was sleeping over and remember you said you wanted see what a '98 party was like?!
So Josephine came over, dressed me up like a prep, and we headed out for a night that would not go quite as expected...
my grey T-shirt looks good on you. Here are some faded Levis.
this is fun!
um, so I got some rum-where is everybody? and I put it in this water bottle but it isn't very much. oh there's Amy
hi, ok now see last time Rick and Steve, see, I think they tried to rip me off what's 3 $ for a 40oz? I mean...
I'm HELLSA DRUNK
40 OUNCES OF

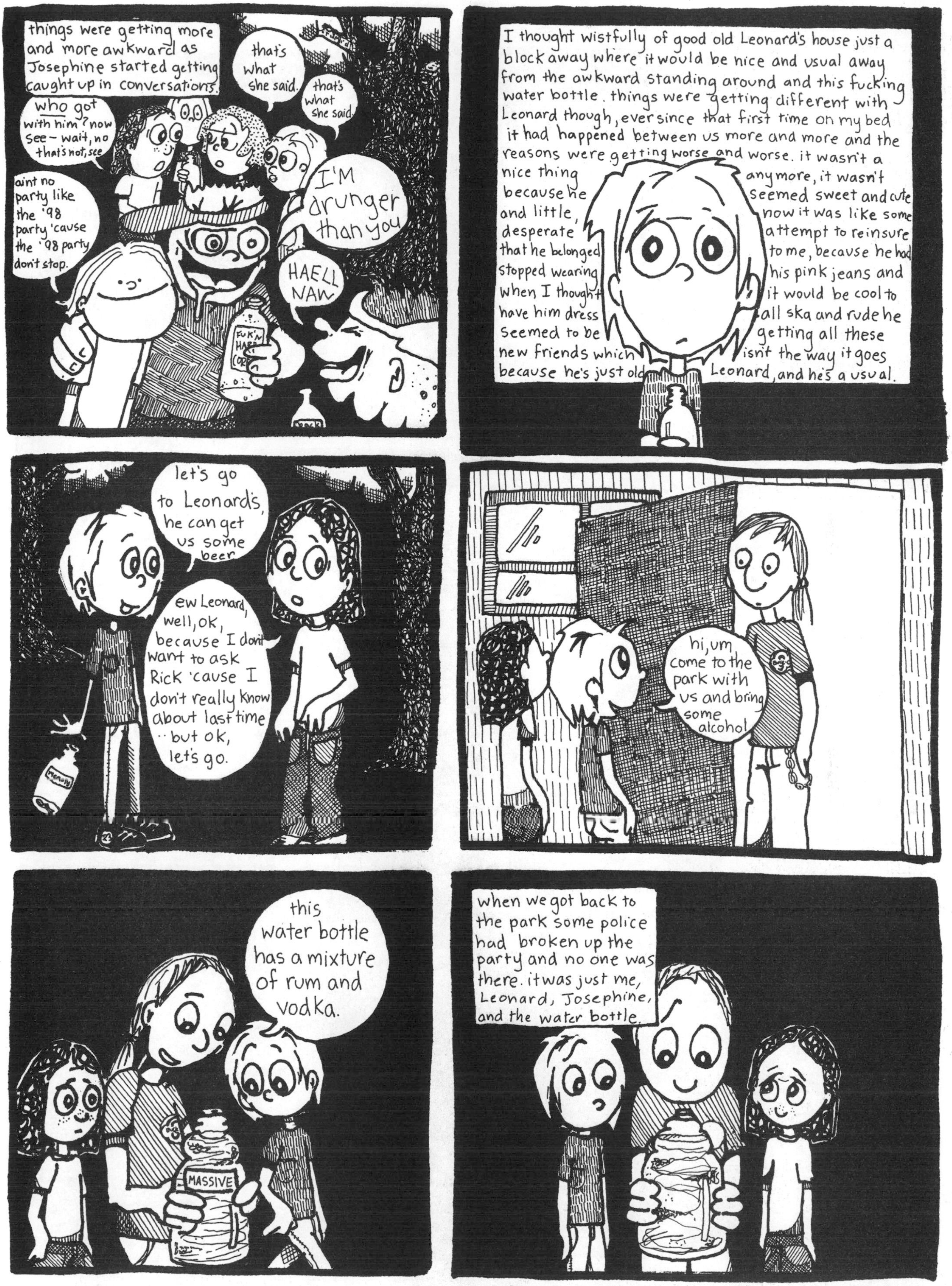
things were getting more and more awkward as Josephine started getting caught up in conversations.
that's what she said.
that's what she said.
who got with him? now see - wait, no that's not, see
aint no party like the '98 party 'cause the '98 party don't stop.
I'M drunger than you
HAELL NAW
I thought wistfully of good old Leonard's house just a block away where it would be nice and usual away from the awkward standing around and this fucking water bottle. things were getting different with Leonard though, ever since that first time on my bed it had happened between us more and more and the reasons were getting worse and worse. it wasn't a nice thing anymore, it wasn't because he seemed sweet and cute and little, now it was like some desperate attempt to reinsure that he belonged to me, because he had stopped wearing his pink jeans and when I thought it would be cool to have him dress all ska and rude he seemed to be getting all these new friends which isn't the way it goes because he's just old Leonard, and he's a usual.
let's go to Leonard's, he can get us some beer
ew Leonard, well, ok, because I don't want to ask Rick 'cause I don't really know about last time .. but ok, let's go.
hi, um come to the park with us and bring some alcohol
this water bottle has a mixture of rum and vodka.
MASSIVE
when we got back to the park some police had broken up the party and no one was there. it was just me, Leonard, Josephine, and the water bottle.

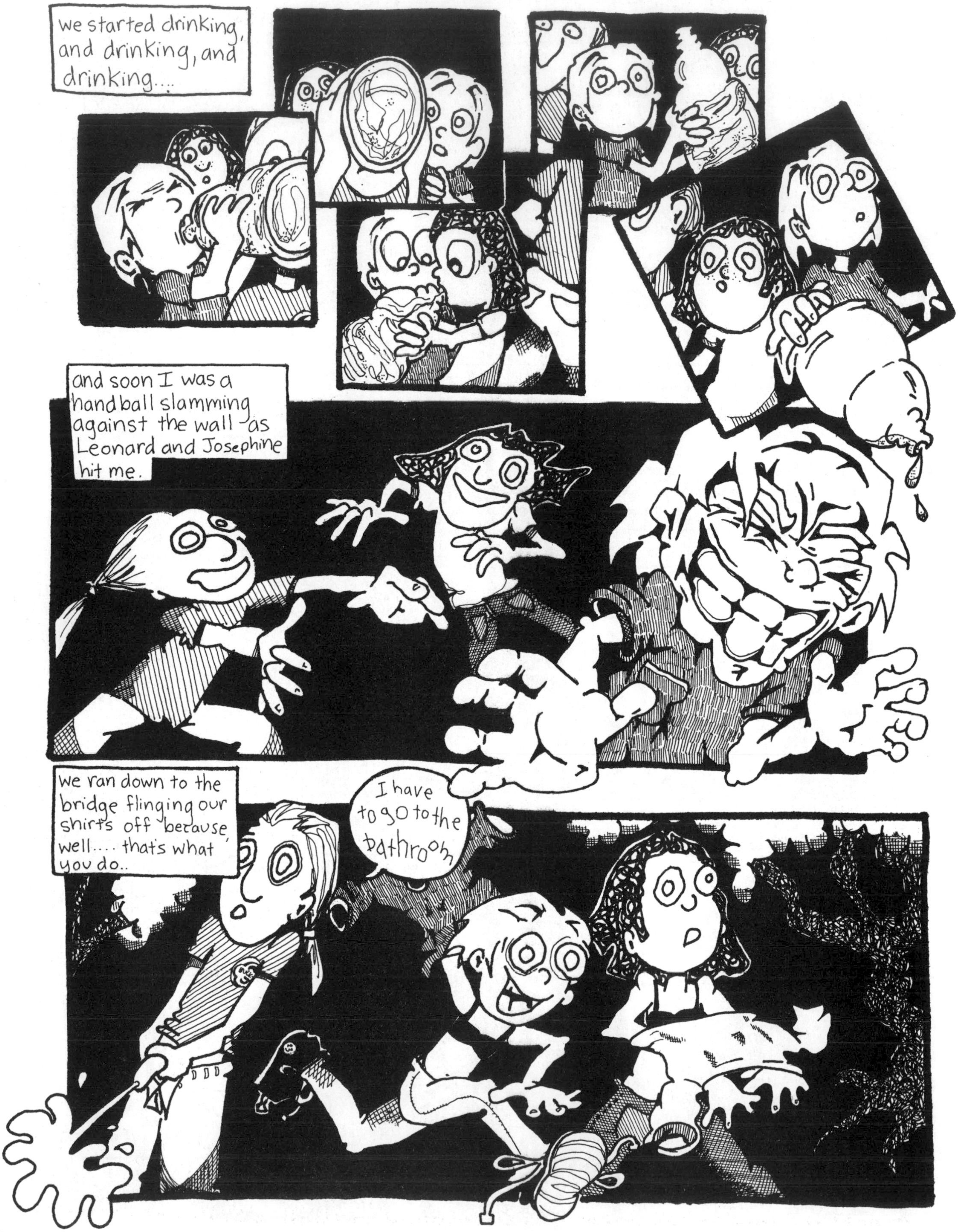
we started drinking, and drinking, and drinking....
and soon I was a handball slamming against the wall as Leonard and Josephine hit me.
We ran down to the bridge flinging our shirts off because, well.... that's what you do..
I have to go to the bathroom

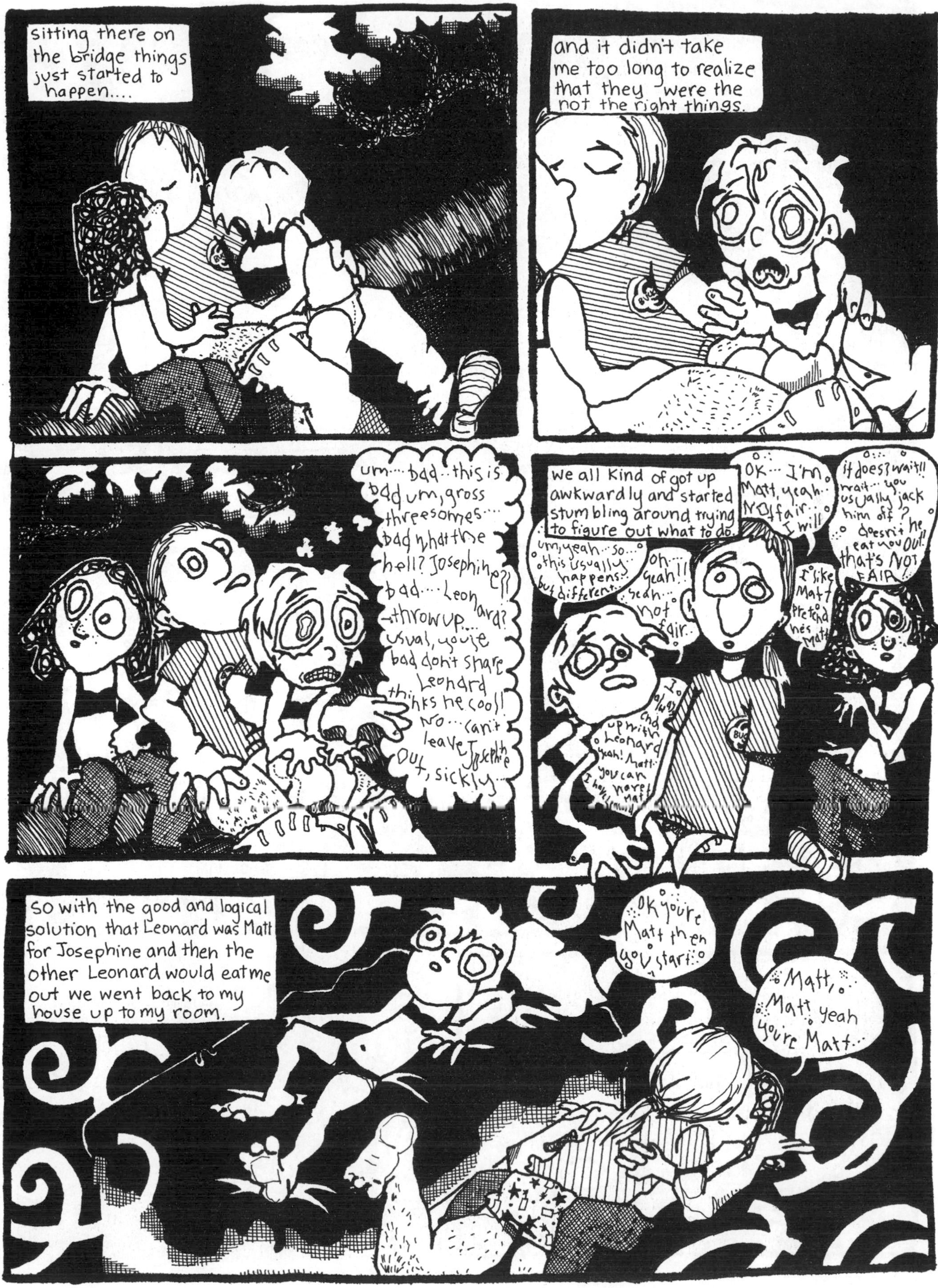

sitting there on the bridge things just started to happen....
and it didn't take me too long to realize that they were the not the right things.
um.... bad.. this is bad um, gross threesomes.... bad what the hell? Josephine?? bad.... Leonard? throw up.... usual, you're bad don't share Leonard thinks he cool! no... can't leave Josephine out, sickly...
we all kind of got up awkwardly and started stumbling around trying to figure out what to do.
um, yeah... so... this usually happens... but different...
oh... yeah!! yeah... not fair...
OK... I'm Matt, yeah.. NOT fair... I will
I like Matt pretend he's Matt
it does? wait!! wait... you usually jack him off? doesn't he eat you out! that's NOT FAIR!
I always end up with Leonard yeah! Matt... you can have Matt
so with the good and logical solution that Leonard was Matt for Josephine and then the other Leonard would eat me out we went back to my house up to my room.
OK you're Matt then you start...
Matt, Matt yeah you're Matt...

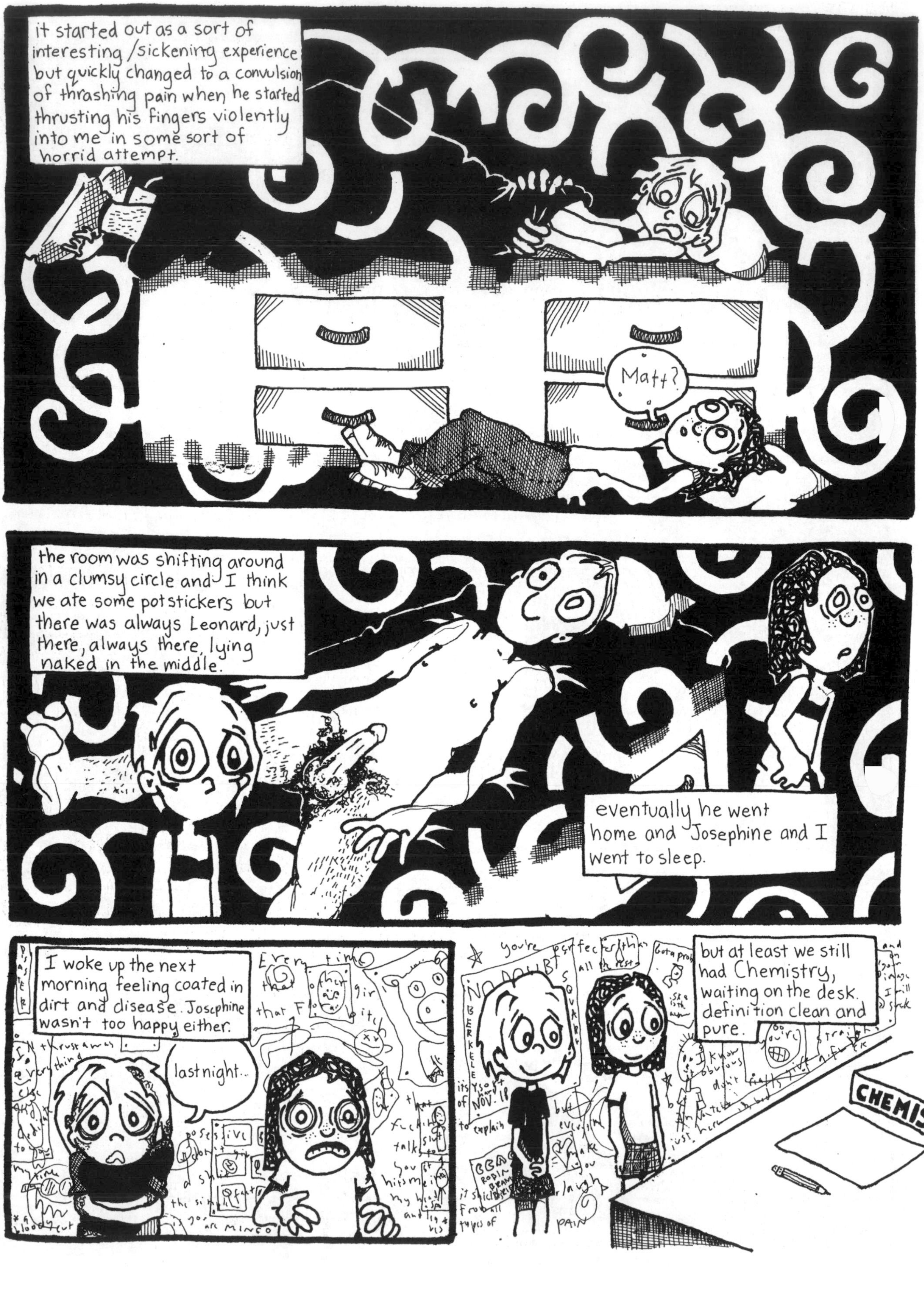
it started out as a sort of interesting/sickening experience but quickly changed to a convulsion of thrashing pain when he started thrusting his fingers violently into me in some sort of horrid attempt.
Matt?
the room was shifting around in a clumsy circle and I think we ate some potstickers but there was always Leonard, just there, always there, lying naked in the middle.
eventually he went home and Josephine and I went to sleep.
I woke up the next morning feeling coated in dirt and disease. Josephine wasn't too happy either.
last night...
but at least we still had Chemistry, waiting on the desk. definition clean and pure.
CHEMIS

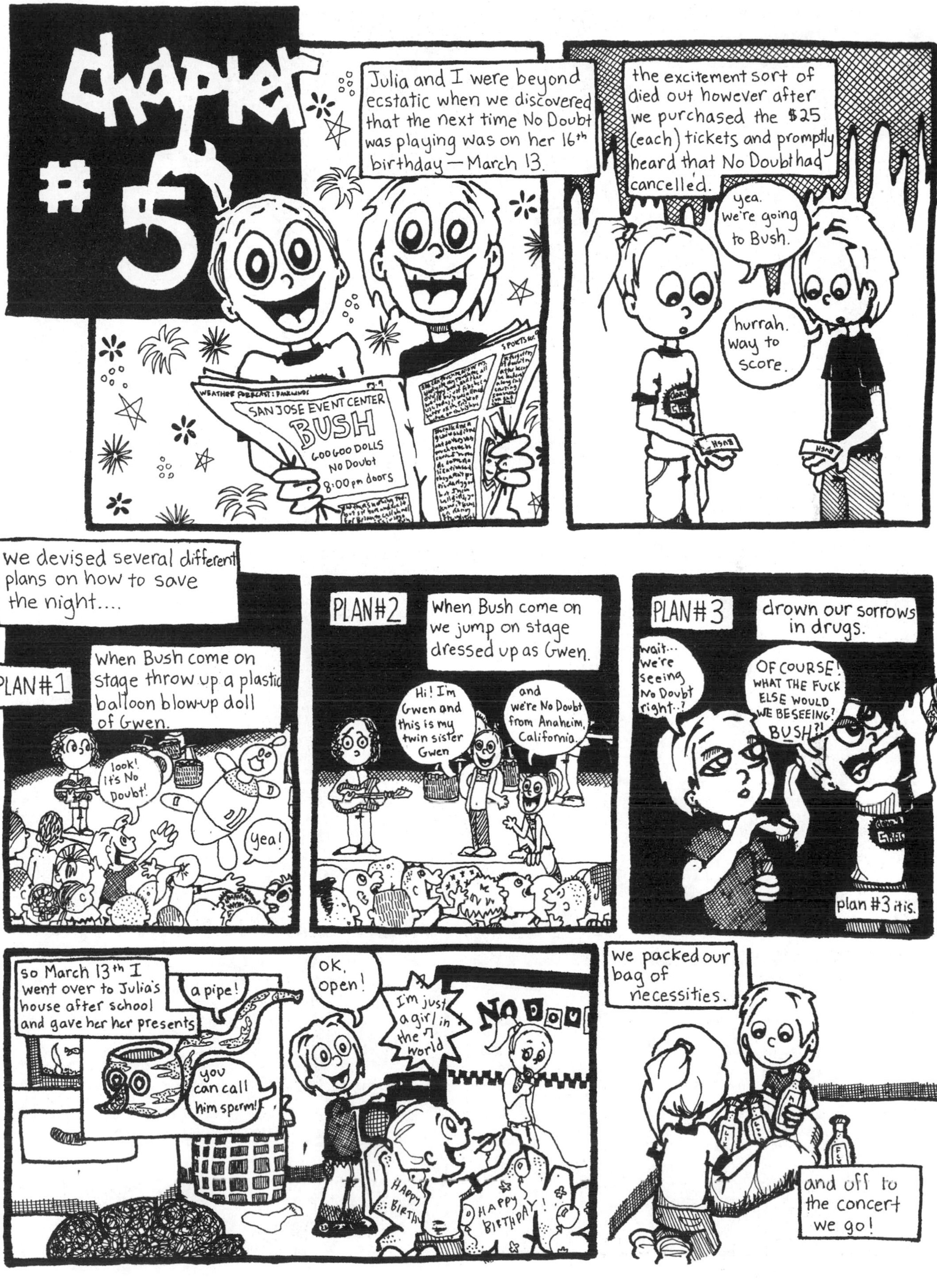
chapter #5
Julia and I were beyond ecstatic when we discovered that the next time No Doubt was playing was on her 16th birthday — March 13.
SAN JOSE EVENT CENTER
BUSH
GOO GOO DOLLS
No Doubt
8:00 pm doors
the excitement sort of died out however after we purchased the $25 (each) tickets and promptly heard that No Doubt had cancelled.
yea. we're going to Bush.
hurrah. way to score.
we devised several different plans on how to save the night....
PLAN #1
When Bush come on stage throw up a plastic balloon blow-up doll of Gwen.
look! it's No Doubt!
yea!
PLAN #2
When Bush come on we jump on stage dressed up as Gwen.
Hi! I'm Gwen and this is my twin sister Gwen
and we're No Doubt from Anaheim, California.
PLAN #3
drown our sorrows in drugs.
wait... we're seeing No Doubt right..?
OF COURSE! WHAT THE FUCK ELSE WOULD WE BE SEEING? BUSH?!
plan #3 it is.
so March 13th I went over to Julia's house after school and gave her her presents
a pipe!
you can call him sperm!
OK, open!
I'm just a girl in the world
HAPPY BIRTH
HAPPY BIRTHDAY!
we packed our bag of necessities.
and off to the concert we go!

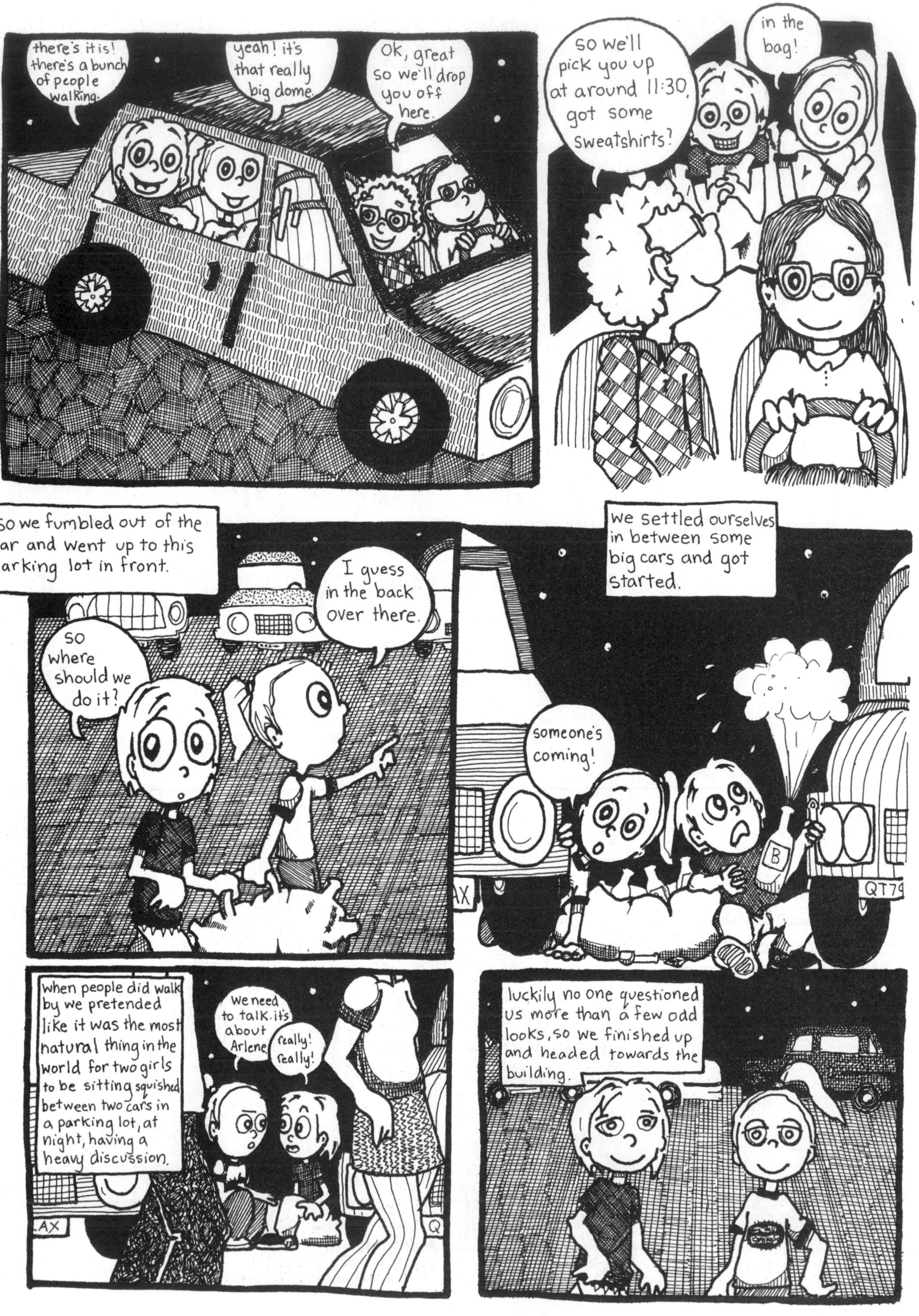

there's it is! there's a bunch of people walking.
yeah! it's that really big dome.
Ok, great so we'll drop you off here.
so we'll pick you up at around 11:30, got some sweatshirts?
in the bag!
so we fumbled out of the car and went up to this parking lot in front.
so where should we do it?
I guess in the back over there.
we settled ourselves in between some big cars and got started.
someone's coming!
B
AX
QT79
when people did walk by we pretended like it was the most natural thing in the world for two girls to be sitting squished between two cars in a parking lot, at night, having a heavy discussion.
We need to talk. it's about Arlene.
really! really!
AX
Q
luckily no one questioned us more than a few odd looks, so we finished up and headed towards the building.

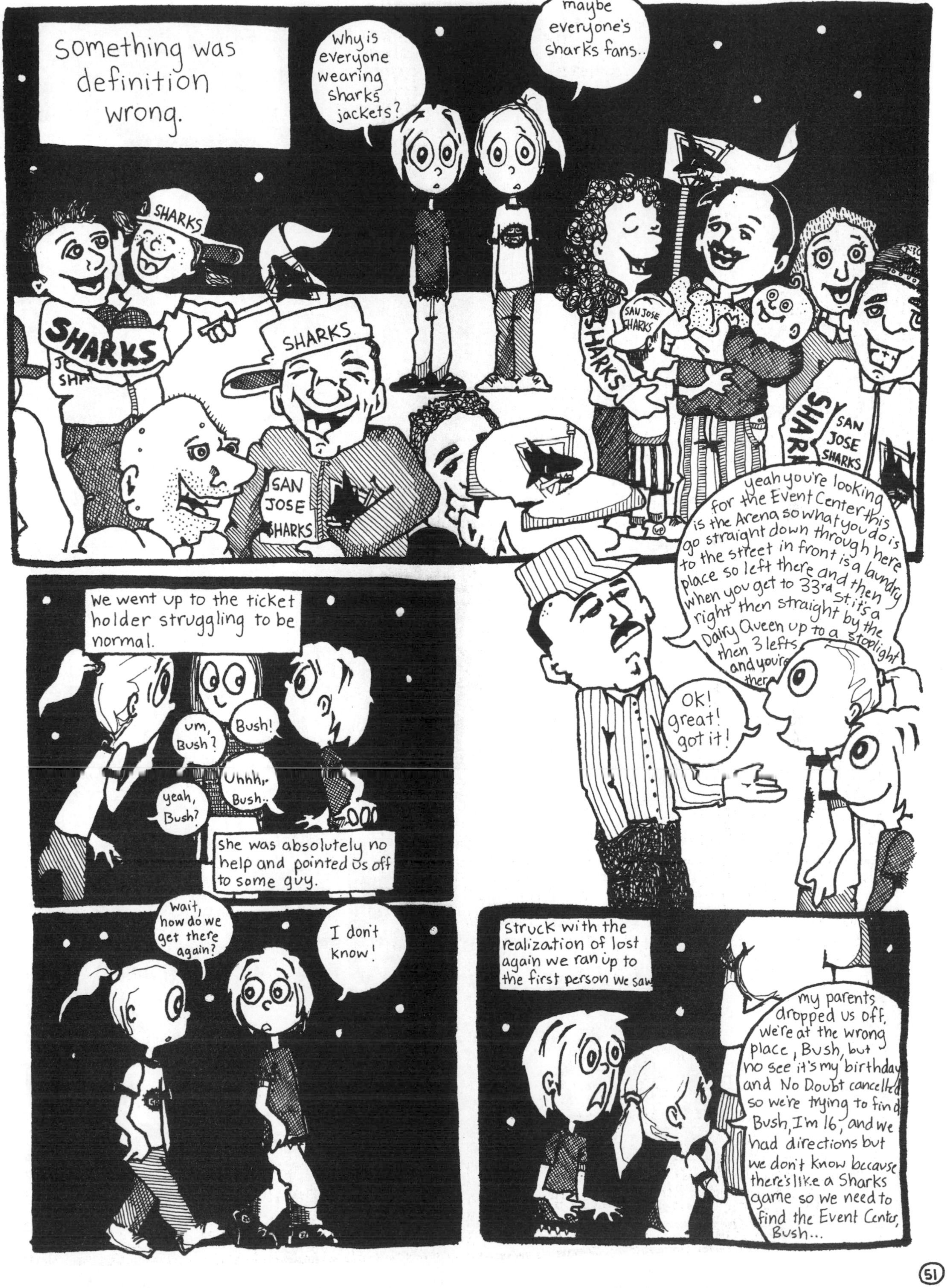

something was definition wrong.
why is everyone wearing sharks jackets?
maybe everyone's sharks fans..
SHARKS
SHARKS
SHARKS
SAN JOSE SHARKS
SHARKS
SAN JOSE SHARKS
SAN JOSE SHARKS
yeah you're looking for the Event Center this is the Arena so what you do is go straight down through here to the street in front is a laundry place so left there and then when you get to 33rd st. it's a right then straight by the Dairy Queen up to a stoplight then 3 lefts and you're there
We went up to the ticket holder struggling to be normal.
um, Bush?
Bush!
Uhhh, Bush..
yeah, Bush?
she was absolutely no help and pointed us off to some guy.
OK! great! got it!
wait, how do we get there again?
I don't know!
struck with the realization of lost again we ran up to the first person we saw
my parents dropped us off. we're at the wrong place, Bush, but no see it's my birthday and No Doubt cancelled so we're trying to find Bush, I'm 16, and we had directions but we don't know because there's like a Sharks game so we need to find the Event Center, Bush...

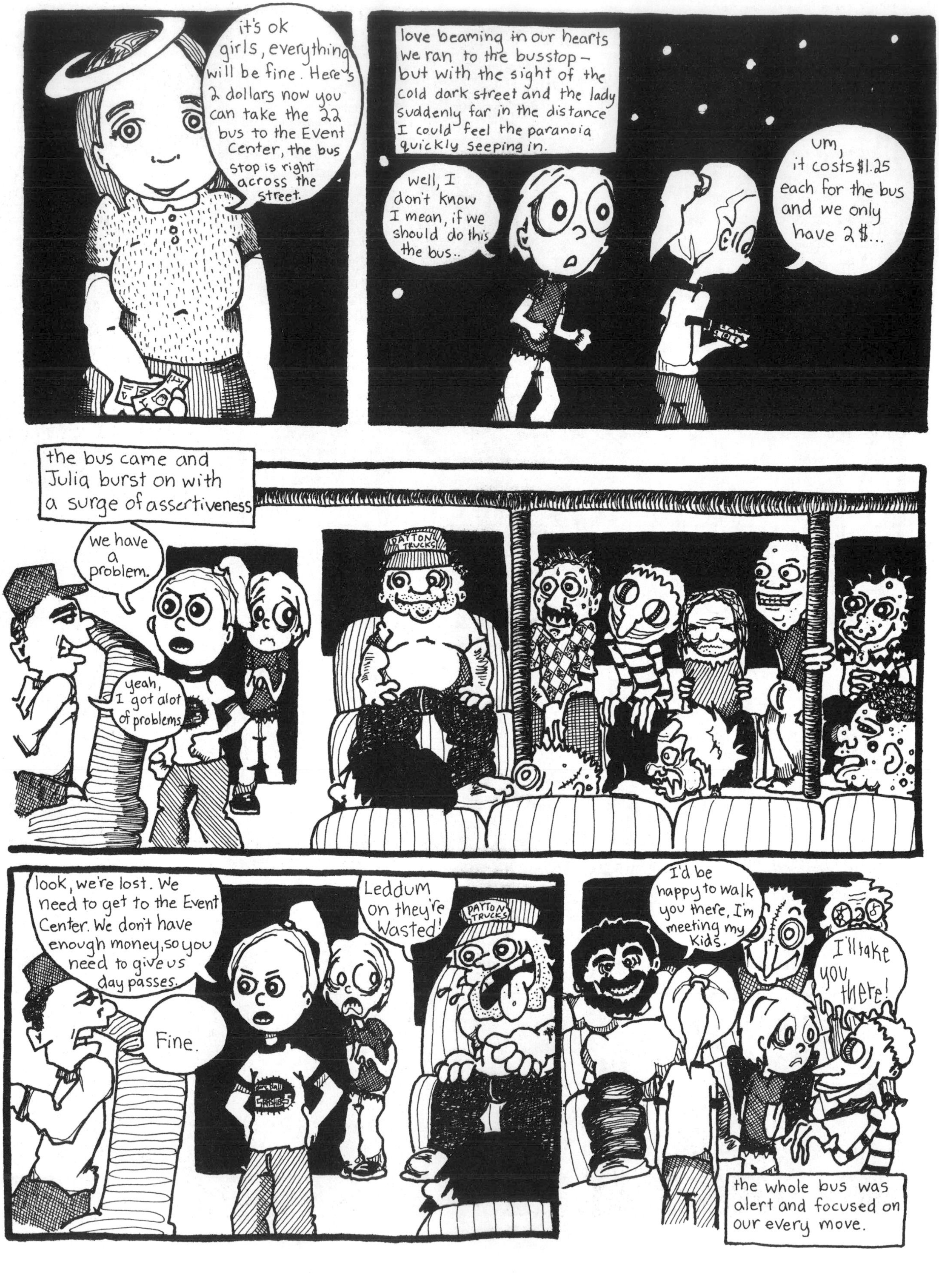

it's ok girls, everything will be fine. Here's 2 dollars now you can take the 22 bus to the Event Center, the bus stop is right across the street.
love beaming in our hearts we ran to the busstop — but with the sight of the cold dark street and the lady suddenly far in the distance I could feel the paranoia quickly seeping in.
well, I don't know I mean, if we should do this the bus..
um, it costs $1.25 each for the bus and we only have 2$...
the bus came and Julia burst on with a surge of assertiveness
We have a problem.
yeah, I got alot of problems.
DAYTON TRUCKS
look, we're lost. We need to get to the Event Center. We don't have enough money, so you need to give us day passes.
Fine.
Leddum on they're Wasted!
DAYTON TRUCKS
I'd be happy to walk you there. I'm meeting my Kids.
I'll take you there!
the whole bus was alert and focused on our every move.

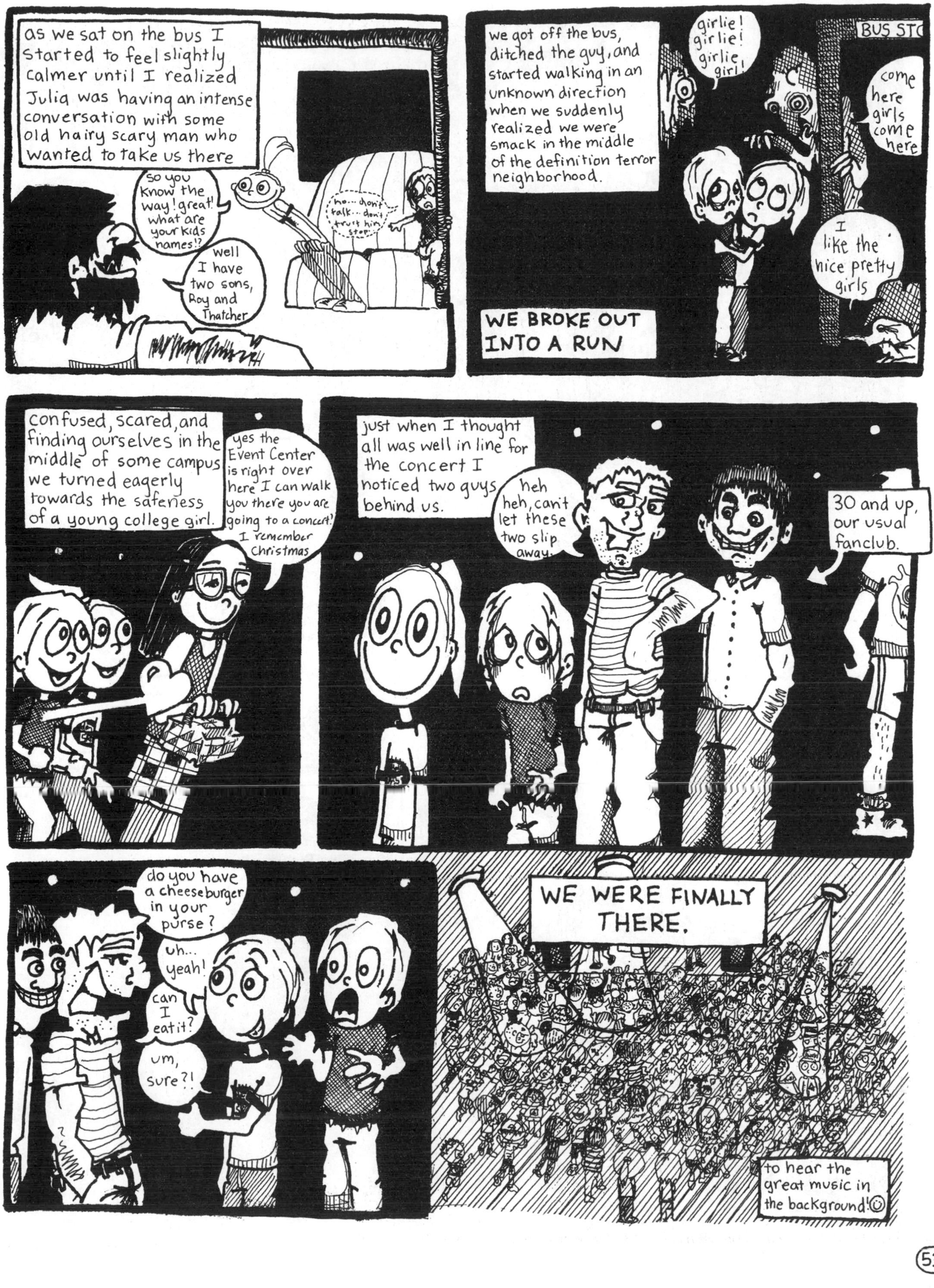
as we sat on the bus I started to feel slightly calmer until I realized Julia was having an intense conversation with some old hairy scary man who wanted to take us there
so you know the way! great! what are your kids names!?
no... don't talk... don't trust him stop.
well I have two sons, Roy and Thatcher
we got off the bus, ditched the guy, and started walking in an unknown direction when we suddenly realized we were smack in the middle of the definition terror neighborhood.
girlie! girlie! girlie girl!
BUS STO
come here girls come here
I like the nice pretty girls
WE BROKE OUT INTO A RUN
confused, scared, and finding ourselves in the middle of some campus we turned eagerly towards the safeness of a young college girl.
yes the Event Center is right over here I can walk you there you are going to a concert! I remember Christmas
just when I thought all was well in line for the concert I noticed two guys behind us.
heh heh, can't let these two slip away.
30 and up, our usual fanclub.
do you have a cheeseburger in your purse?
uh... yeah!
can I eat it?
um, sure?!
WE WERE FINALLY THERE.
to hear the great music in the background! ☺

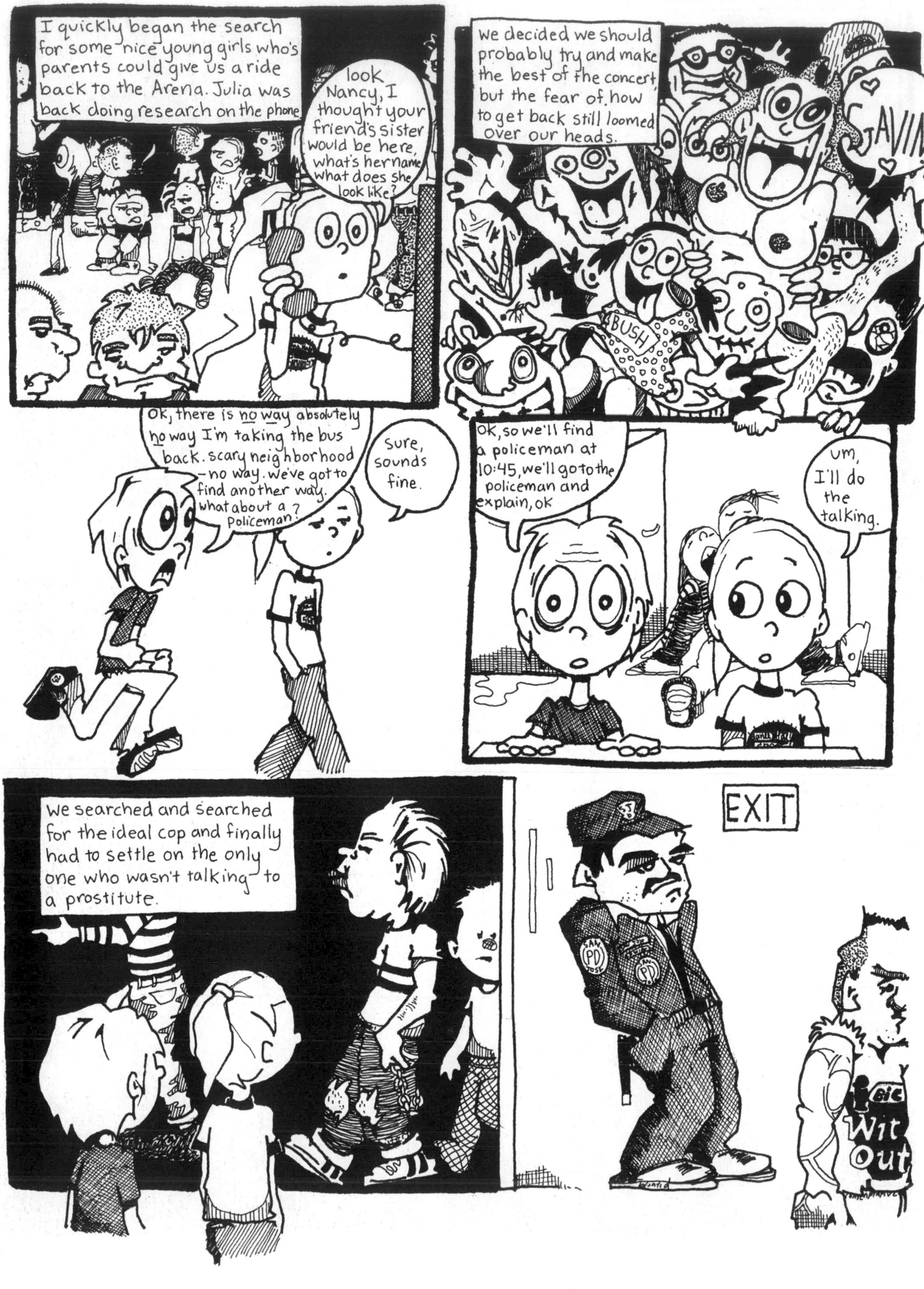
I quickly began the search for some nice young girls who's parents could give us a ride back to the Arena. Julia was back doing research on the phone
look Nancy, I thought your friend's sister would be here, what's her name, what does she look like?
We decided we should probably try and make the best of the concert, but the fear of how to get back still loomed over our heads.
SAVING
BUSH
Ok, there is no way absolutely no way I'm taking the bus back. scary neighborhood — no way. we've got to find another way. what about a policeman?
sure, sounds fine.
Ok, so we'll find a policeman at 10:45, we'll go to the policeman and explain, ok
um, I'll do the talking.
We searched and searched for the ideal cop and finally had to settle on the only one who wasn't talking to a prostitute.
EXIT
Wit out

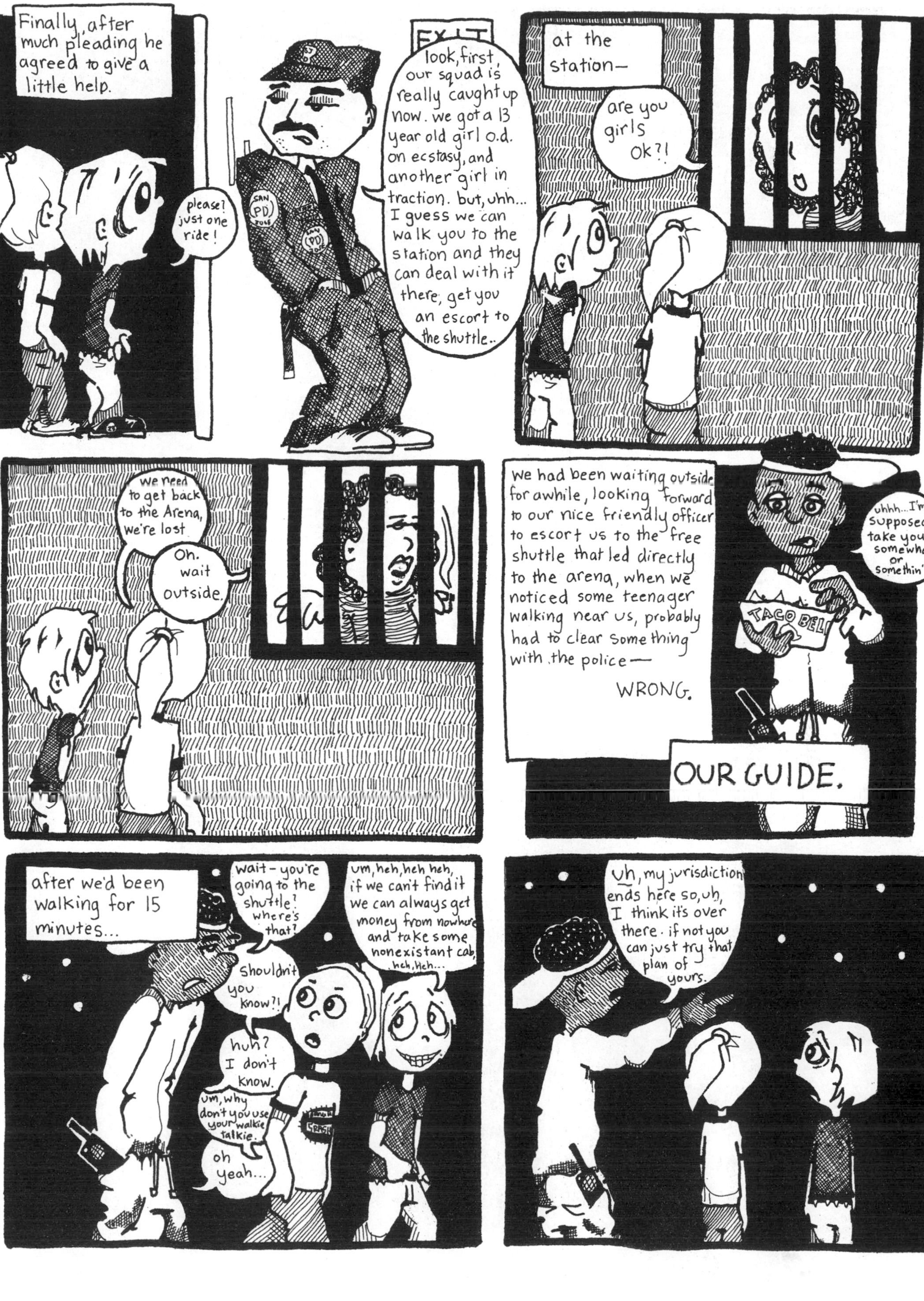
Finally, after much pleading he agreed to give a little help.
please? just one ride!
EXIT
look, first, our squad is really caught up now. we got a 13 year old girl o.d. on ecstasy, and another girl in traction. but, uhh... I guess we can walk you to the station and they can deal with it there; get you an escort to the shuttle..
SAN PD
at the station—
are you girls Ok?!
we need to get back to the Arena, we're lost
Oh. wait outside.
We had been waiting outside for awhile, looking forward to our nice friendly officer to escort us to the free shuttle that led directly to the arena, when we noticed some teenager walking near us, probably had to clear some thing with the police— WRONG.
uhhh... I'm supposed to take you somewhere or somethin'?
TACO BELL
OUR GUIDE.
after we'd been walking for 15 minutes...
wait- you're going to the shuttle? where's that?
Shouldn't you know?!
huh? I don't know.
um, why don't you use your walkie talkie.
oh yeah...
um, heh, heh heh, if we can't find it we can always get money from nowhere and take some nonexistant cab, heh, heh...
uh, my jurisdiction ends here so, uh, I think it's over there. if not you can just try that plan of yours.

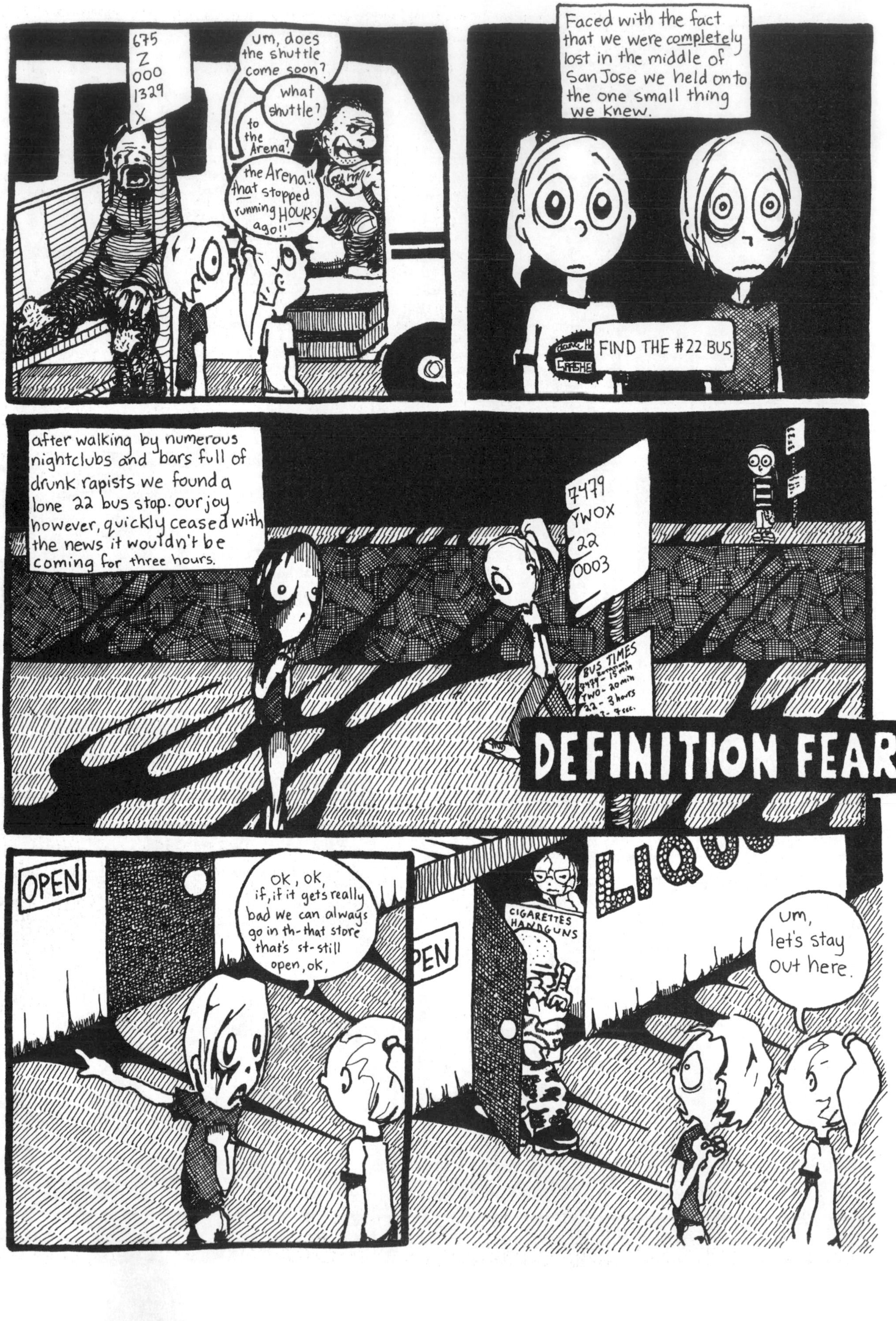
675
Z
000
1329
X
um, does the shuttle come soon?
what shuttle?
to the Arena?
the Arena!! that stopped running HOURS ago!!
Faced with the fact that we were completely lost in the middle of San Jose we held on to the one small thing we knew.
FIND THE #22 BUS.
after walking by numerous nightclubs and bars full of drunk rapists we found a lone 22 bus stop. our joy however, quickly ceased with the news it wouldn't be coming for three hours.
7479
YWOX
22
0003
BUS TIMES
DEFINITION FEAR
OPEN
ok, ok, if, if it gets really bad we can always go in th-that store that's st-still open, ok,
CIGARETTES
HANDGUNS
PEN
um, let's stay out here.

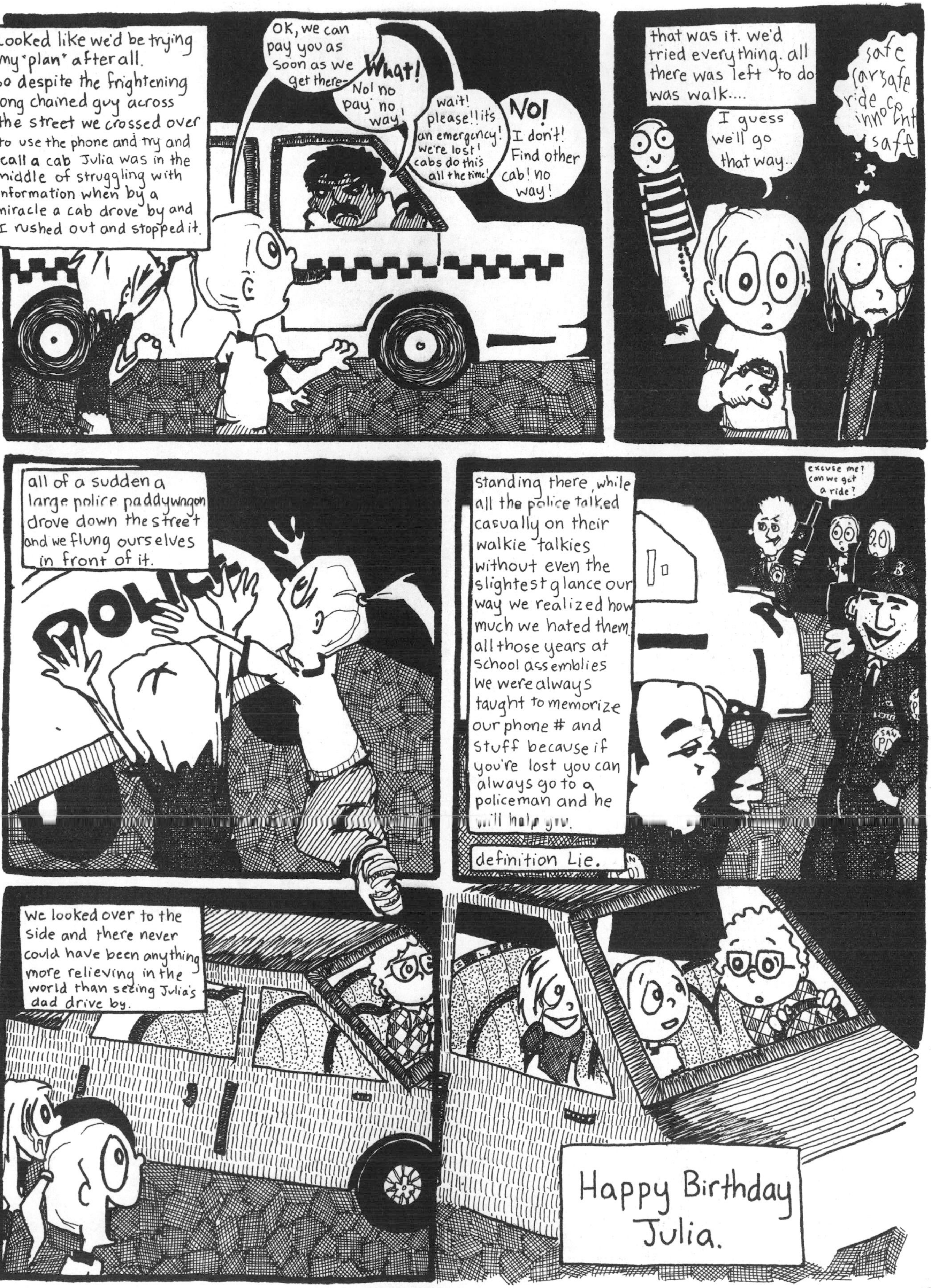
Looked like we'd be trying my "plan" after all. so despite the frightening long chained guy across the street we crossed over to use the phone and try and call a cab Julia was in the middle of struggling with information when by a miracle a cab drove by and I rushed out and stopped it.
OK, we can pay you as soon as we get there—
What! No! no pay no way!
wait! please!! it's an emergency! we're lost! cabs do this all the time!
NO! I don't! Find other cab! no way!
that was it. we'd tried everything. all there was left to do was walk....
I guess we'll go that way..
safe
car safe
ride co
innocent
safe
all of a sudden a large police paddywagon drove down the street and we flung ourselves in front of it.
POLIC
standing there, while all the police talked casually on their walkie talkies without even the slightest glance our way we realized how much we hated them. all those years at school assemblies we were always taught to memorize our phone # and stuff because if you're lost you can always go to a policeman and he will help you.
definition Lie.
excuse me? can we get a ride?
We looked over to the side and there never could have been anything more relieving in the world than seeing Julia's dad drive by.
Happy Birthday Julia.

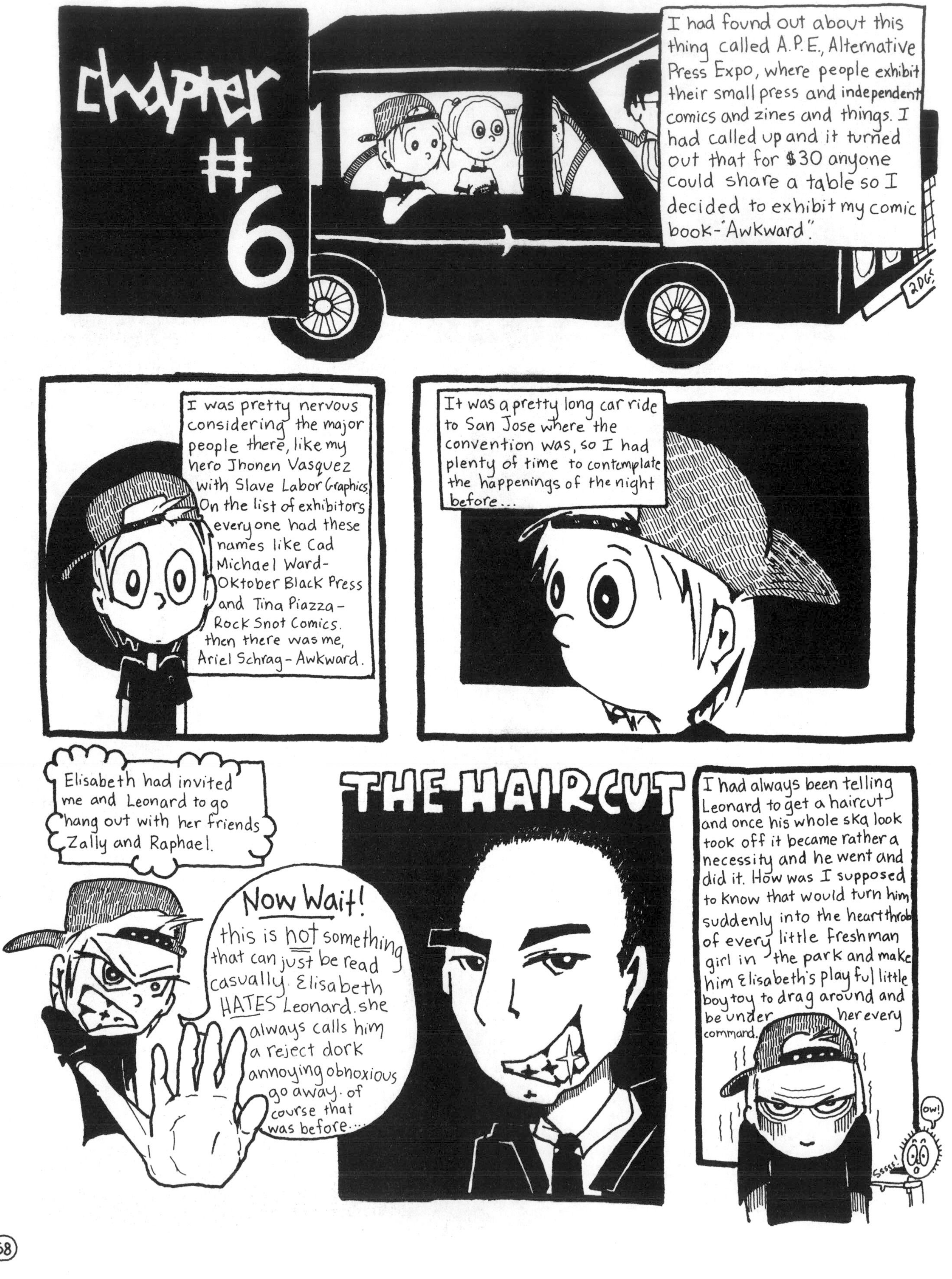
chapter #6
I had found out about this thing called A.P.E., Alternative Press Expo, where people exhibit their small press and independent comics and zines and things. I had called up and it turned out that for $30 anyone could share a table so I decided to exhibit my comic book-"Awkward".
I was pretty nervous considering the major people there, like my hero Jhonen Vasquez with Slave Labor Graphics. On the list of exhibitors everyone had these names like Cad Michael Ward-Oktober Black Press and Tina Piazza-Rock Snot Comics. then there was me, Ariel Schrag-Awkward.
It was a pretty long car ride to San Jose where the convention was, so I had plenty of time to contemplate the happenings of the night before...
Elisabeth had invited me and Leonard to go hang out with her friends Zally and Raphael.
Now Wait! this is not something that can just be read casually. Elisabeth HATES Leonard. she always calls him a reject dork annoying obnoxious go away. of course that was before....
THE HAIRCUT
I had always been telling Leonard to get a haircut and once his whole ska look took off it became rather a necessity and he went and did it. How was I supposed to know that would turn him suddenly into the heartthrob of every little freshman girl in the park and make him Elisabeth's playful little boy toy to drag around and be under her every command.
ow!
Sssss!

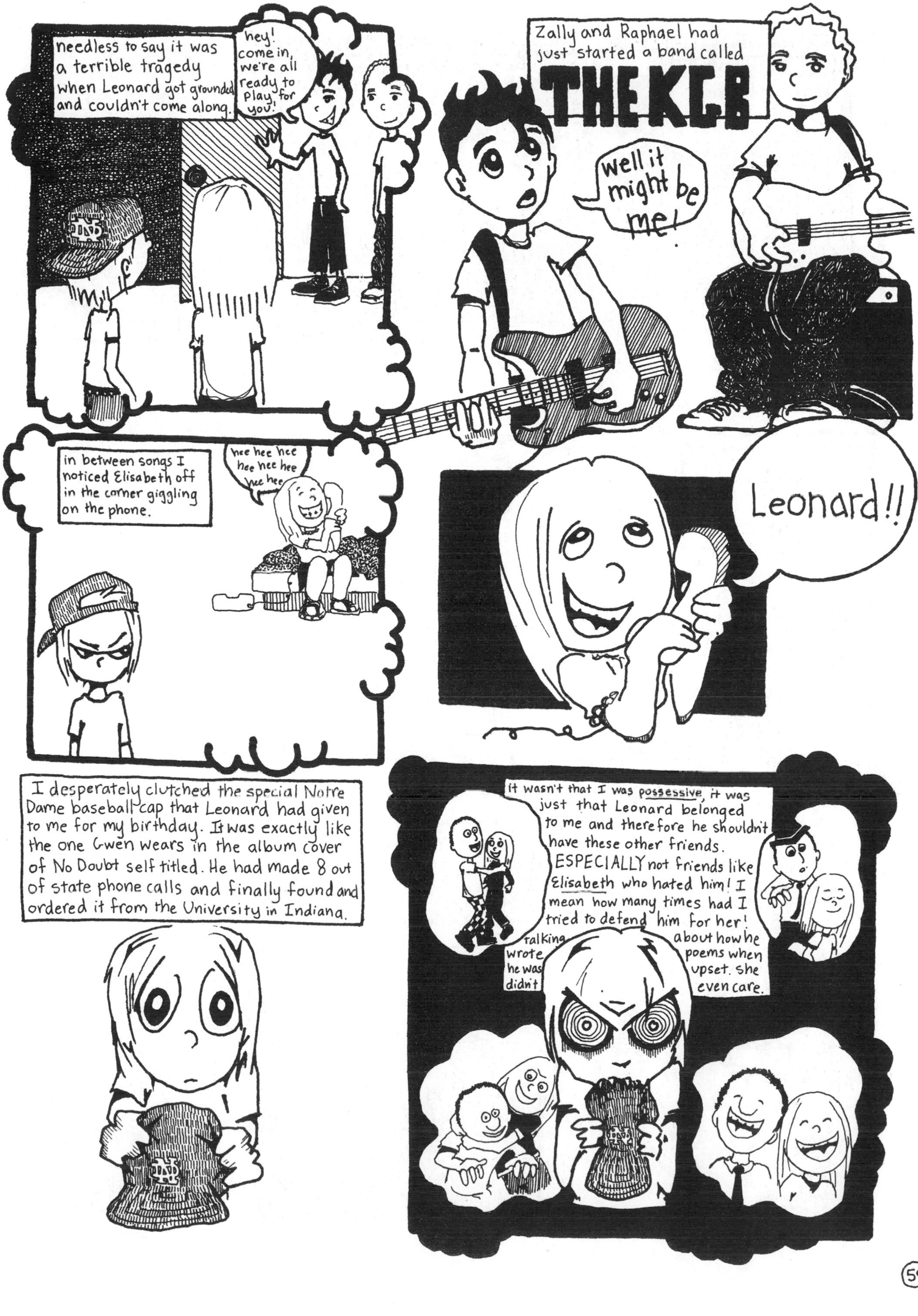
needless to say it was a terrible tragedy when Leonard got grounded and couldn't come along.
hey! come in, we're all ready to play for you!
Zally and Raphael had just started a band called
THE K.G.B
well it might be me!
in between songs I noticed Elisabeth off in the corner giggling on the phone.
hee hee hee hee hee hee hee hee
Leonard!!
I desperately clutched the special Notre Dame baseball cap that Leonard had given to me for my birthday. It was exactly like the one Gwen wears in the album cover of No Doubt self titled. He had made 8 out of state phone calls and finally found and ordered it from the University in Indiana.
it wasn't that I was possessive, it was just that Leonard belonged to me and therefore he shouldn't have these other friends. ESPECIALLY not friends like Elisabeth who hated him! I mean how many times had I tried to defend him for her! talking about how he wrote poems when he was upset. she didn't even care.

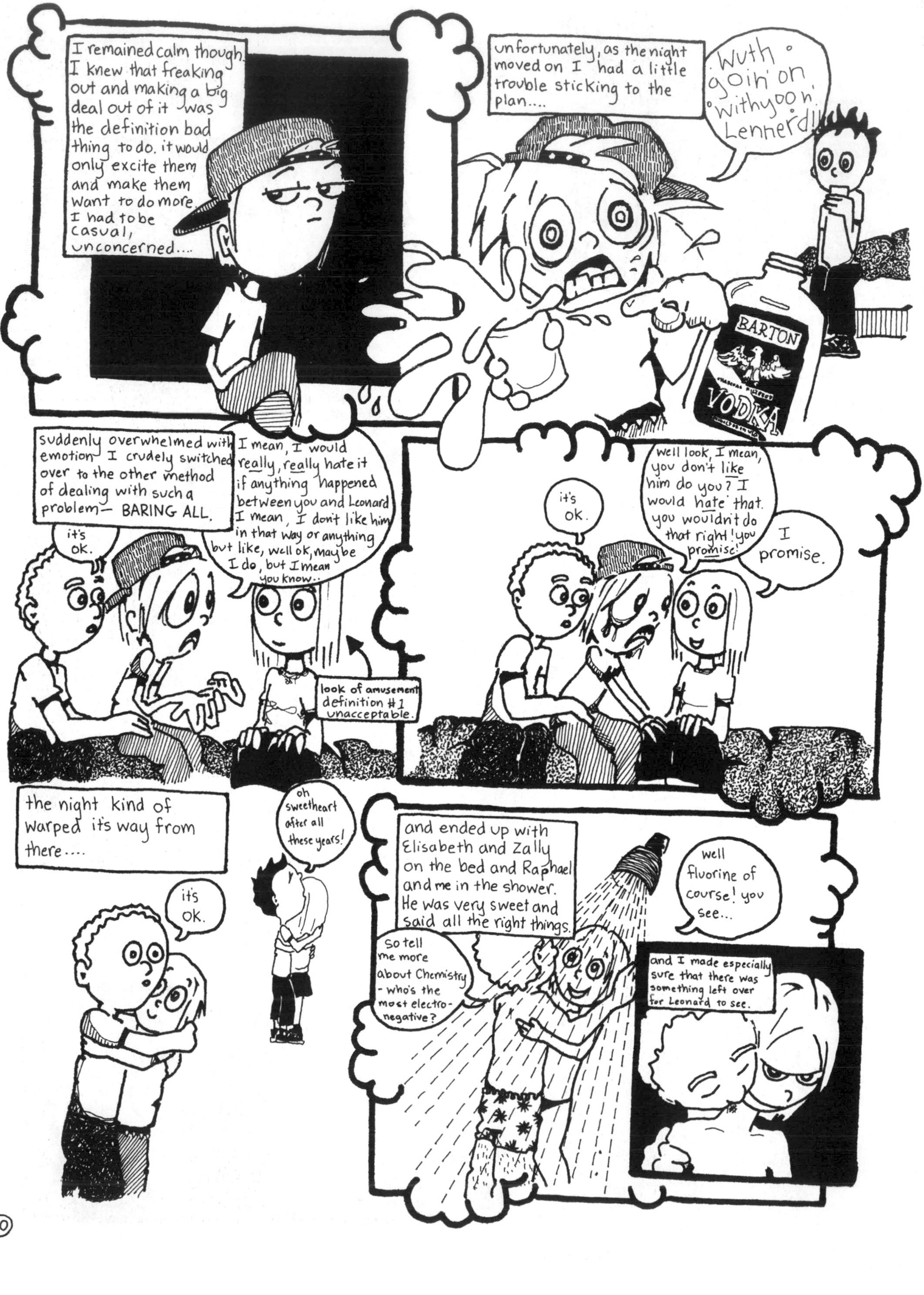
I remained calm though. I knew that freaking out and making a big deal out of it was the definition bad thing to do. it would only excite them and make them want to do more. I had to be casual, unconcerned....
unfortunately, as the night moved on I had a little trouble sticking to the plan....
wuth goin' on withyoo n' Lennerd!!
BARTON
VODKA
suddenly overwhelmed with emotion I crudely switched over to the other method of dealing with such a problem— BARING ALL.
I mean, I would really, really hate it if anything happened between you and Leonard I mean, I don't like him in that way or anything but like, well ok, maybe I do, but I mean you know..
it's ok.
look of amusement definition #1 unacceptable.
it's ok.
well look, I mean, you don't like him do you? I would hate that. you wouldn't do that right! you promise!
I promise.
the night kind of warped its way from there....
oh sweetheart after all these years!
it's ok.
and ended up with Elisabeth and Zally on the bed and Raphael and me in the shower. He was very sweet and said all the right things.
well fluorine of course! you see...
so tell me more about Chemistry - who's the most electro-negative?
and I made especially sure that there was something left over for Leonard to see.

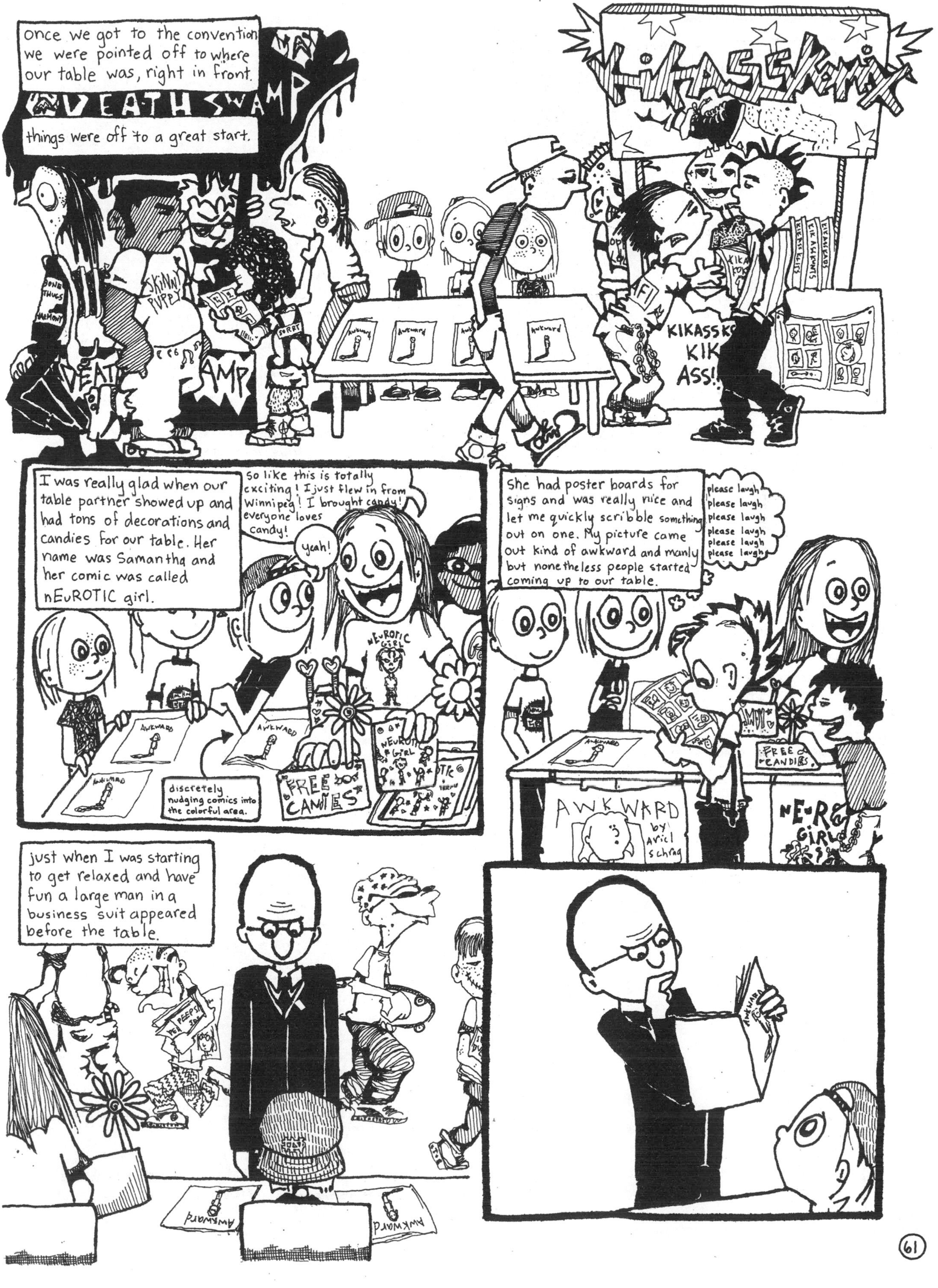
once we got to the convention we were pointed off to where our table was, right in front.
DEATH SWAMP
things were off to a great start.
KIKASSKOMIX
SKINNY PUPPY
SORRY
Awkward
KIKASSKO KIK ASS!
I was really glad when our table partner showed up and had tons of decorations and candies for our table. Her name was Samantha and her comic was called nEuROTIC girl.
So like this is totally exciting! I just flew in from Winnipeg! I brought candy! everyone loves candy!
yeah!
NEUROTIC GIRL
AWKWARD
discretely nudging comics into the colorful area.
FREE CANDIES
She had poster boards for signs and was really nice and let me quickly scribble something out on one. My picture came out kind of awkward and manly but nonetheless people started coming up to our table.
please laugh
please laugh
please laugh
please laugh
please laugh
please laugh
FREE CANDIES
AWKWARD by Ariel Schrag
NEURO GIRL
just when I was starting to get relaxed and have fun a large man in a business suit appeared before the table.
AWKWARD

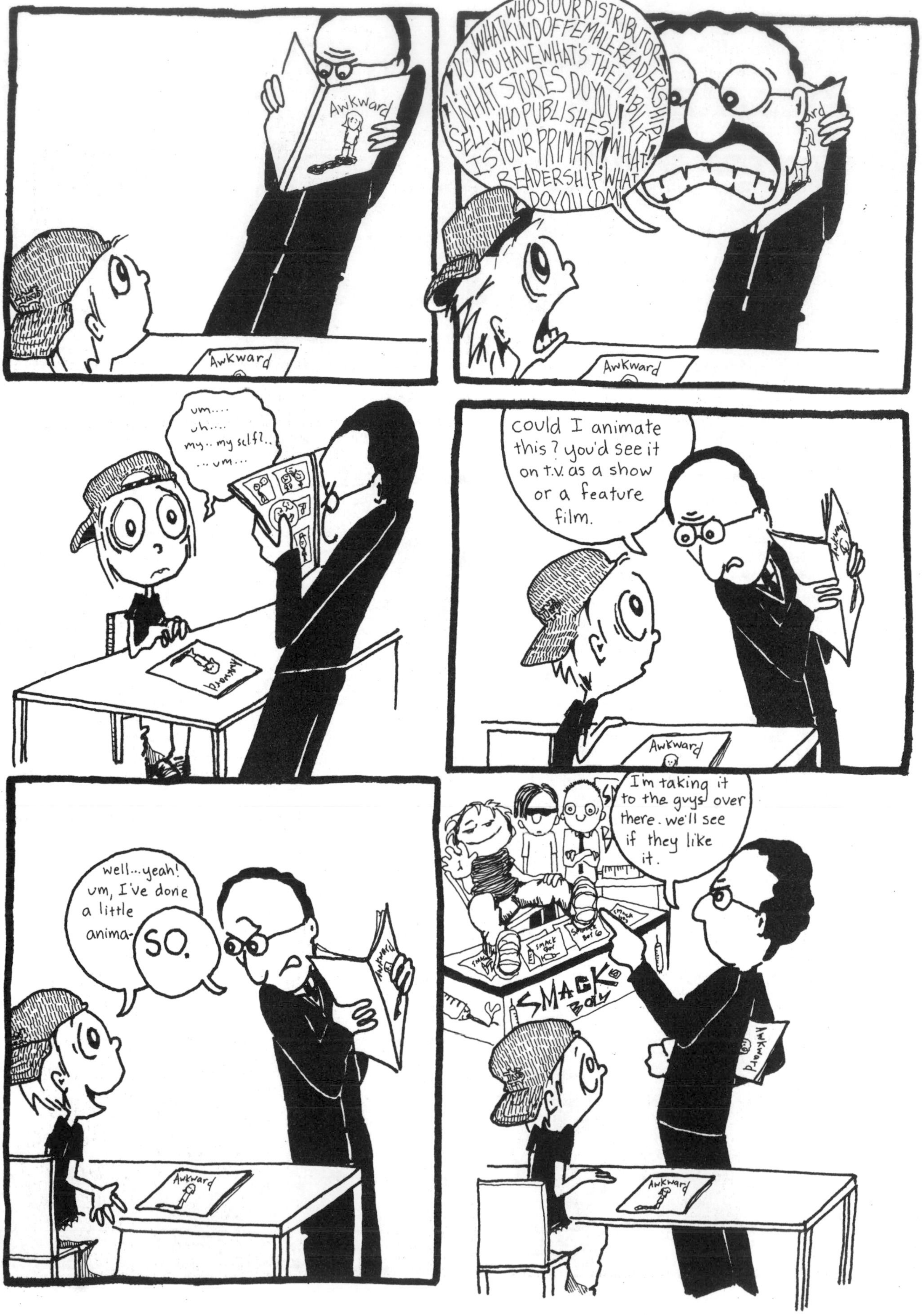
Awkward
Awkward
WHO'S YOUR DISTRIBUTOR! WHAT KIND OF FEMALE READERSHIP! DO YOU HAVE WHAT'S THE LIABILITY! WHAT STORES DO YOU SELL WHO PUBLISHES! IS YOUR PRIMARY! WHAT! READERSHIP WHAT DO YOU COM
Awkward
um.... uh.... my.. my self?.. ...um...
Awkward
could I animate this? you'd see it on t.v. as a show or a feature film.
Awkward
Awkward
well...yeah! um, I've done a little anima-
SO.
Awkward
Awkward
I'm taking it to the guys over there. we'll see if they like it.
SMACK BOY
Awkward
Awkward

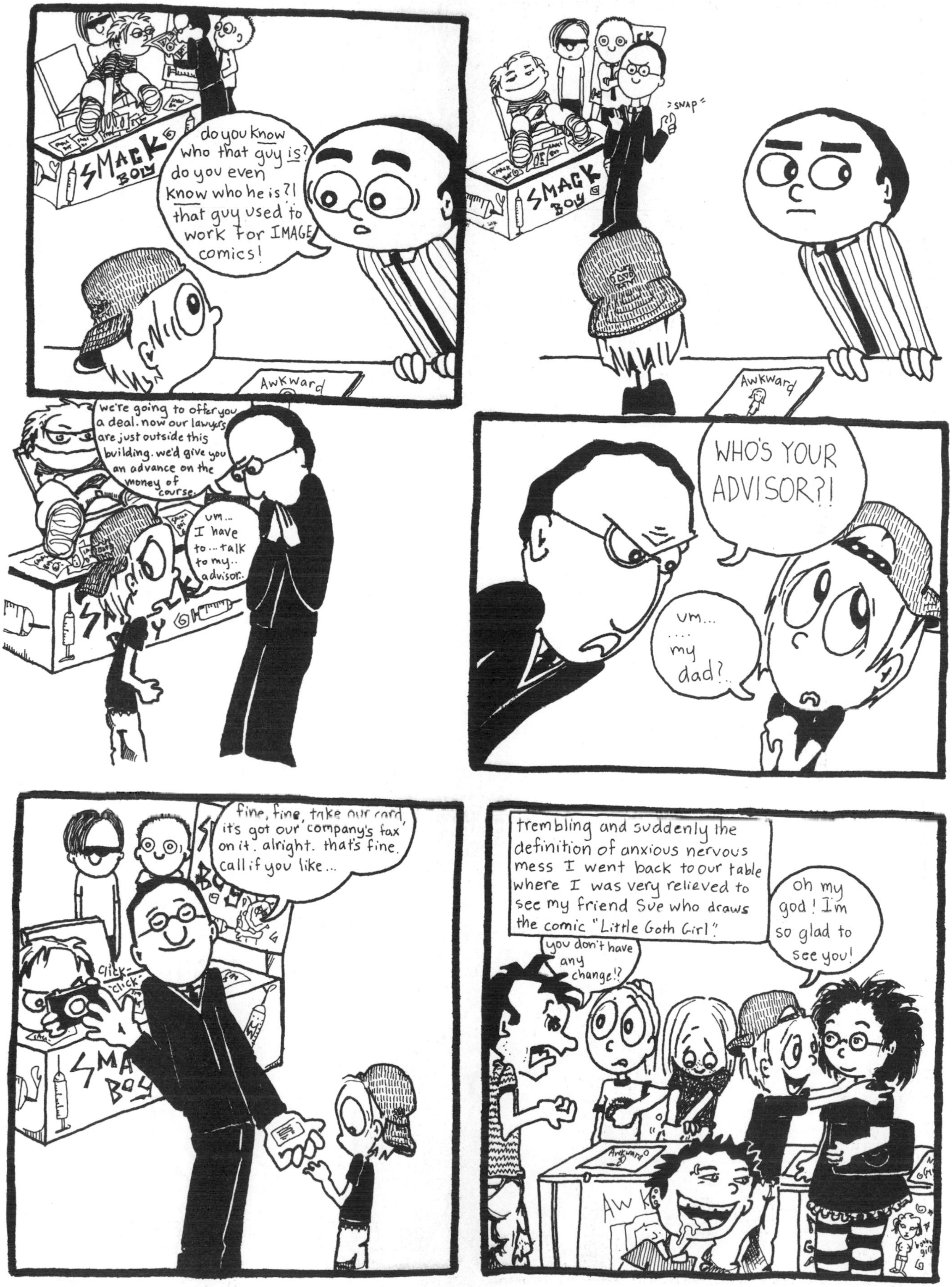
do you know who that guy is? do you even know who he is?! that guy used to work for IMAGE comics!
SMACK BOY
Awkward
SNAP
we're going to offer you a deal. now our lawyers are just outside this building. we'd give you an advance on the money of course.
um... I have to... talk to my.. advisor..
WHO'S YOUR ADVISOR?!
um... .... my dad?..
fine, fine, take our card, it's got our company's fax on it. alright. that's fine. call if you like...
click-click
trembling and suddenly the definition of anxious nervous mess I went back to our table where I was very relieved to see my friend Sue who draws the comic "Little Goth Girl".
you don't have any change!?
oh my god! I'm so glad to see you!

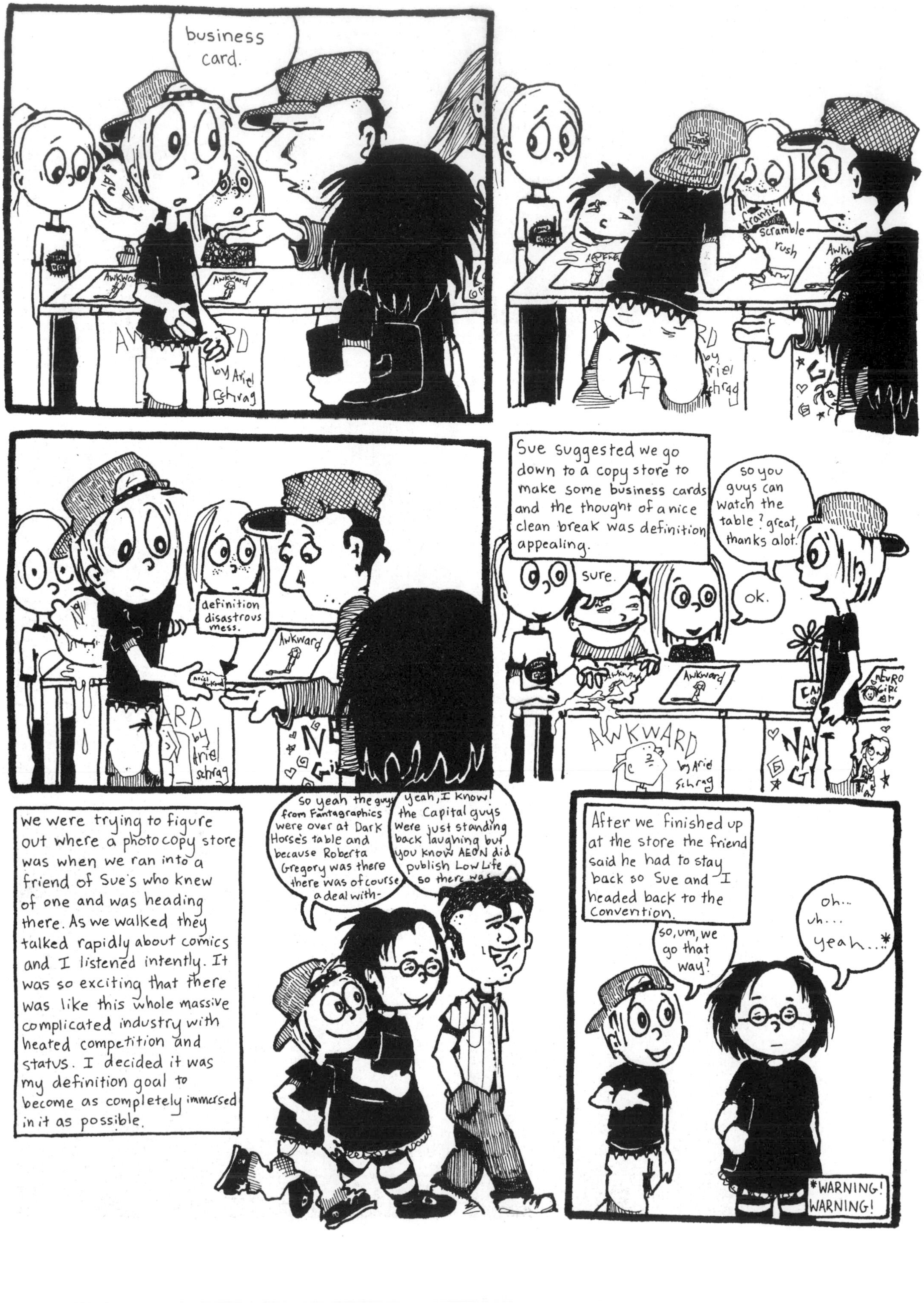
business card.
AWKWARD
by Ariel Schrag
frantic scramble rush
definition disastrous mess.
Sue suggested we go down to a copy store to make some business cards and the thought of a nice clean break was definition appealing.
so you guys can watch the table? great, thanks alot.
sure.
ok.
we were trying to figure out where a photocopy store was when we ran into a friend of Sue's who knew of one and was heading there. As we walked they talked rapidly about comics and I listened intently. It was so exciting that there was like this whole massive complicated industry with heated competition and status. I decided it was my definition goal to become as completely immersed in it as possible.
So yeah the guys from Fantagraphics were over at Dark Horse's table and because Roberta Gregory was there there was of course a deal with-
yeah, I know! the Capital guys were just standing back laughing but you know AEON did publish Low Life so there was
After we finished up at the store the friend said he had to stay back so Sue and I headed back to the Convention.
so, um, we go that way?
oh... uh... yeah...*
*WARNING! WARNING!

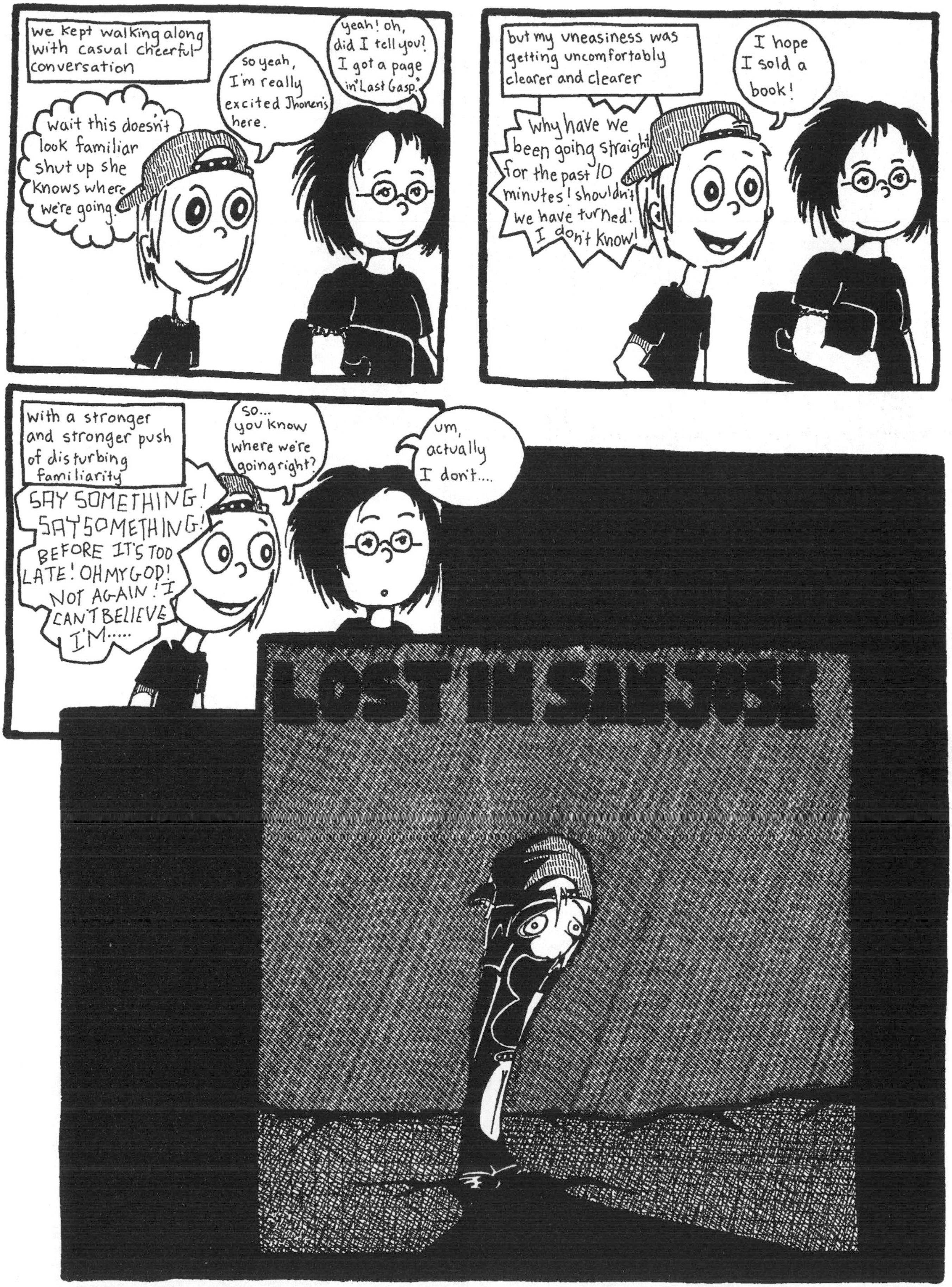

we kept walking along with casual cheerful conversation
wait this doesn't look familiar shut up she knows where we're going.
so yeah, I'm really excited Jhonen's here.
yeah! oh, did I tell you? I got a page in "Last Gasp."
but my uneasiness was getting uncomfortably clearer and clearer
why have we been going straight for the past 10 minutes! shouldn't we have turned! I don't know!
I hope I sold a book!
with a stronger and stronger push of disturbing familiarity
SAY SOMETHING! SAY SOMETHING! BEFORE IT'S TOO LATE! OHMYGOD! NOT AGAIN! I CAN'T BELIEVE I'M.....
so... you know where we're going right?
um, actually I don't....
LOST IN SAN JOSE

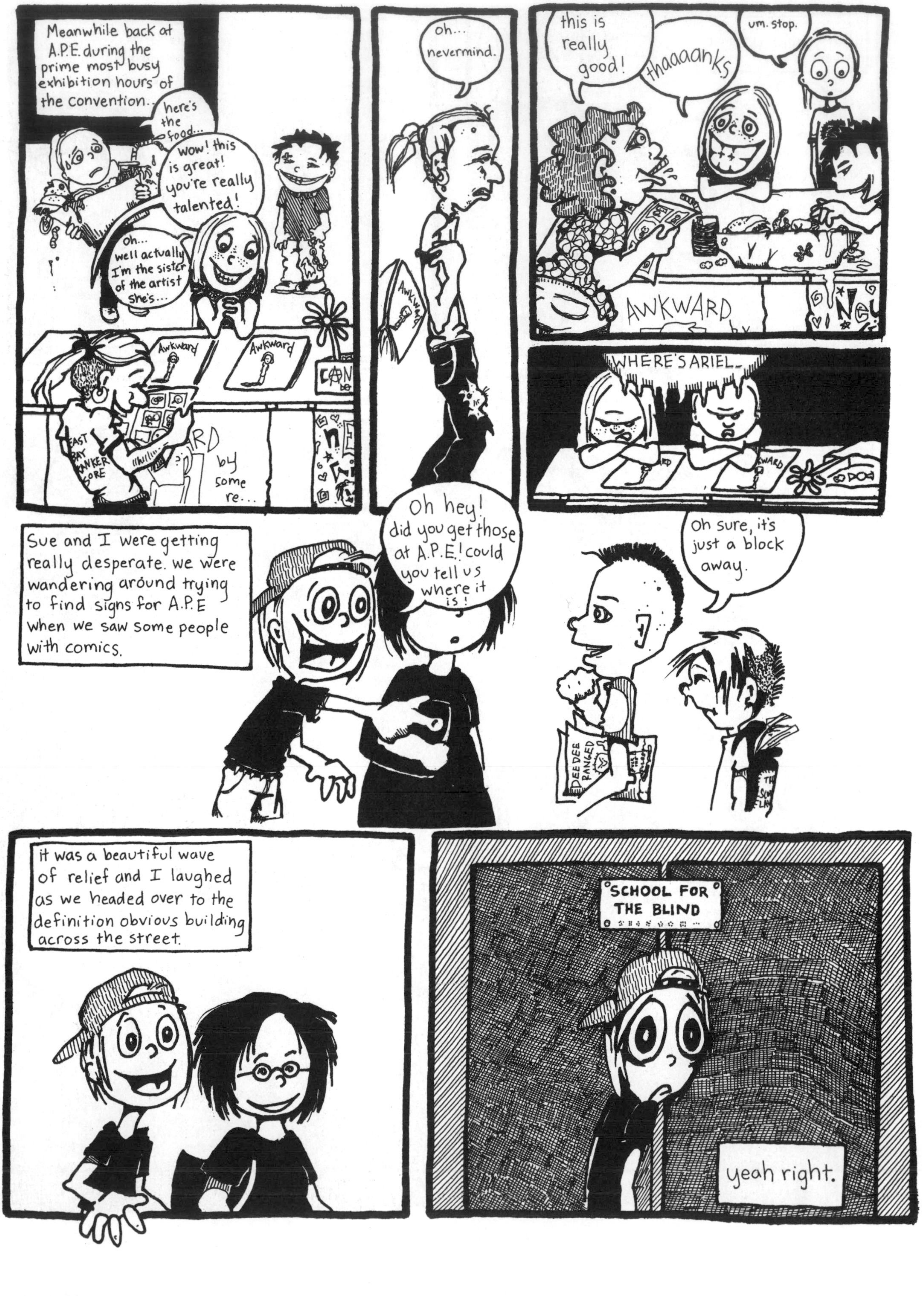

Meanwhile back at A.P.E. during the prime most busy exhibition hours of the convention...
here's the food...
wow! this is great! you're really talented!
oh... well actually I'm the sister of the artist she's...
Awkward
Awkward
by some re...
oh... nevermind.
this is really good!
thaaaanks
um. stop.
AWKWARD by
WHERE'S ARIEL
Sue and I were getting really desperate. we were wandering around trying to find signs for A.P.E when we saw some people with comics.
Oh hey! did you get those at A.P.E.! could you tell us where it is!
Oh sure, it's just a block away.
it was a beautiful wave of relief and I laughed as we headed over to the definition obvious building across the street.
SCHOOL FOR THE BLIND
yeah right.

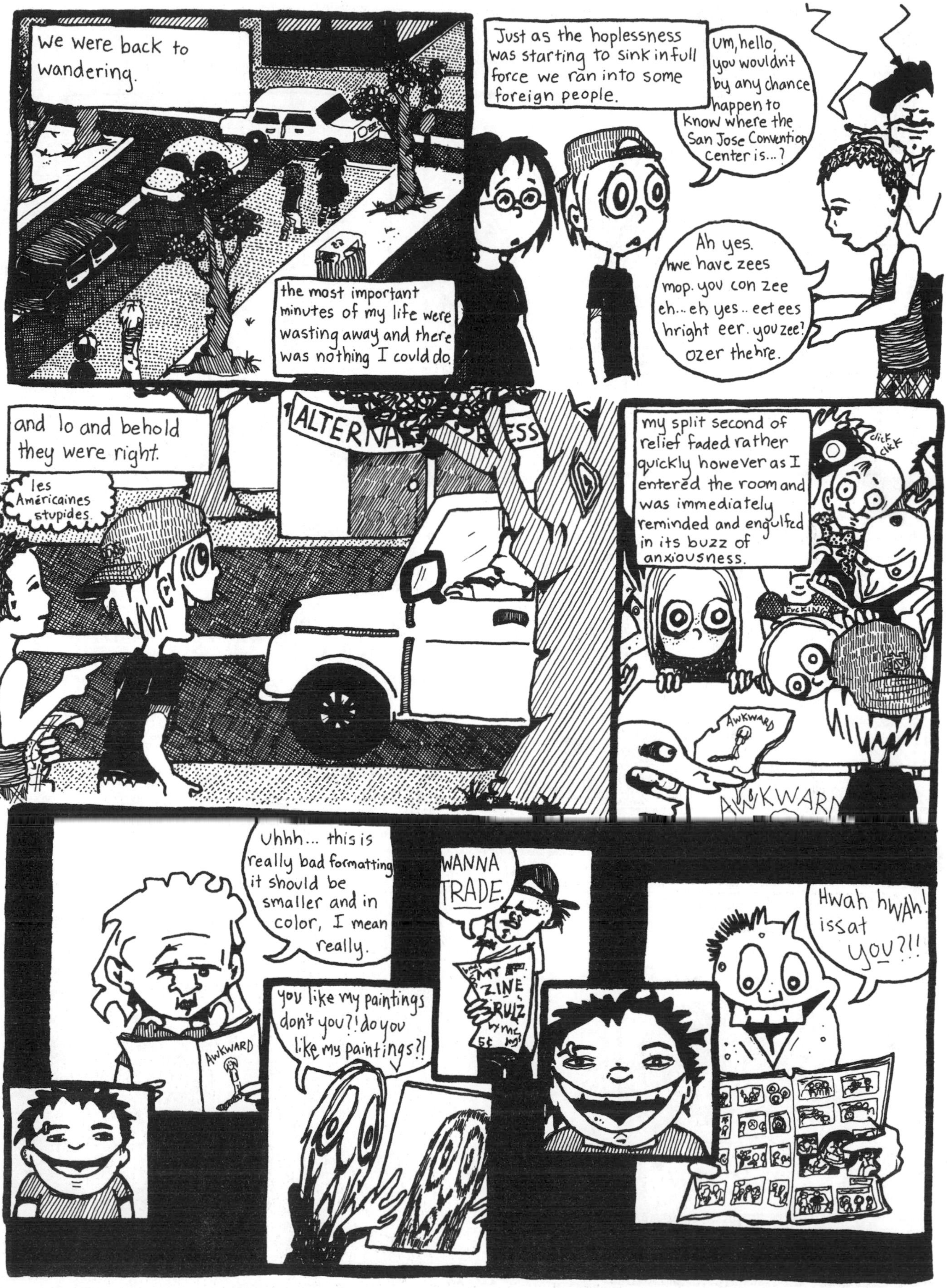
We were back to wandering.
the most important minutes of my life were wasting away and there was nothing I could do.
Just as the hoplessness was starting to sink in full force we ran into some foreign people.
Um, hello, you wouldn't by any chance happen to know where the San Jose Convention center is...?
Ah yes. hwe have zees mop. you con zee eh... eh yes.. eet ees hright eer. you zee? ozer thehre.
and lo and behold they were right.
les Américaines stupides.
ALTERNA
RESS
my split second of relief faded rather quickly however as I entered the room and was immediately reminded and engulfed in its buzz of anxiousness.
click click
AWKWARD
AWKWARD
Uhhh... this is really bad formatting it should be smaller and in color, I mean really.
AWKWARD
WANNA TRADE.
MY ZINE RULZ
you like my paintings don't you?! do you like my paintings?!
Hwah hwAh! issat you?!!

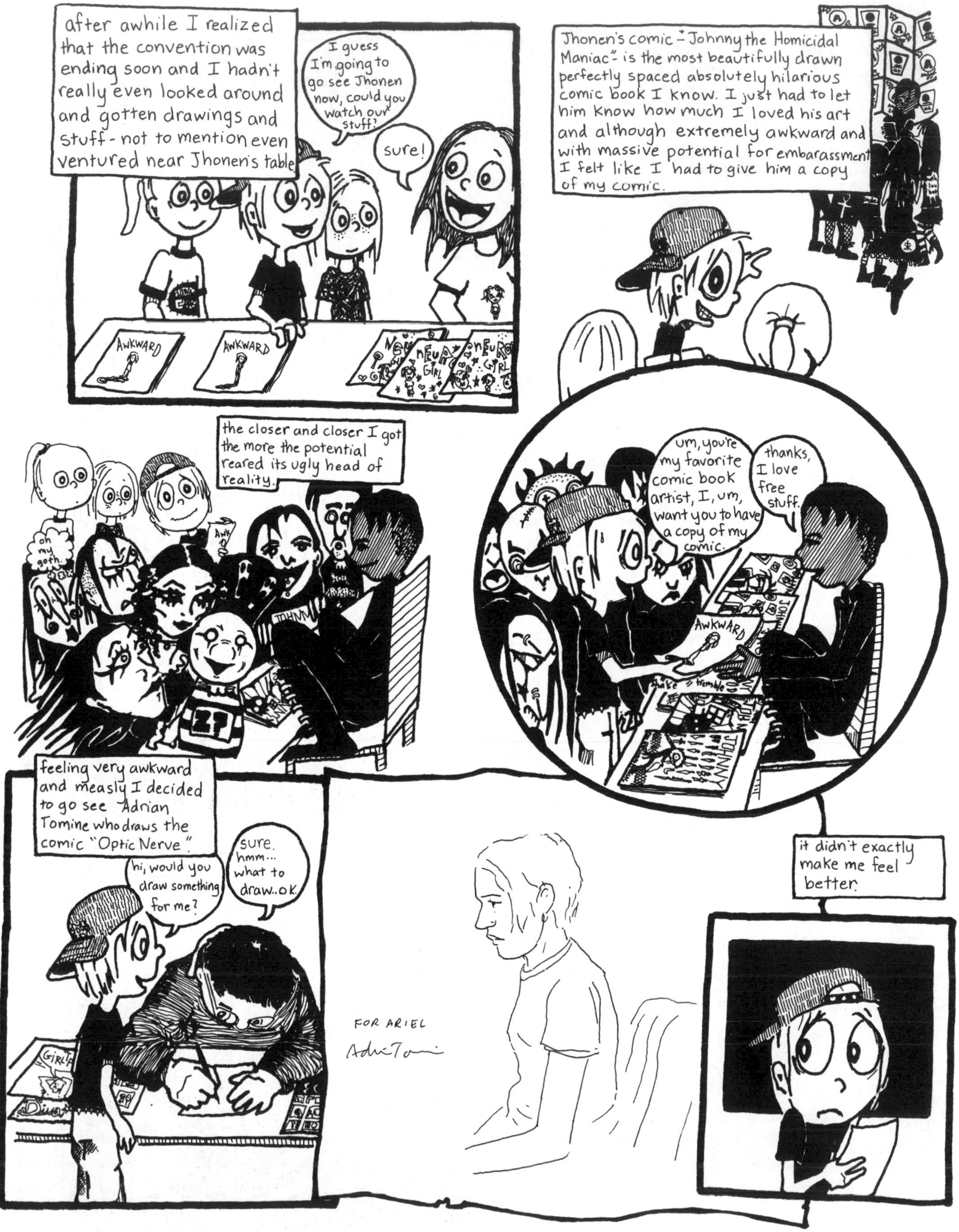

after awhile I realized that the convention was ending soon and I hadn't really even looked around and gotten drawings and stuff - not to mention even ventured near Jhonen's table
I guess I'm going to go see Jhonen now, could you watch our stuff?
sure!
AWKWARD
AWKWARD
Jhonen's comic - "Johnny the Homicidal Maniac" - is the most beautifully drawn perfectly spaced absolutely hilarious comic book I know. I just had to let him know how much I loved his art and although extremely awkward and with massive potential for embarassment I felt like I had to give him a copy of my comic.
the closer and closer I got the more the potential reared its ugly head of reality.
oh my goth.
um, you're my favorite comic book artist, I, um, want you to have a copy of my comic.
thanks, I love free stuff.
AWKWARD
shake tremble
feeling very awkward and measly I decided to go see Adrian Tomine who draws the comic "Optic Nerve".
hi, would you draw something for me?
sure. hmm... what to draw..OK.
FOR ARIEL
it didn't exactly make me feel better.

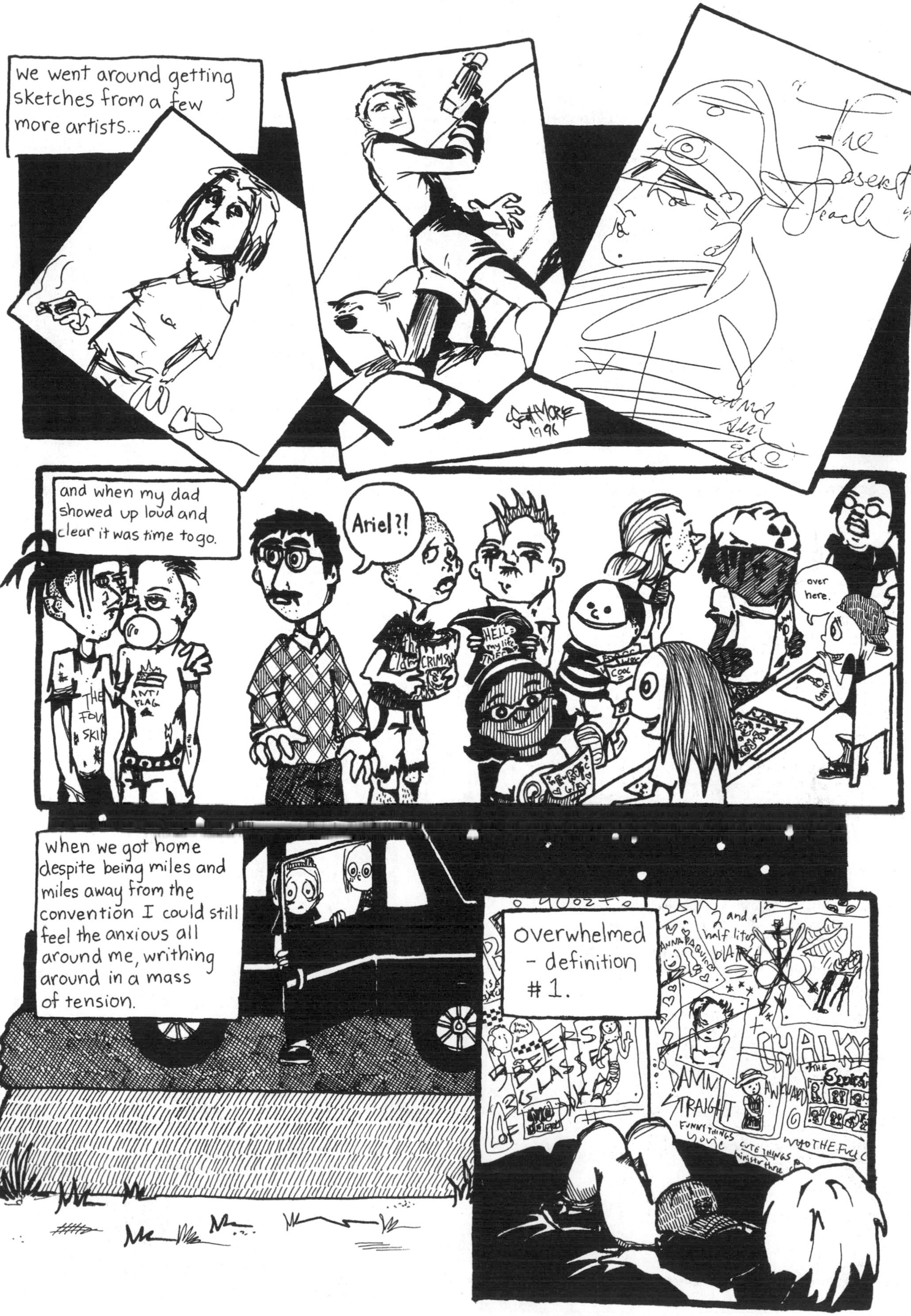

we went around getting sketches from a few more artists...
The Desert Peach
and when my dad showed up loud and clear it was time to go.
Ariel?!
over here.
when we got home despite being miles and miles away from the convention I could still feel the anxious all around me, writhing around in a mass of tension.
Overwhelmed - definition #1.

Chapter #7

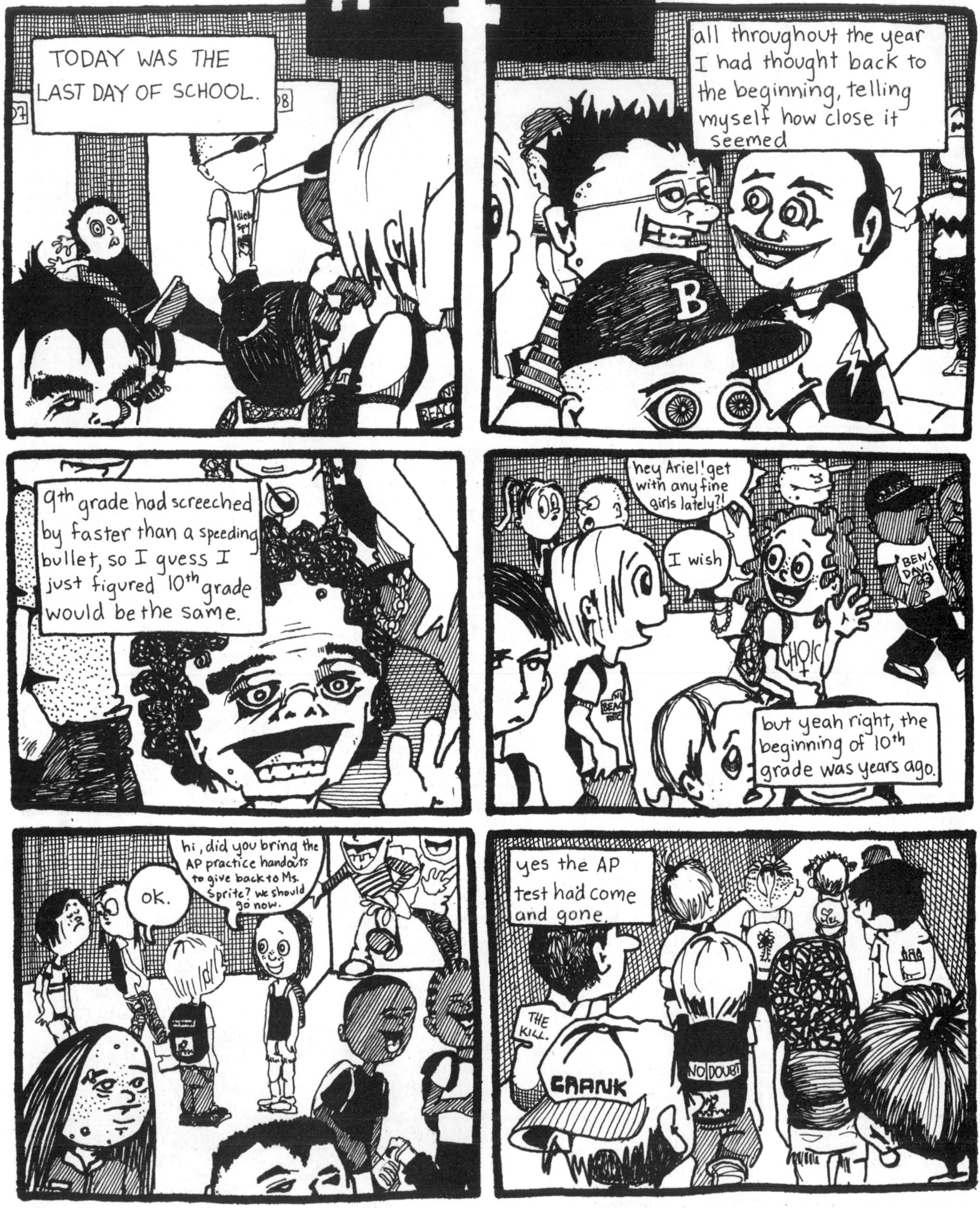

TODAY WAS THE LAST DAY OF SCHOOL.
all throughout the year I had thought back to the beginning, telling myself how close it seemed
9th grade had screeched by faster than a speeding bullet, so I guess I just figured 10th grade would be the same.
hey Ariel! get with any fine girls lately?!
I wish
BEN DAVIS
but yeah right, the beginning of 10th grade was years ago.
ok.
hi, did you bring the AP practice handouts to give back to Ms. Sprite? we should go now.
yes the AP test had come and gone.
THE KILL.
CRANK
NO DOUBT

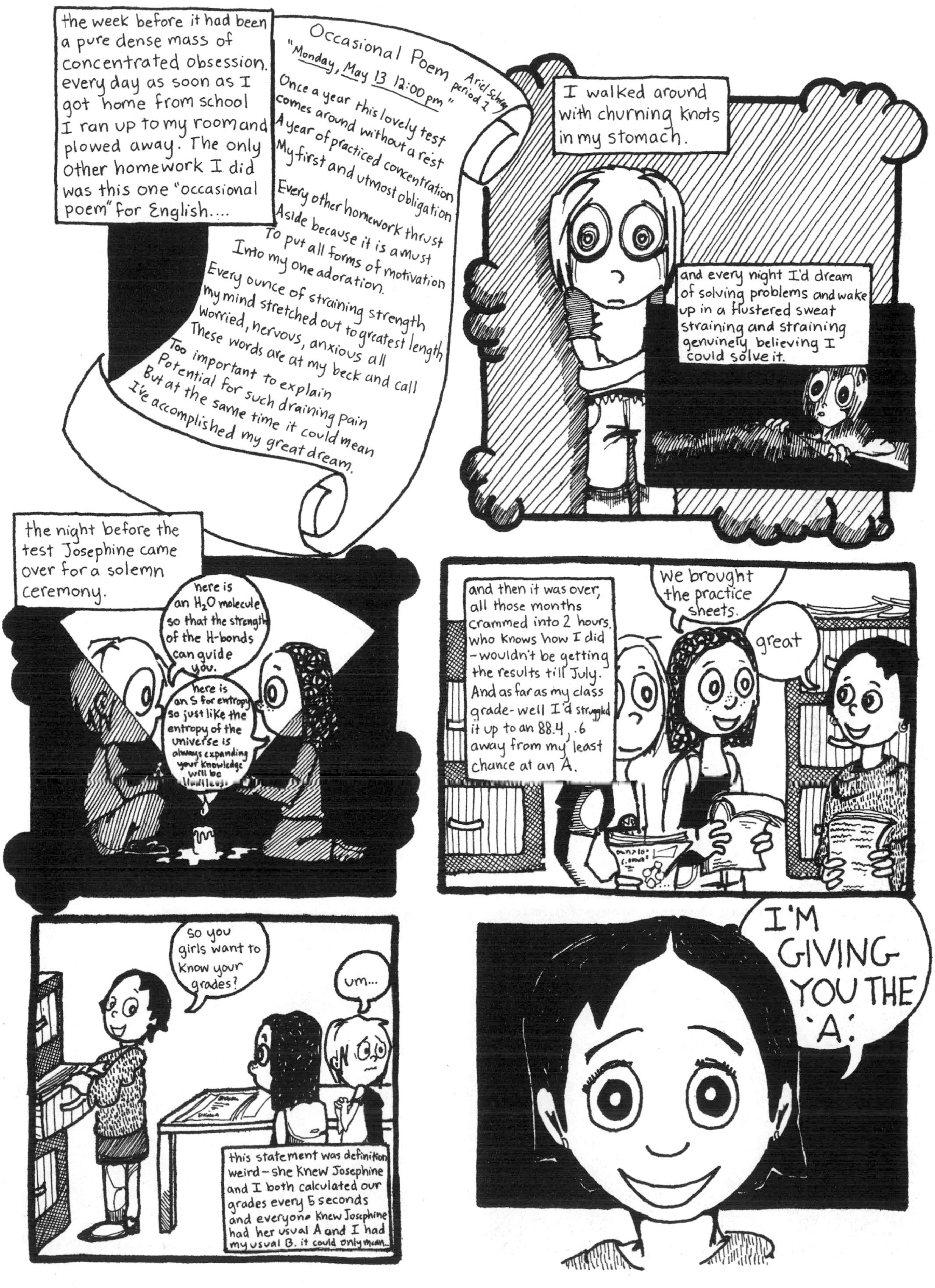

the week before it had been a pure dense mass of concentrated obsession. every day as soon as I got home from school I ran up to my room and plowed away. The only other homework I did was this one "occasional poem" for English....
Occasional Poem
"Monday, May 13 12:00 pm"
Ariel Schrag period 1
Once a year this lovely test
Comes around without a rest
A year of practiced concentration
My first and utmost obligation
Every other homework thrust
Aside because it is a must
To put all forms of motivation
Into my one adoration.
Every ounce of straining strength
My mind stretched out to greatest length
Worried, nervous, anxious all
These words are at my beck and call
Too important to explain
Potential for such draining pain
But at the same time it could mean
I've accomplished my great dream.
I walked around with churning knots in my stomach.
and every night I'd dream of solving problems and wake up in a flustered sweat straining and straining genuinely believing I could solve it.
the night before the test Josephine came over for a solemn ceremony.
here is an H_2O molecule so that the strength of the H-bonds can guide you.
here is an S for entropy so just like the entropy of the universe is always expanding your knowledge will be
and then it was over, all those months crammed into 2 hours. who knows how I did - wouldn't be getting the results till July. And as far as my class grade - well I'd struggled it up to an 88.4, .6 away from my least chance at an A.
We brought the practice sheets.
great
so you girls want to know your grades?
um...
this statement was definition weird - she knew Josephine and I both calculated our grades every 5 seconds and everyone knew Josephine had her usual A and I had my usual B. it could only mean...
I'M GIVING YOU THE 'A.'

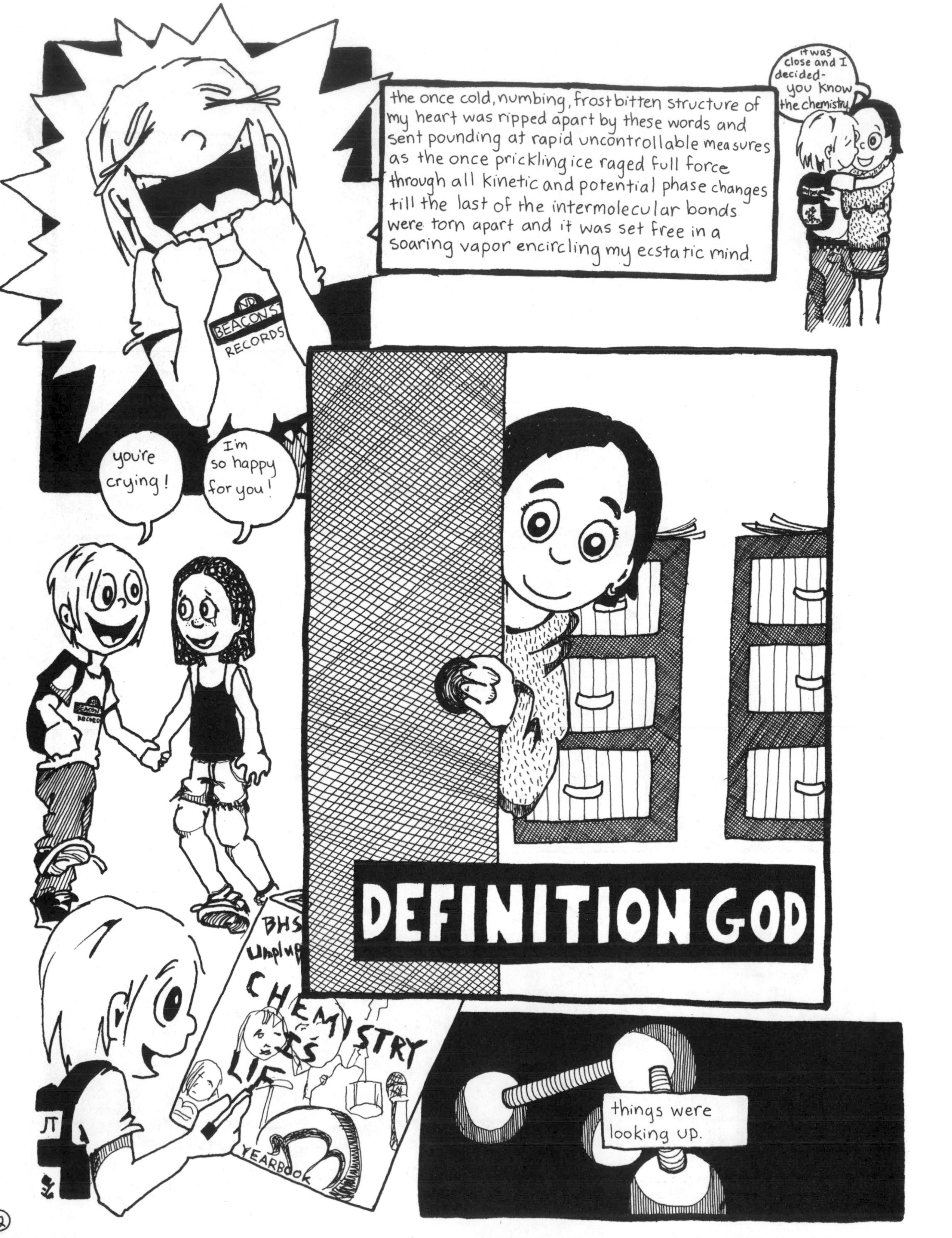
the once cold, numbing, frostbitten structure of my heart was ripped apart by these words and sent pounding at rapid uncontrollable measures as the once prickling ice raged full force through all kinetic and potential phase changes till the last of the intermolecular bonds were torn apart and it was set free in a soaring vapor encircling my ecstatic mind.
it was close and I decided- you know the chemistry.
BEACON ST RECORDS
you're crying!
I'm so happy for you!
DEFINITION GOD
BHS
CHEMISTRY IS LIFE
YEARBOOK
things were looking up.

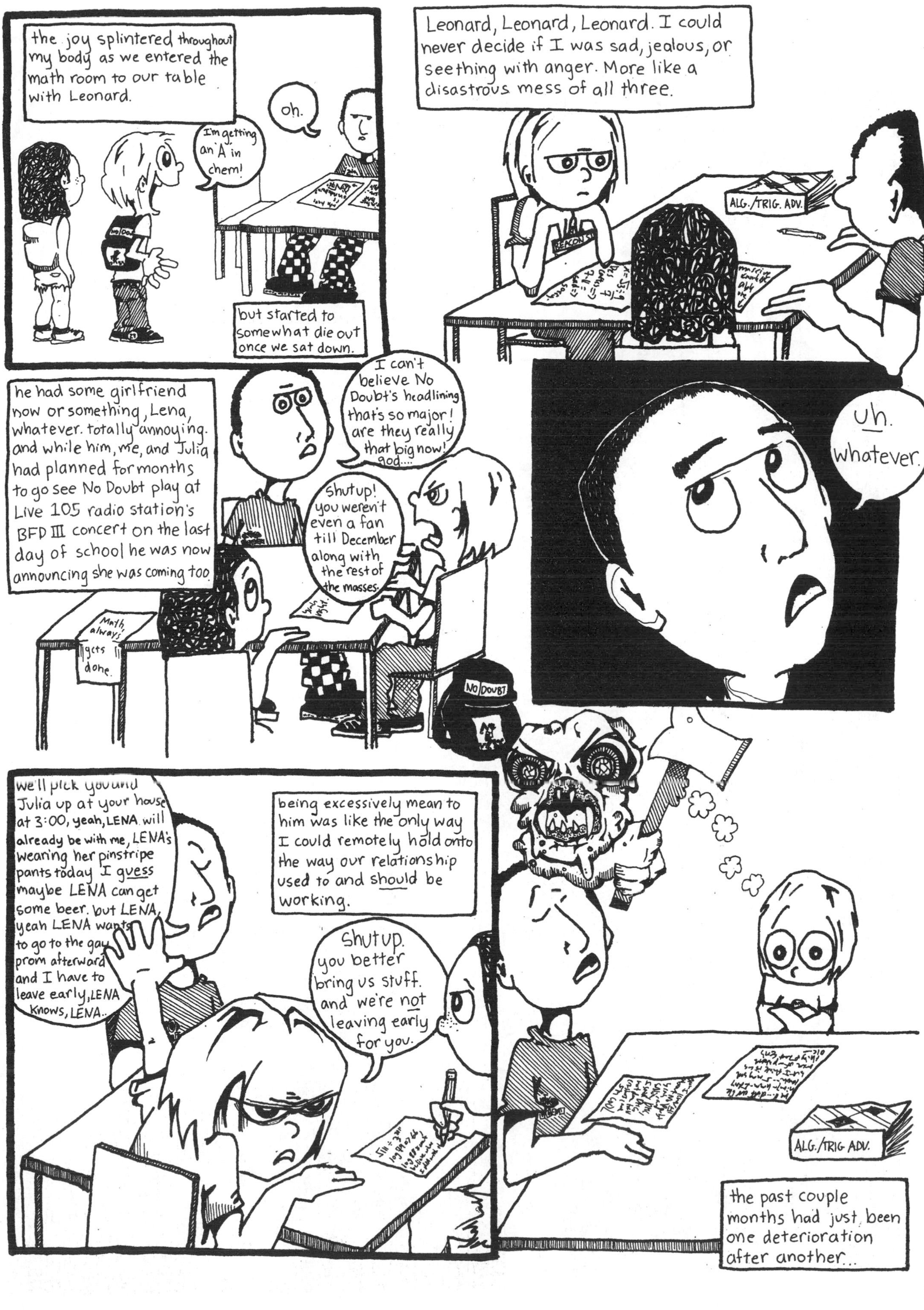
the joy splintered throughout my body as we entered the math room to our table with Leonard.
I'm getting an A in chem!
oh.
but started to somewhat die out once we sat down.
Leonard, Leonard, Leonard. I could never decide if I was sad, jealous, or seething with anger. More like a disastrous mess of all three.
ALG./TRIG. ADV.
he had some girlfriend now or something, Lena, whatever. totally annoying. and while him, me, and Julia had planned for months to go see No Doubt play at Live 105 radio station's BFD III concert on the last day of school he was now announcing she was coming too.
I can't believe No Doubt's headlining that's so major! are they really that big now! god....
Shutup! you weren't even a fan till December along with the rest of the masses.
Math always gets done.
NO DOUBT
uh. whatever.
we'll pick you and Julia up at your house at 3:00, yeah, LENA will already be with me, LENA's wearing her pinstripe pants today I guess maybe LENA can get some beer. but LENA, yeah LENA wants to go to the gay prom afterward and I have to leave early, LENA knows, LENA..
being excessively mean to him was like the only way I could remotely hold onto the way our relationship used to and should be working.
Shut up. you better bring us stuff. and we're not leaving early for you.
ALG./TRIG ADV.
the past couple months had just been one deterioration after another..

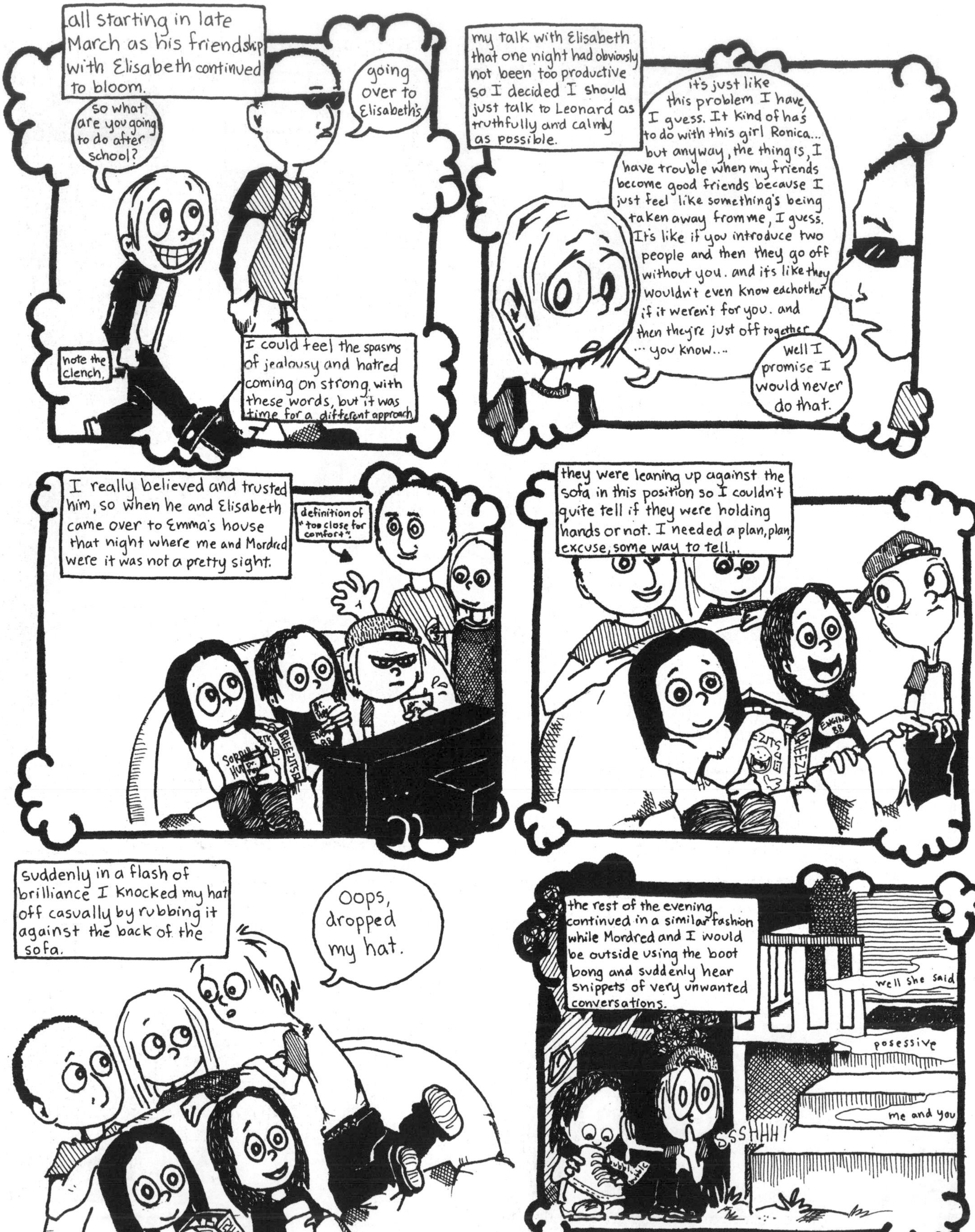

all starting in late March as his friendship with Elisabeth continued to bloom.
so what are you going to do after school?
going over to Elisabeth's.
note the clench.
I could feel the spasms of jealousy and hatred coming on strong with these words, but it was time for a different approach.
my talk with Elisabeth that one night had obviously not been too productive so I decided I should just talk to Leonard as truthfully and calmly as possible.
it's just like this problem I have I guess. It kind of has to do with this girl Ronica... but anyway, the thing is, I have trouble when my friends become good friends because I just feel like something's being taken away from me, I guess. It's like if you introduce two people and then they go off without you. and it's like they wouldn't even know eachother if it weren't for you. and then they're just off together ... you know...
Well I promise I would never do that.
I really believed and trusted him, so when he and Elisabeth came over to Emma's house that night where me and Mordred were it was not a pretty sight.
definition of "too close for comfort".
they were leaning up against the sofa in this position so I couldn't quite tell if they were holding hands or not. I needed a plan, plan, excuse, some way to tell...
suddenly in a flash of brilliance I knocked my hat off casually by rubbing it against the back of the sofa.
Oops, dropped my hat.
the rest of the evening continued in a similar fashion while Mordred and I would be outside using the boot bong and suddenly hear snippets of very unwanted conversations.
well she said
posessive
me and you
SSSHHH!

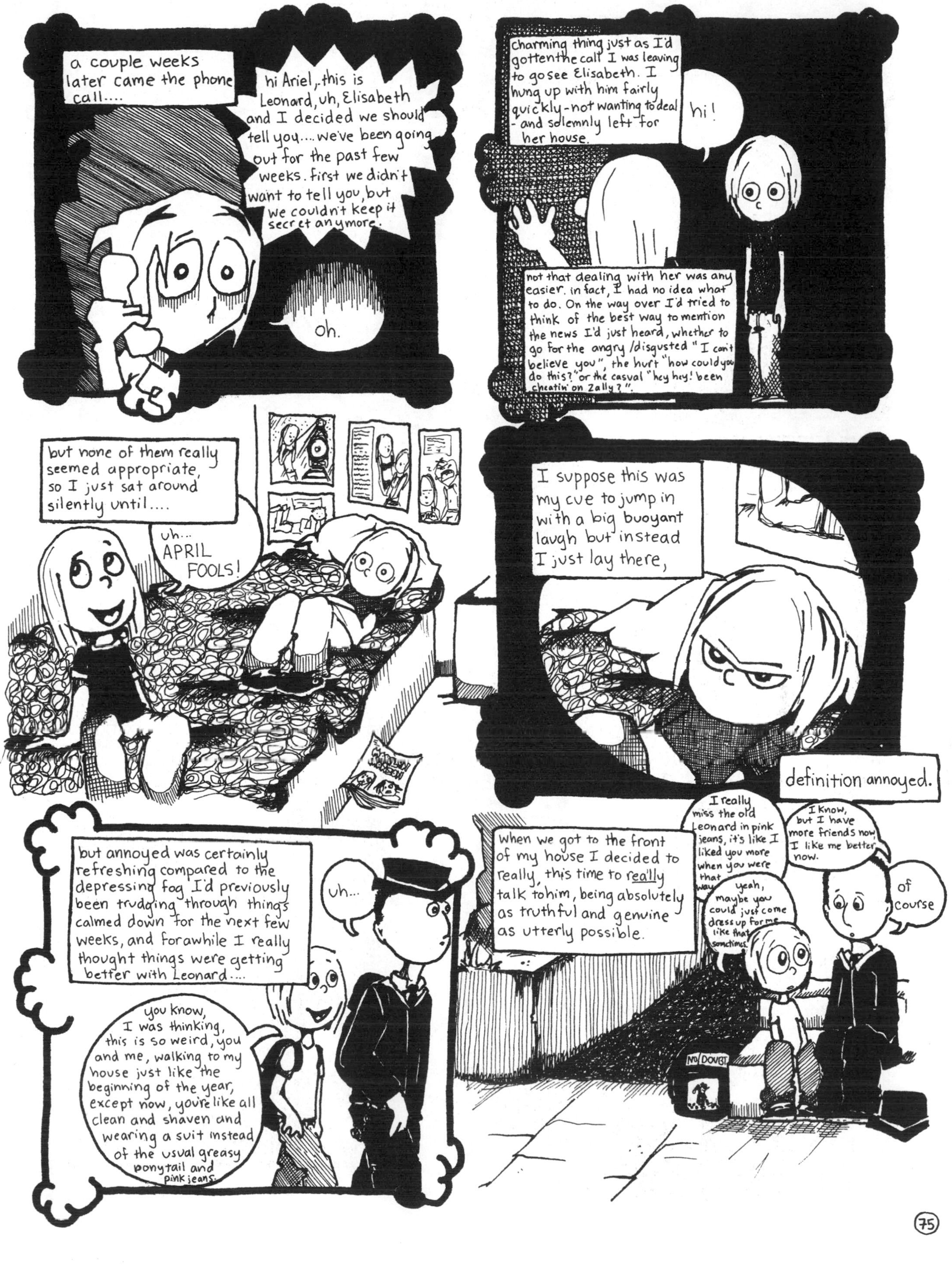

a couple weeks later came the phone call....
hi Ariel, this is Leonard, uh, Elisabeth and I decided we should tell you.... we've been going out for the past few weeks. first we didn't want to tell you, but we couldn't keep it secret anymore.
oh.
charming thing just as I'd gotten the call I was leaving to go see Elisabeth. I hung up with him fairly quickly - not wanting to deal - and solemnly left for her house.
hi!
not that dealing with her was any easier. in fact, I had no idea what to do. On the way over I'd tried to think of the best way to mention the news I'd just heard, whether to go for the angry/disgusted "I can't believe you", the hurt "how could you do this?" or the casual "hey hey! been cheatin' on Zally?".
but none of them really seemed appropriate, so I just sat around silently until....
uh... APRIL FOOLS!
I suppose this was my cue to jump in with a big buoyant laugh but instead I just lay there,
definition annoyed.
but annoyed was certainly refreshing compared to the depressing fog I'd previously been trudging through things calmed down for the next few weeks, and forawhile I really thought things were getting better with Leonard....
uh...
you know, I was thinking, this is so weird, you and me, walking to my house just like the beginning of the year, except now, you're like all clean and shaven and wearing a suit instead of the usual greasy ponytail and pink jeans.
when we got to the front of my house I decided to really, this time to really talk to him, being absolutely as truthful and genuine as utterly possible.
I really miss the old Leonard in pink jeans, it's like I liked you more when you were that way
I know, but I have more friends now, I like me better now.
yeah, maybe you could just come dress up for me like that sometimes
of course
NO DOUBT

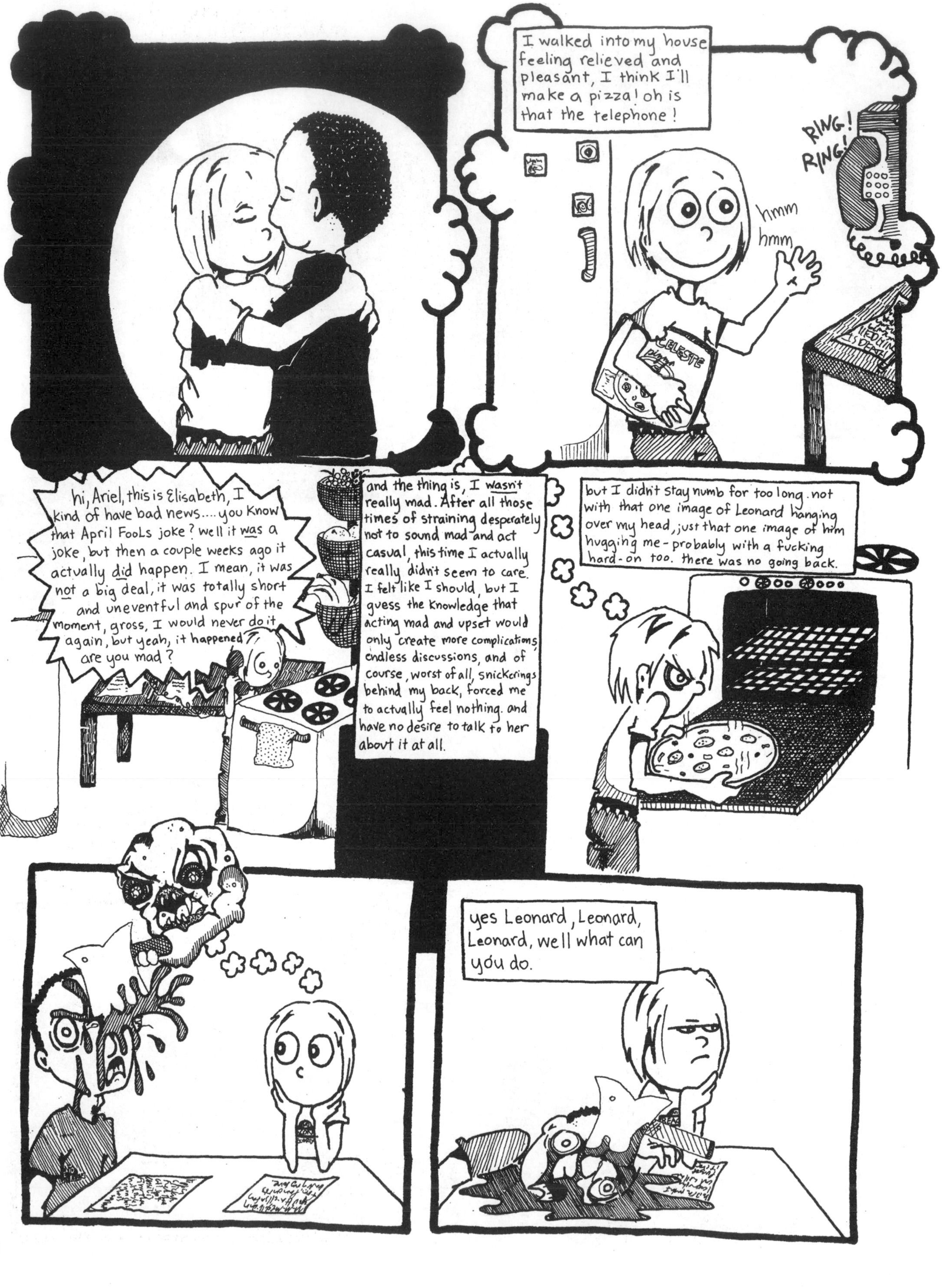
I walked into my house feeling relieved and pleasant, I think I'll make a pizza! oh is that the telephone!
RING! RING!
hmm hmm
CELESTE
hi, Ariel, this is Elisabeth, I kind of have bad news.... you know that April Fools joke? well it was a joke, but then a couple weeks ago it actually did happen. I mean, it was not a big deal, it was totally short and uneventful and spur of the moment, gross, I would never do it again, but yeah, it happened are you mad?
and the thing is, I wasn't really mad. After all those times of straining desperately not to sound mad and act casual, this time I actually really didn't seem to care. I felt like I should, but I guess the knowledge that acting mad and upset would only create more complications, endless discussions, and of course, worst of all, snickerings behind my back, forced me to actually feel nothing. and have no desire to talk to her about it at all.
but I didn't stay numb for too long. not with that one image of Leonard hanging over my head, just that one image of him hugging me - probably with a fucking hard-on too. there was no going back.
yes Leonard, Leonard, Leonard, well what can you do.

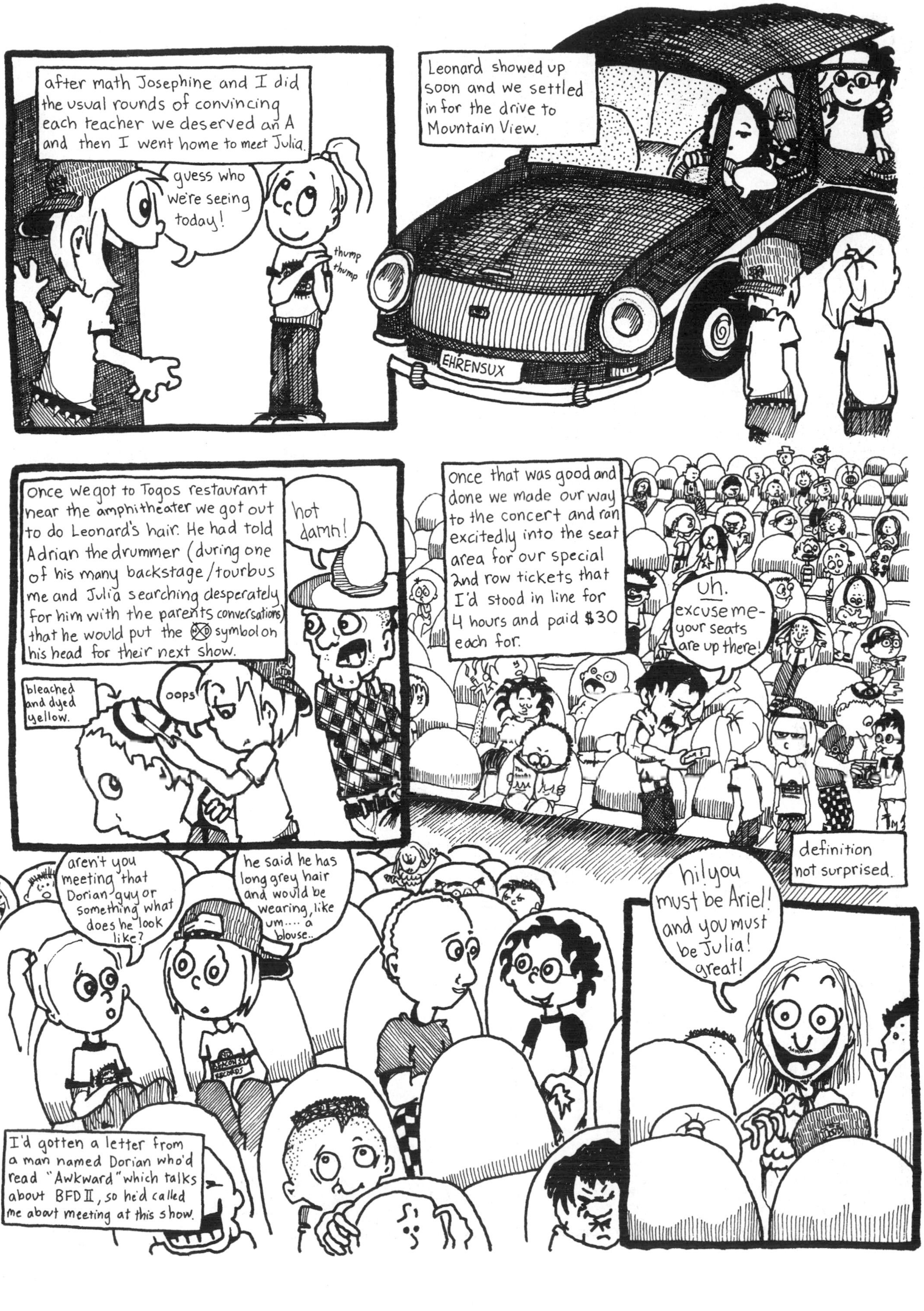

after math Josephine and I did the usual rounds of convincing each teacher we deserved an A and then I went home to meet Julia.
guess who we're seeing today!
thump thump
Leonard showed up soon and we settled in for the drive to Mountain View.
EHRENSUX
Once we got to Togos restaurant near the amphitheater we got out to do Leonard's hair. He had told Adrian the drummer (during one of his many backstage/tourbus conversations) me and Julia searching desperately for him with the parents that he would put the symbol on his head for their next show.
hot damn!
bleached and dyed yellow.
oops
Once that was good and done we made our way to the concert and ran excitedly into the seat area for our special 2nd row tickets that I'd stood in line for 4 hours and paid $30 each for.
uh. excuse me- your seats are up there!
definition not surprised.
aren't you meeting that Dorian guy or something what does he look like?
he said he has long grey hair and would be wearing, like um.... a blouse..
I'd gotten a letter from a man named Dorian who'd read "Awkward" which talks about BFD II, so he'd called me about meeting at this show.
hi! you must be Ariel! and you must be Julia! great!

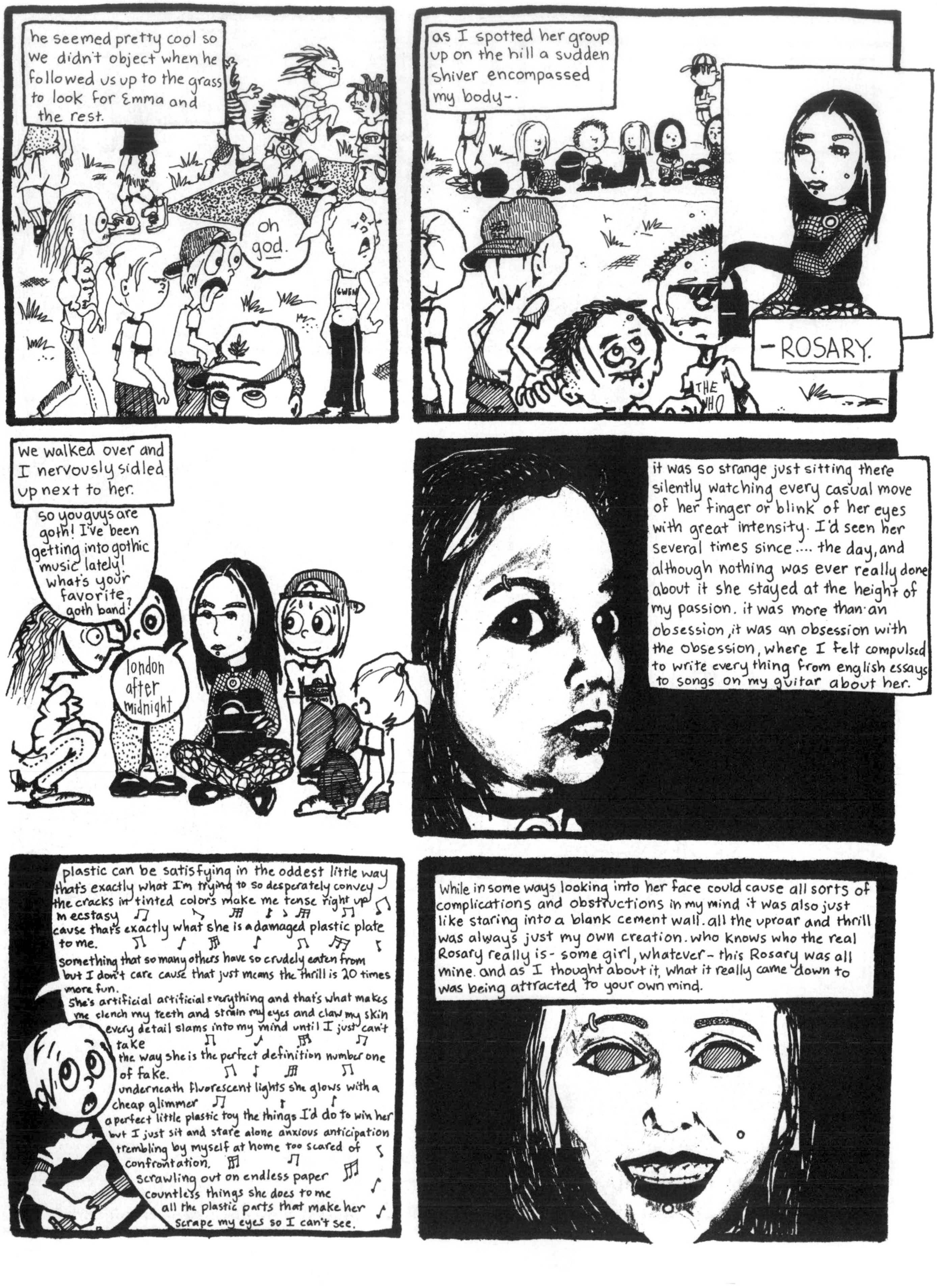
he seemed pretty cool so we didn't object when he followed us up to the grass to look for Emma and the rest.
oh god.
GWEN
as I spotted her group up on the hill a sudden shiver encompassed my body-.
-ROSARY.
THE WHO
We walked over and I nervously sidled up next to her.
so you guys are goth! I've been getting into gothic music lately! what's your favorite goth band?
london after midnight
it was so strange just sitting there silently watching every casual move of her finger or blink of her eyes with great intensity. I'd seen her several times since .... the day, and although nothing was ever really done about it she stayed at the height of my passion. it was more than an obsession, it was an obsession with the obsession, where I felt compulsed to write everything from english essays to songs on my guitar about her.
plastic can be satisfying in the oddest little way
that's exactly what I'm trying to so desperately convey
the cracks in tinted colors make me tense right up
in ecstasy
cause that's exactly what she is a damaged plastic plate
to me.
something that so many others have so crudely eaten from
but I don't care cause that just means the thrill is 20 times
more fun.
She's artificial artificial everything and that's what makes
me clench my teeth and strain my eyes and claw my skin
every detail slams into my mind until I just can't
take
the way she is the perfect definition number one
of fake.
underneath fluorescent lights she glows with a
cheap glimmer
a perfect little plastic toy the things I'd do to win her
but I just sit and stare alone anxious anticipation
trembling by myself at home too scared of
confrontation.
scrawling out on endless paper
countless things she does to me
all the plastic parts that make her
scrape my eyes so I can't see.
While in some ways looking into her face could cause all sorts of complications and obstructions in my mind it was also just like staring into a blank cement wall. all the uproar and thrill was always just my own creation. who knows who the real Rosary really is - some girl, whatever - this Rosary was all mine. and as I thought about it, what it really came down to was being attracted to your own mind.

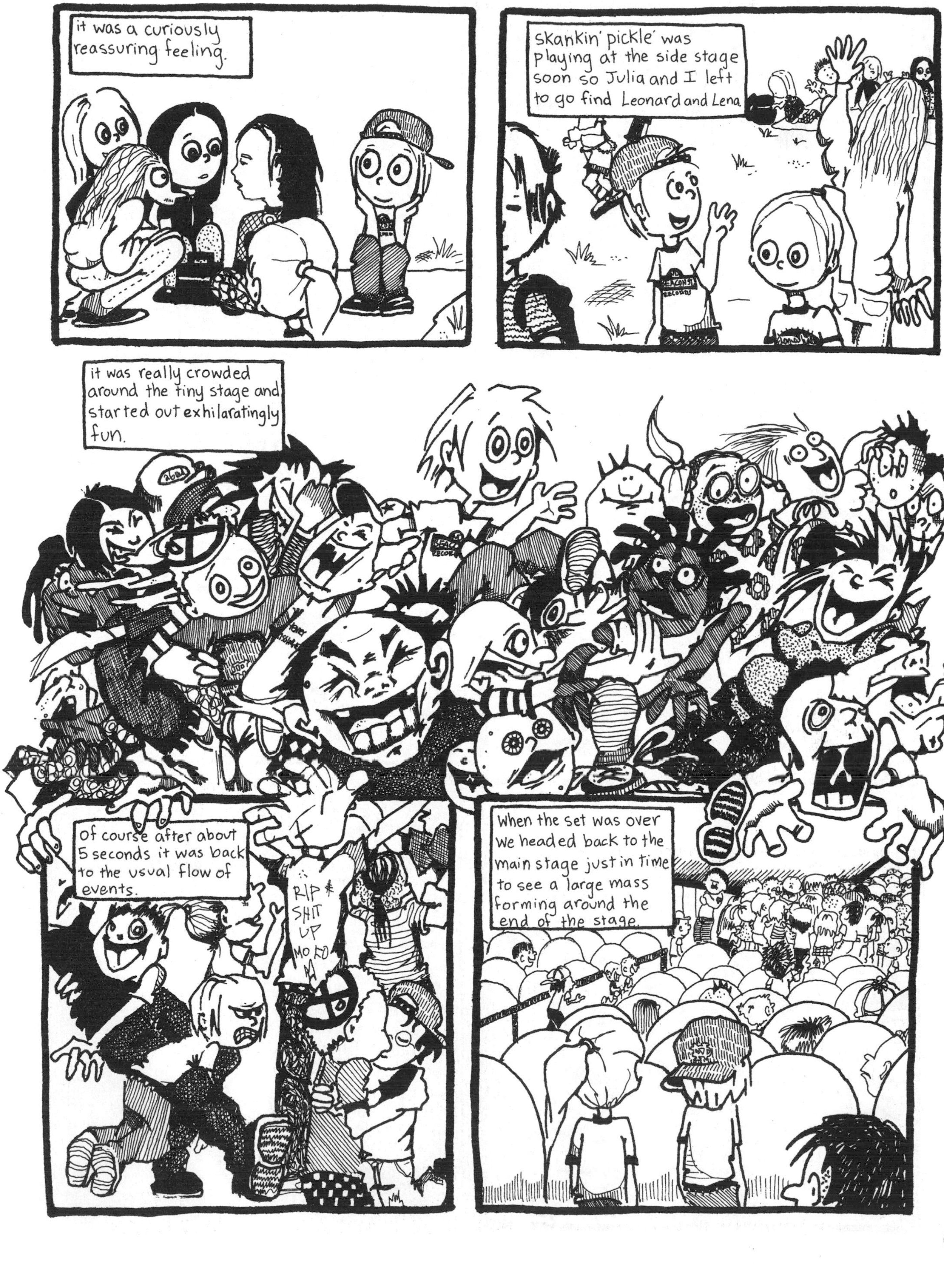
it was a curiously reassuring feeling.
skankin' pickle' was playing at the side stage soon so Julia and I left to go find Leonard and Lena
it was really crowded around the tiny stage and started out exhilaratingly fun.
of course after about 5 seconds it was back to the usual flow of events.
RIP $ SHIT UP
When the set was over we headed back to the main stage just in time to see a large mass forming around the end of the stage.

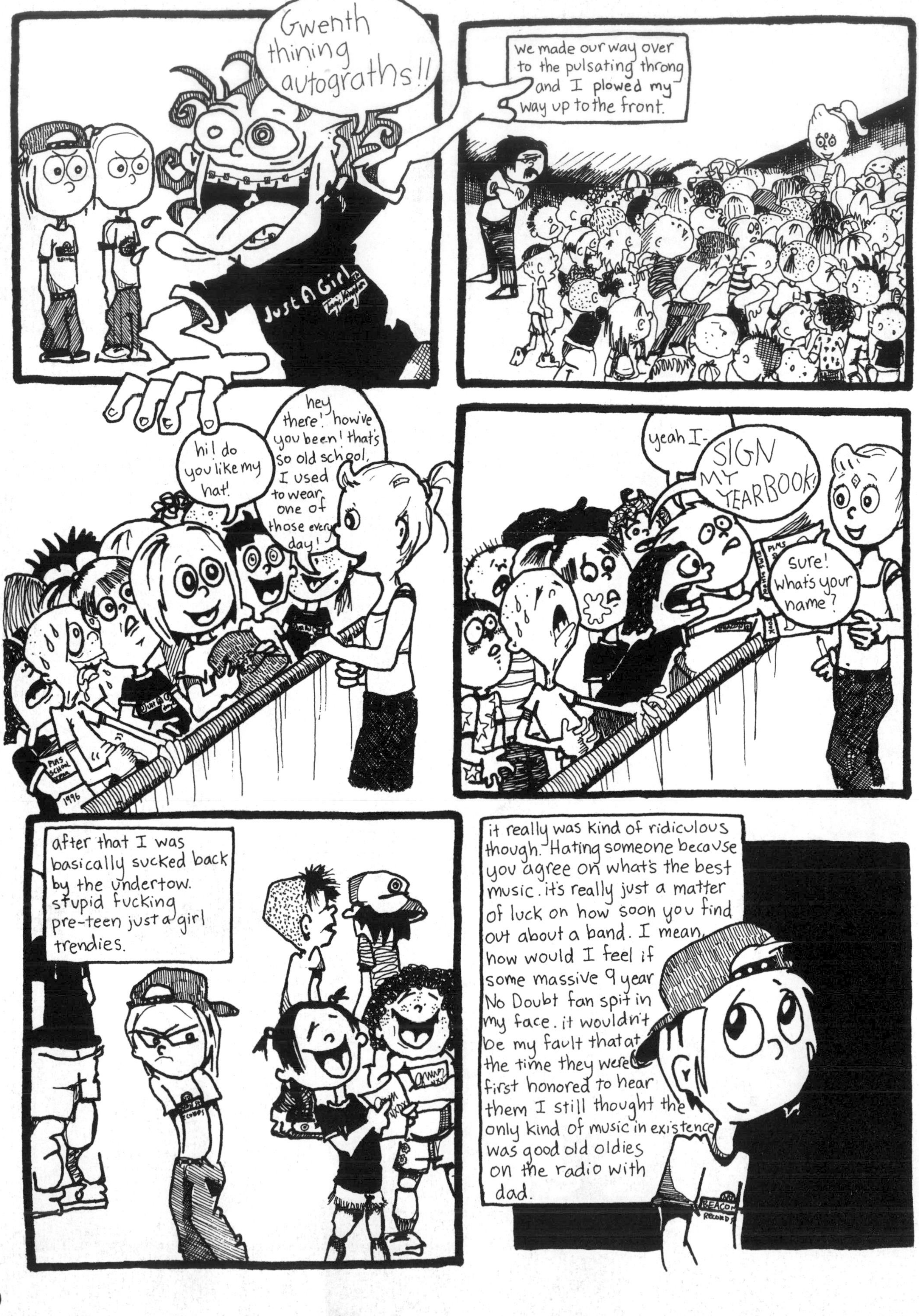
Gwenth thining autograths!!
Just A Girl
We made our way over to the pulsating throng and I plowed my way up to the front.
hi! do you like my hat!
hey there! how've you been! that's so old school, I used to wear one of those every day!
1996
yeah I-
SIGN MY YEARBOOK!
Sure! What's your name?
after that I was basically sucked back by the undertow. stupid fucking pre-teen just a girl trendies.
it really was kind of ridiculous though. Hating someone because you agree on what's the best music. it's really just a matter of luck on how soon you find out about a band. I mean, how would I feel if some massive 9 year No Doubt fan spit in my face. it wouldn't be my fault that at the time they were first honored to hear them I still thought the only kind of music in existence was good old oldies on the radio with dad.
BEACON RECORDS

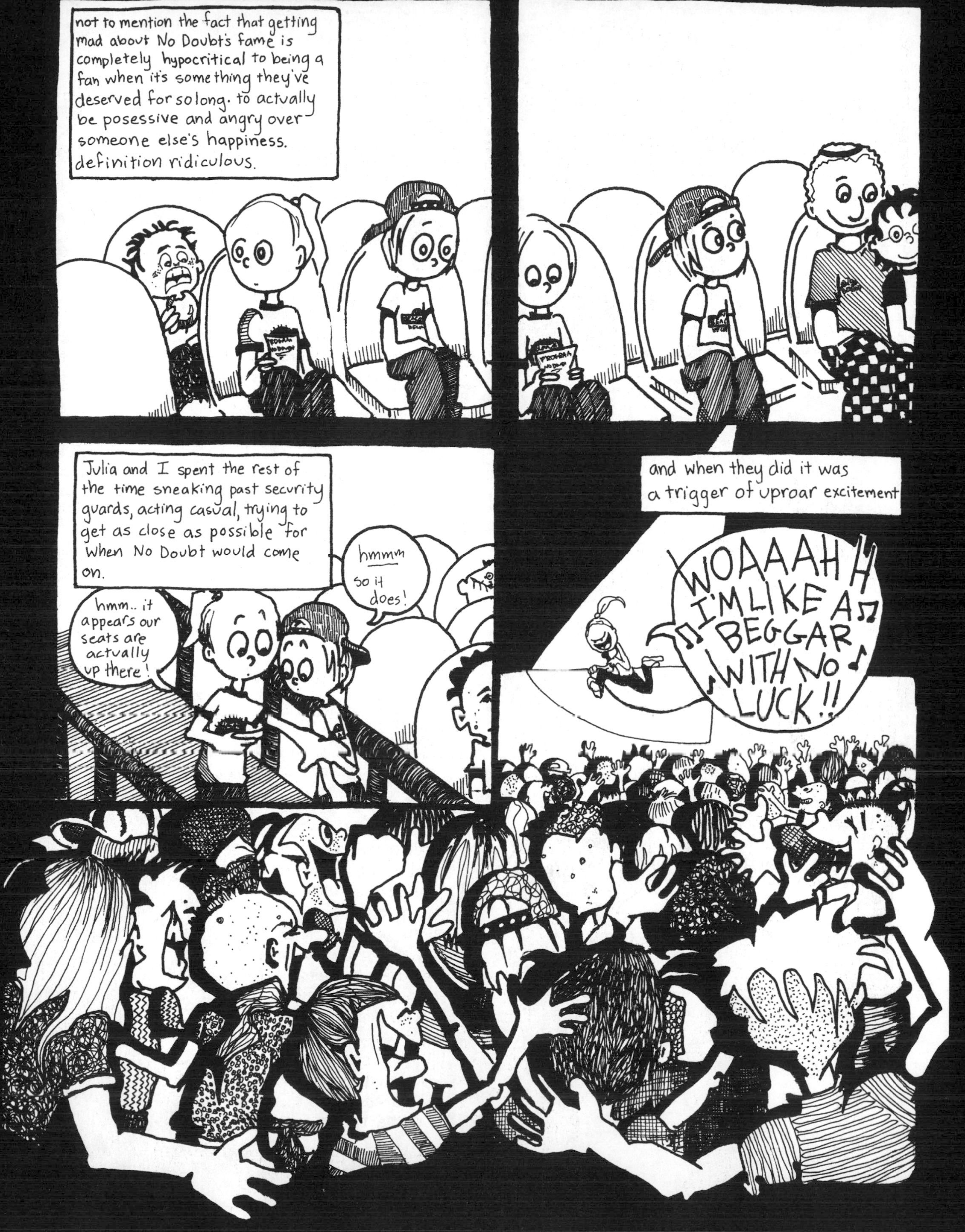
not to mention the fact that getting mad about No Doubt's fame is completely hypocritical to being a fan when it's something they've deserved for so long. to actually be posessive and angry over someone else's happiness. definition ridiculous.
Julia and I spent the rest of the time sneaking past security guards, acting casual, trying to get as close as possible for when No Doubt would come on.
hmm.. it appears our seats are actually up there!
hmmm so it does!
and when they did it was a trigger of uproar excitement
WOAAAHH I'M LIKE A BEGGAR WITH NO LUCK!!

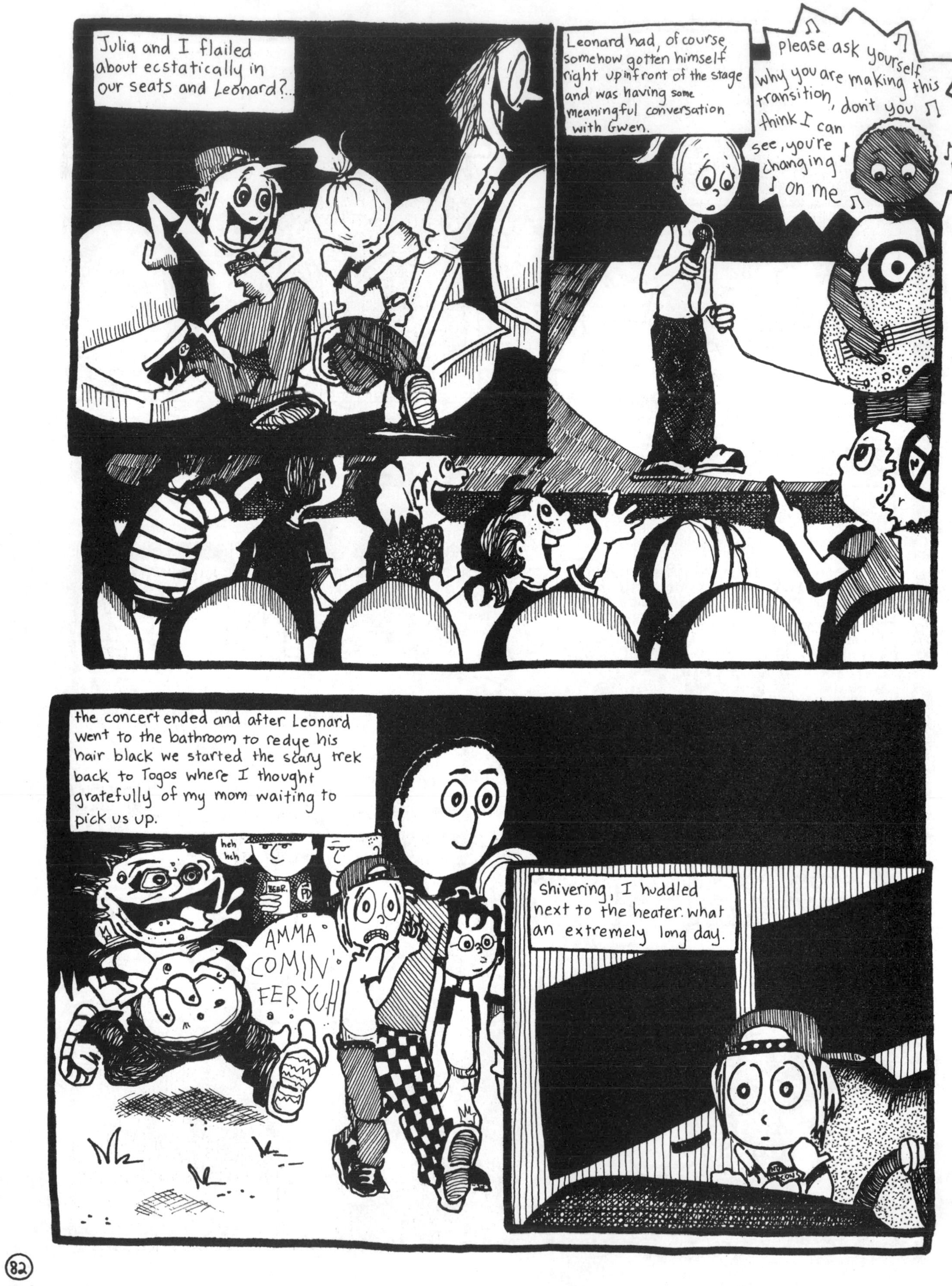

Julia and I flailed about ecstatically in our seats and Leonard?...
Leonard had, of course, somehow gotten himself right up in front of the stage and was having some meaningful conversation with Gwen.
Please ask yourself why you are making this transition, dont you think I can see, you're changing on me
the concert ended and after Leonard went to the bathroom to redye his hair black we started the scary trek back to Togos where I thought gratefully of my mom waiting to pick us up.
heh heh
AMMA COMIN' FER YUH
Shivering, I huddled next to the heater. what an extremely long day.

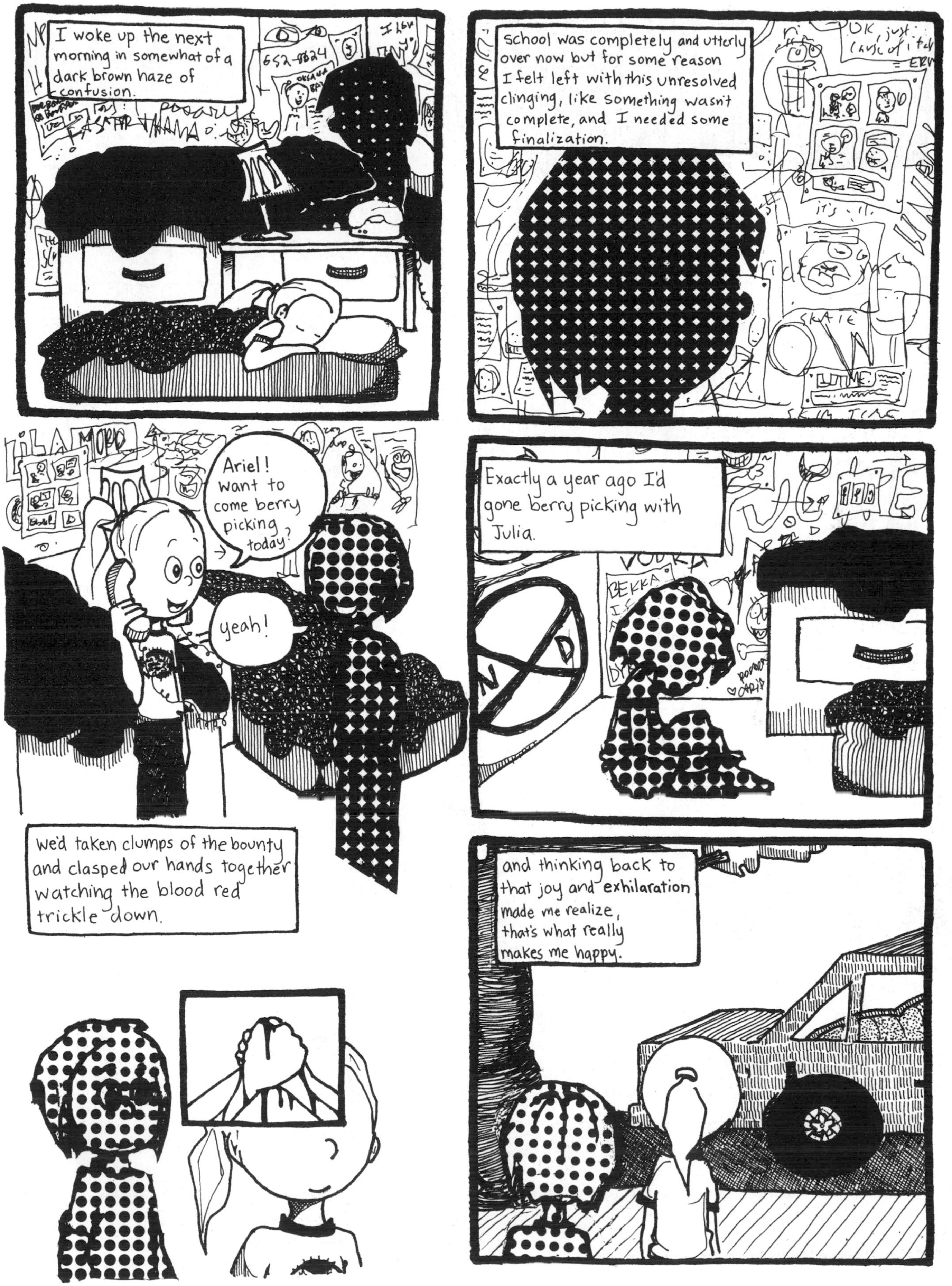

I woke up the next morning in somewhat of a dark brown haze of confusion.
School was completely and utterly over now but for some reason I felt left with this unresolved clinging, like something wasn't complete, and I needed some finalization.
Ariel! Want to come berry picking today?
Yeah!
Exactly a year ago I'd gone berry picking with Julia.
We'd taken clumps of the bounty and clasped our hands together watching the blood red trickle down.
and thinking back to that joy and exhilaration made me realize, that's what really makes me happy.

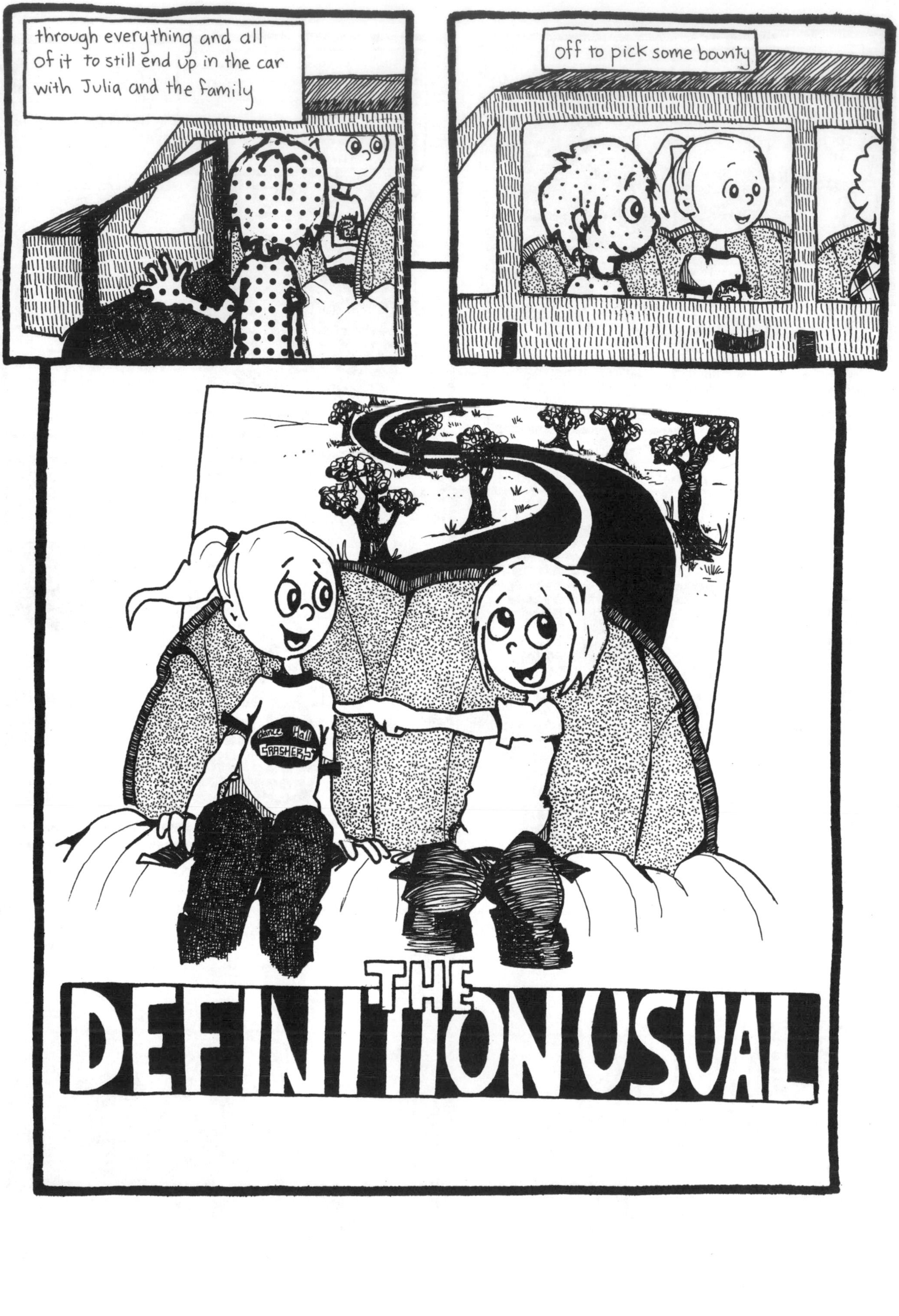
through everything and all of it to still end up in the car with Julia and the family
off to pick some bounty
dance Hall CRASHERS
THE
DEFINITION USUAL

a few weeks later one night at Gilman....

hey look, it's the bassist to the Dance Hall Crashers! let's go say hi!
oh wow! yeah!

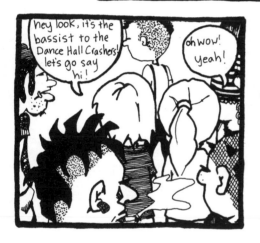

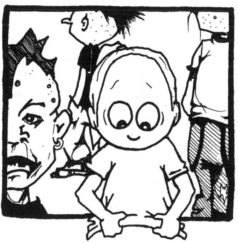

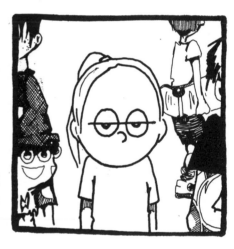

Chapter #5 with help from Julia Fuller
pg. #66 with help from Tania Schrag

and a very special thanks to
Ehren Reilly
and the definition truth

The High School Comic Chronicles of

Ariel Schrag

AWKWARD
AND
DEFINITION
The High School Comic Chronicles of
Ariel Schrag
Author of POTENTIAL

9th Grade

it seemed like we waited at the bus stop for hours
So Marie, um, I was thinking
yes?
So like Tissy's friend got hooked up with like a fuckin' pound so that means Tissy's hooked up with a pound so that means I'm hooked up with a pound so..
well, um. I'll pay for your bus fare.
um, ok. yeah, yeah alright.
I couldn't stop staring at these people who had just come out of some group therapy class. the guy was like making his move.

10th Grade

675
Z
000
1329
X
um, does the shuttle come soon?
what shuttle?
to the Arena?
the Arena!! that stopped running HOURS ago!!

POTENTIAL
The High School Comic Chronicles of
ARIEL SCHRAG

11th Grade

the blatant fact of the matter was, that as sad as it was, and as much as I would rather hop on Sally over any guy in the world...
67
604
605
51
9
15
43
AC TRANS

12th Grade

51

LIKEWISE
The High School Comic Chronicles of
ARIEL SCHRAG
Author of POTENTIAL

Coming Fall 2008

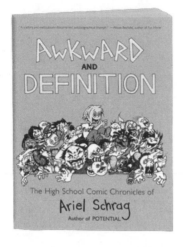

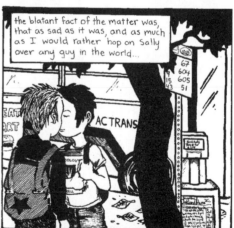

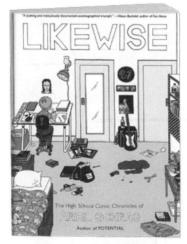

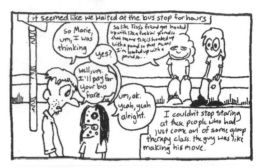

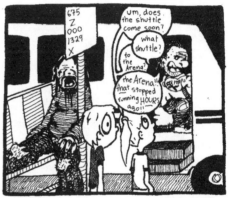

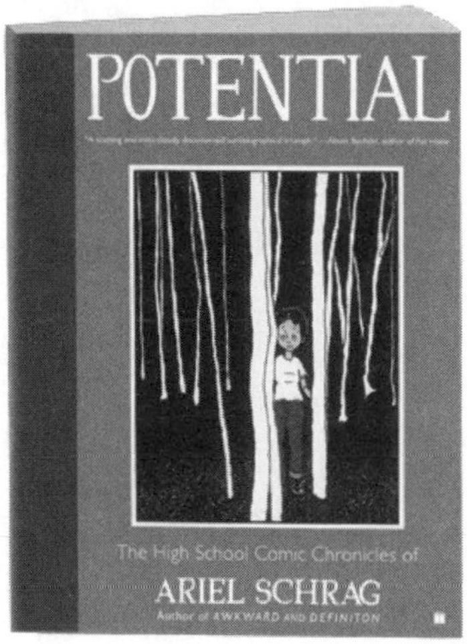

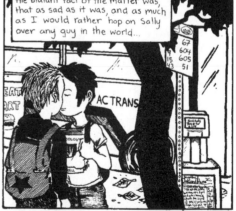

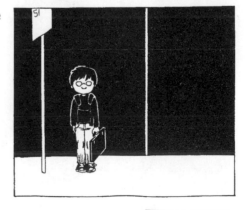